Chilling Out

**Recent Title in
The Psychology of Everyday Life**

Working Out: The Psychology of Sport and Exercise
Justine J. Reel

CHILLING OUT

The Psychology of Relaxation

Christine L. B. Selby

The Psychology of Everyday Life

An Imprint of ABC-CLIO, LLC
Santa Barbara, California • Denver, Colorado

Copyright © 2015 by ABC-CLIO, LLC

All rights reserved. No part of this publication may be reproduced, stored in a retrieval system, or transmitted, in any form or by any means, electronic, mechanical, photocopying, recording, or otherwise, except for the inclusion of brief quotations in a review, without prior permission in writing from the publisher.

Library of Congress Cataloging-in-Publication Data

Selby, Christine L. B.
 Chilling out : the psychology of relaxation / Christine L. B. Selby.
  pages cm. — (The psychology of everyday life)
 Includes bibliographical references and index.
 ISBN 978–1–61069–769–9 (hardcopy : alk. paper) — ISBN 978–1–61069–770–5 (ebook) 1. Stress management. I. Title.
RA785.S456   2015
155.9′042—dc23   2015009859

ISBN: 978–1–61069–769–9
EISBN: 978–1–61069–770–5

19 18 17 16 15   1 2 3 4 5

This book is also available on the World Wide Web as an eBook.
Visit www.abc-clio.com for details.

Greenwood
An Imprint of ABC-CLIO, LLC

ABC-CLIO, LLC
130 Cremona Drive, P.O. Box 1911
Santa Barbara, California 93116-1911

This book is printed on acid-free paper ∞

Manufactured in the United States of America

This book is dedicated to my husband and best friend. It could not have been completed without his unyielding support.

Contents

Series Foreword	ix
Preface	xiii
Acknowledgments	xv
Part I: Relaxation in Everyday Life	1
1 What: The Many Forms of Relaxation	3
2 Why: The Importance of Relaxation in Our Lives	27
3 How: The Positive and Negative Effects of Relaxation	45
4 Who: Psychologists' Theories about Relaxation	61
5 When: Relaxation throughout the Life Cycle	81
6 Where: Relaxation around the World	101
Part II: Scenarios	121
Part III: Controversies and Debates	135
Directory of Resources	159
Glossary	161

Bibliography	165
About the Author and Contributors	171
Index	175

Series Foreword

Psychology is the science of behavior; it is the field that examines how and why people do, feel, and think the things that they do. However, in a very real way, everyone is a psychologist. Each of us observes and tries to understand the thoughts, feelings, and behaviors of people we are around, as well as trying to understand ourselves. Have you ever thought, "I wonder why she did that?" Or perhaps, "Why did I do that; it makes no sense." If you have, then you are asking psychological questions. Most people enjoy being "students of human behavior" and observing and thinking about people, human nature, and all of the variants of the human condition. The difference between "most people" and psychologists is that the psychologist has spent many years in school studying and learning about people.

In addition to studying and doing research, psychologists also work directly with people in many settings. For example, clinical and counseling psychologists work with people who are dealing with psychological disorders or are having problems in their lives that require professional assistance, but there are many other branches of psychology as well. Sport psychologists work with athletes and teams to improve performance and team functioning. Industrial/organizational psychologists help workers, managers, and organizations function more effectively and efficiently. Military psychologists deal with military personnel and organizations. Forensic psychologists work with police and other law enforcement organizations to help solve crimes and assist law enforcement personnel. In addition to all of the things that psychologists know about people, for any person, understanding psychology can help take advantage of what psychologists have learned to help all people live better and healthier lives and to deal more effectively with others.

The Psychology of Everyday Life is a series of books that will address many different and important psychological issues and areas, the goal being to provide information and examples of how psychology touches all of our lives on a daily basis. The series will also show ways in which psychological knowledge can help us. These books will address psychological concerns with the most up-to-date and relevant knowledge from the field of psychology. Information from the laboratories, classrooms, clinics, hospitals, and other settings will be brought together to help make sense out of some important and often complex ideas. However, these books will be directed toward readers who are not psychologists, but are interested in learning more about the field and what it has to offer. Thus, the language is not technical but is common language addressing "regular" people. There will be times when professional and technical language may be used, but only if thoroughly explained and related to the issues being discussed.

This series of books will focus on specific facets of our daily lives and show how psychology can help us understand and deal with these issues. A wide range of topics will be covered, from eating to exercising to relaxing to interpersonal conflict. Each book will consist of three distinct parts. Part I will answer the "who/what/where/when/why/how" questions related to the topic. These chapters will examine everything from how the subject manifests in our day-to-day lives and how it impacts our psychological well-being to differences across the life span and cultures to what famous psychologists have to say on the subject.

Part II in each book will focus on "real-life" examples and will address many of the issues that were introduced in each book in Part I, but will do so with examples and explanations that will make the issues even clearer. It is one thing to have knowledge, but it is an entirely different thing to be able to apply and use that knowledge, and this is what will be covered by the scenarios and interpretative analyses in Part II. When people read Part II they will begin to see many of the ways in which our daily lives are touched by psychology, and the many ways that psychology can be used to support and help people.

Part III in each book will address the controversial issues related to the book's subject. Like any academic and professional discipline, psychology has many areas where there are spirited disagreements among academics, practitioners, and researchers about important issues in the field. It will be very instructive for people to understand these issues and to see the careful and systematic ways that scholars think about and conceptualize various topics, and to see how they debate, discuss, and resolve some of their differences of opinion. For non-psychologists these controversial issues and how they are addressed will lead to a greater understanding of psychological matters, but also a better grasp of how scientists and professionals deal with differences and controversies and how these disagreements are addressed.

Psychology is a broad and diverse field with many different approaches, theories, methods, and ideas, and to capture this field in its breadth and depth would be impossible in a single book. This series of books, however, will serve as an introductory journey through psychology as it relates to the daily lives of ordinary people. I have been teaching, studying, and practicing psychology for many decades, and I can hardly wait to read each of the books in this very exciting series, and I welcome readers to take this journey with me.

Rudy Nydegger, PhD, ABPP

Preface

Chilling Out: The Psychology of Relaxation is one of the books in a series on *Psychology in Everyday Life*. This book is of particular interest for those who struggle with managing stress and finding effective ways to relax. It is also for those who want to learn more about how our bodies respond to both being stressed and being relaxed. In fact, these are the same things that drew me to this topic area. Although I have improved my ability to recognize and manage my levels of stress, I continue to struggle with finding ways to help quiet my mind and body on a consistent basis. Thus, researching and writing this book was as much about sharing what is known about the science and practice of relaxation as it was instructional for me personally.

As already noted, this book covers both the science and the practice of relaxation. The book is organized into three parts. Part I includes several chapters on the nature of relaxation, including specific techniques, what is good and not so good about relaxation, what relaxation looks like throughout the life span, and how various cultures across the globe practice relaxation. The reader is eased into the subject of relaxation via Chapter 1, which discusses ways in which one may already relax, followed by Chapter 2, on what professionals recommend as effective forms of relaxation. Chapter 3 focuses on the positive and negative effects of relaxation, and Chapter 4 introduces readers to a few theories that have been put forth regarding relaxation—how it works and why it is important. Chapters 5 and 6, respectively, encourage readers to contemplate how the use of relaxation can be tailored to an individual's needs depending on how old they are, and what people who live in cultures different from that of the United States do in order to reach a state of relaxation.

Part II is devoted to five different scenarios and their interpretations. Readers are presented with a description of various situations that occur in real life and how they can be handled. The first scenario describes an elementary school-aged boy's struggle to go to school. The second scenario involves an adult toward the end of middle age coming to terms with receiving a serious medical diagnosis. The third scenario illustrates how a high school girl struggles to handle the pressure of performing. The fourth scenario describes a middle-aged, married mother who begins to abuse caffeine and alcohol in an effort to manage stress and sleep. Finally, the fifth scenario involves a high school girl who is struggling in school but is unable to handle this without being disruptive in class and eventually mildly explosive. Each scenario is followed by an interpretation of what occurred in the scenario and what was done to help each person cope more effectively.

Part III addresses debates and controversies in the area of relaxation. Although it may seem as if relaxation is not a terribly controversial subject nor that there would be areas rife for debate, three questions are posed with answers on either side of the issue presented by six different scholars. The initial debate addresses the question of whether or not relaxation drinks actually work. Relaxation drinks are the counterparts of energy drinks, and the two essays addressing this topic effectively tackle an issue to which much scientific effort has not been devoted. One scholar takes the position that these drinks can help people relax, whereas the other takes the position that they cannot. Debate number two addresses the idea of whether or not American culture encourages or discourages relaxation. Readers may have their own immediate answer to this issue but are encouraged to read both sides of the debate, which are effectively addressed by two professionals. The third debate addresses whether or not medication should be used to help people relax or whether or not new behaviors should be learned. The two scholars responding to this debate question are practitioners in their respective fields and present compelling arguments for their respective side in this debate.

Finally, this book includes a resource section containing both online and print sources, a glossary of terms that may be unfamiliar to readers, and a bibliography of sources from which information included in this book was gleaned.

I hope you enjoy learning about the science behind both stress and relaxation and experimenting with various forms of relaxation that work for you!

Acknowledgments

Completing this project could not have been possible without a great deal of support. I would like to thank Husson University for granting me a sabbatical during which I was able to work on this book. Without their support it would not have been feasible for me to take on a project of this scope. I would also like to thank Dr. Justine Reel, who has been an informal mentor to me in my quest to become a published writer. She has trusted me to contribute to her published works and has supported me in my efforts to develop and publish my own work. I would also like to recognize the support I have received from my psychology colleagues at Husson University: Rachelle Smith, Chris Howard, and Lauren Holleb. They have been a joy to work with over the past several years and have also supported and encouraged me despite the amount of time I spent behind a closed office door endeavoring to meet my deadlines. I would also like to thank Maxine Taylor of ABC-CLIO. She has been instrumental in keeping me on track with deadlines and content throughout the process of writing this book while also providing encouragement along the way.

Part I

Relaxation in Everyday Life

1

What: The Many Forms of Relaxation

Relaxation, or the lack thereof, is a mind and body phenomenon. Scientific evidence in many areas of health has consistently recognized the connection between the health of the body and the health of the mind. The conclusion is that if your body is not healthy, your mental health can also suffer, and if you are struggling with mental health concerns, your body may also show signs of distress. Throughout this book the use of the term *relax* and all of its forms (e.g., relaxation, relaxing) is intended to refer to both the mind and the body. That is, in order to be relaxed, one must have a quiet mind and a quiet body. These ideas will be discussed in more detail in later sections of this book.

WAYS YOU MAY ALREADY RELAX

As the title of this chapter indicates, there are a multitude of ways to relax. There are things that you and/or your friends and family may already be doing that you may not have realized are forms of relaxation. There are also specific techniques that professionals recommend and that have been found scientifically to be effective. To begin, we'll look at the various ways you may already relax in your daily life.

Hanging Out on the Couch

Now more than ever people spend much of their time inside, often sitting in front of a screen of some type or another. This has been a source of concern for some, and in fact, increasingly more evidence is showing that too much time sitting can have a significantly negative impact on one's physical health, especially for adults. So, in this case, it *is* possible to do too much of this particular form of relaxation. When done appropriately, however, and in moderation, sitting can be an effective relaxation strategy especially for those who do not routinely allow themselves to slow down.

Many people live highly stressful lives, not just adults. They are constantly doing something for themselves or others and often are going from one activity to the next without much time in between. As a result, their minds and bodies rarely have time to slow down. For some even going to sleep is not a rejuvenating activity as they may be unable to sleep due to being preoccupied by what needs to be accomplished. For these folks it is critical that they learn how to relax, and one way to do that is by physically sitting in a chair (or on a couch) and giving their mind something else on which it can focus.

Watching a television show, surfing the Internet, or playing a video game of some type can be activities that are absorbing enough that the worries of one's daily life fade into the background, at least temporarily. It is common for people engaged in these types of activities to be aware that their minds *go blank*, and some even talk about *being in the zone*, meaning that they are so focused on what is going on in front of them that they are unaware of anything else going on around them. This experience allows them to enter a relaxed state.

To be fair, some people report that some screen-based activities can be highly stressful. A new area of scientific study is the effect of social media on well-being. Increasingly, scientists are finding that engaging in certain types of social media can lead to a decrease in self-esteem and additionally can lead to having a stressful experience. So it is certainly important to be aware of how such activities affect you. If you are a highly competitive person, playing video games that allow you to compete with others may not be relaxing. If you often compare yourself to others and end up feeling like your life is terrible, social media will not likely be a relaxing activity. Finally, some television shows are specifically designed to evoke emotional reactions in the viewer. If you are particularly sensitive to dramas or action/thriller-type shows, a different genre may be more relaxing for you.

Many of us already spend a lot of time sitting. If you do, and you do not find that you are relaxed as a result, it is recommended that you take a look at whether you can change what you're doing when you are sitting so you can feel more relaxed. If this method of relaxation is just not effective for you, then it is likely that you'll need to employ a different method to encourage your mind and body to slow down.

Hugging

Maybe you just need a hug. Yes, seriously. According to neurophysiologist Jürgen Sandkühler, who is head of the Centre for Brain Research at the Medical University of Vienna, hugging someone has been scientifically shown to increase the production of the hormone oxytocin, which increases the bond that exists between people who care about one another. Dr. Sandkühler also noted that when this hormone is released into your system, you can also experience a decrease in stress and anxiety as well as lower blood pressure and an improvement in mood.

An important factor when using hugs to de-stress, however, is that you can't just go around randomly hugging people. In order to get the benefits of a hug, it is important to hug only someone you trust and who wants to be hugged. If you can remember a time you hugged someone under these circumstances, chances are good that your recollection will be that the hug felt good to you and you may even remember feeling calmer afterward. By contrast, if you ever received an unwanted hug (i.e., by someone you didn't know, or you weren't in the mood for one) or a hug that felt more like an obligation than a sign of affection, it probably felt awkward and may have even made you feel a little worse than before.

A hug can be a quick and easy way to experience a reduction in stress and therefore an increase in relaxation. Find someone you care about and who cares about you back and ask for a hug. Chances are good you'll both feel better.

Time with Your Pets

Time with pets can be considered "pet therapy." While technically this is not true in the sense that spending time with pets does not *cure* mental illness (nor does this term refer to therapy *for* pets), time with pets can be very therapeutic (i.e., have beneficial effects).

Research in this area routinely shows that those who have another living thing to care for report having a higher degree of life satisfaction and increased self-esteem. Research also shows that the act of petting an animal can lower one's blood pressure. Many people with pets talk about them as being members of their family, of being their best friends, or use other terms of endearment. Thus, those with pets already know how beneficial having a pet can be.

Spending time with pets can include holding a pet and petting them, talking with them, playing with them, or just watching them. With some pets, of course, you can do all of those things. Dogs and cats being among the most popular pets can provide a great deal of comfort and joy. For those with allergies or those living in places that do not allow such pets, other living creatures can still provide similar beneficial experiences, such as smaller furry creatures including hamsters, gerbils, and guinea pigs. Although fish do not allow for the same types of interactions that mammals can, watching a fish swim around a tank can be soothing. Moreover, some fish are able to learn and may interact with those who regularly feed and/or watch them.

There are, of course, many things to consider when bringing a pet into your life, including whether or not you have the time, space, and money to ensure your pet is properly cared for. When those things are in place, pets can bring a lot of joy to people's lives, including serenity and relaxation.

Expressing Your Own Creativity

Not everyone believes they are creative. Usually that assessment is based on the notion that one's creative efforts have to be *good* and/or that others think what they've created has value. When we divorce ourselves from the expectations or evaluations of others and allow ourselves to just create, we give ourselves the opportunity not only to engage in self-expression but also to lose ourselves in something that can take us away from the stressors of daily life.

The kind of creativity indicated here is not attached to a grade or a paycheck but to an activity that you do just for yourself. You can do something as simple as taking a blank piece of paper and drawing a continuous line with a black crayon that curves and twists across the page and crosses itself many times. You can then choose different colors and fill in the various white spaces created by the line drawing. Pick random colors or a theme of colors (e.g., yellows and greens, or blues and pinks). Of course, for some this might sound like an awful waste of time or something quite boring. The point is that creativity doesn't have to be something elaborate. Ideally it should be something you enjoy. The act of drawing and coloring something like this allows you to create anything you want for no particular purpose other than enjoyment. Crayons aren't just for kids. If the idea of a box of brand new crayons is appealing, go buy some and create something just because you can.

You can use blank pieces of printer/copy paper, or find pages from a magazine or newspaper. Draw whatever you want; use various colors (or stick to monochromatic) from pens, crayons, pencils, chalk, markers, paint, or charcoal. For those who have no interest whatsoever in this type of outlet, consider using clay to sculpt, natural materials from your yard to craft almost anything, or broken pottery or glass recycled into something else. You can sing in the shower, in your car, or with a group that gets together every now and then. Experiment with playing an instrument or take lessons. The point is there are myriad ways to be creative. You certainly don't have to do what everyone else is doing or in the way they are doing it. But if you're not sure where to begin, figure out what materials/instruments you need if any and if you need to spend money to get started (around the start of the school year, you can find 24 packs of crayons for less than $0.25). You can also consult the Internet and sites such as *Pinterest* for simple or more challenging projects.

It doesn't matter what you do. It doesn't matter if you're any good. The act of creating something can be rewarding in a multitude of ways.

Experiencing Other People's Creativity

If embarking on your own creative adventure is too intimidating or simply not appealing, you can enjoy the fruits of other people's creativity. Listening to music is something that most people do and enjoy. Indeed, music is a part of many other things we do: watching television and movies involves listening to music, there is nearly always music at sporting events, and people usually play music during social gatherings.

Music is an art, like most other forms, that is often designed to evoke a particular emotion or state of being. This can be done through lyrics or through the tune itself. When people ask what kind of music you like, you may find that difficult to answer because what may be a favorite piece of music today is not tomorrow and may be dependent on your state of mind. You may also like one song for its lyrics or another for the melody. Some types of music may energize you while other types may help you to wind down. As with most other things, what is soothing and calming to you may not be to someone else and vice versa.

In addition to music, there are, of course, other forms of art that can be relaxing. Walking through the halls of a museum to look at and think about paintings, sculptures, mosaics, and armaments is often peaceful in part because people tend to speak in hushed voices or not at all. The distractions are minimal, so it is possible to get lost in a work of art and therefore pulled away from the concerns and stressors of daily life. A similar experience can be found walking through an arboretum, or an elaborate garden. Attending a concert, play, or musical theater can have a similar effect. Similar to the music we choose to listen to, the performance one chooses to attend may not result in a sense of relaxation particularly if the theme or tone of the performance is intense or highly emotional.

Finally, reading a book can be a wonderful way to focus on nothing but the story being told. It is not that uncommon for people to fall asleep while reading, not because the story or topic is boring (although that can certainly be the case), but because the brain has been allowed to slow down and focus only on one thing, thereby allowing the body to relax as well.

Long Hot Baths

Taking hot baths is not a modern phenomenon. Bath houses were abundant in Ancient Rome long before heating water was a relatively simple endeavor. There are bath houses today that are often connected to what many of us know as a spa. These are places where people go to be pampered and to relax. Although a spa will employ a multitude of services to help patrons relax, using heat is among one of the most common mediums.

Saunas, hot stone massage, and hot baths can have very therapeutic effects. The heat can reduce muscle tightness and cramps. Soaking in a tub of hot water in the comfort of your own home will have these effects as well. Hot baths can have the same effects as a massage. Muscle tissue becomes more elastic and a reduction in overall tension can diminish headaches. Moreover, heated water can facilitate blood flow, thereby aiding in the healing process for injured tissue. Readers who are athletes will likely understand the calming and healing effects of warm water therapy as many athletic training rooms across the country are equipped with small whirlpool baths sized for an arm or a leg to be submerged or baths large enough for one's entire body.

Taking a long bath in water hot enough to reduce tension can contribute to overall relaxation. It is important to note, however, that taking a hot bath is not safe for all conditions. In some cases, taking a cold bath will be more healing for one's ailment but will not likely be relaxing since the water temperature is usually set to more than 40 degrees below body temperature. A physician or other credentialed medical professional can determine whether or not it is safe for you to take a hot bath. If you get the go-ahead, it is a highly recommended way to relax.

Yoga and Stretching

Yoga studios seem to be increasing in abundance and popularity. The increase in the mainstream practice of yoga seems to coincide with the increase in the scientific study of the effects of this ancient practice.

Some studies indicate that yoga may reduce risk factors for cardiovascular disease, and it may affect the brain such that improvements in depression and anxiety can be experienced. Various traditions of yoga exist (e.g., Buddhist, Hindu), but all seem to exist for the purpose of attaining peace or stillness.

An additional factor in the increase in popularity of yoga may be that many professional athletes have publicly acknowledged that they practice yoga. A recent article published online identified several professional athletes, coaches, and teams that practice yoga. Among them is New Zealand's rugby team All Blacks. This is an aggressive team known for performing the *Haka*, the traditional Maori war dance, to intimidate their opponents—probably not the first on most people's list of who would use yoga. Elite athletes have recognized the benefits of yoga not only as an exercise technique but also as an activity that can help with stretching, balance, mindfulness, and relaxation.

There are many how-to videos available online, streaming, and DVDs in addition to the classes in which students can enroll for in-person instruction. To the novice, yoga may appear to be easy. After all it is just a series of breathing techniques, stretches, and poses; however, there is beginner yoga and advanced yoga. Those who have never practiced yoga are encouraged to find a beginner's class no matter your level of fitness. As many professional athletes will attest, yoga is a lot more difficult than it looks.

When practiced appropriately, and with the proper mind-set, yoga can not only aid in your ability to find a sense of peace and relaxation but will also improve your body's ability to function more efficiently and effortlessly.

Massage

The word *massage* has multiple origins, all of which refer to kneading, touch, dough, or to feel. Indeed, a massage involves the manipulation of muscle and connective tissue not unlike kneading bread dough. For those of you who have had a massage, this analogy probably makes sense.

A massage can certainly be performed by a friend or family member. In fact, it is not uncommon for people to give one another a shoulder or back rub without any formal training. Most who receive this type of massage are likely to characterize it as relaxing. A massage performed by a professional masseuse/masseur is a very different experience and can help get you to a deeper state of relaxation. Seeking a massage from a respected professional means that they will take into account any medical concerns and particular areas of tension or soreness and, perhaps most importantly for some, will respect your modesty and with what state of undress you are most comfortable.

Professionals have an in-depth knowledge of the musculoskeletal system and will therefore know which muscles to manipulate in order to help alleviate joint pain, other aches, and overall muscle tightness. They will also be well trained and experienced to know how much pressure to apply for maximum relief and relaxation. Although there are myriad forms of massage, a common form in this country is the Swedish massage, which includes long, flowing movement and kneading. Some professionals may also specialize in massage for athletes or pregnant women.

Massage is a well-known technique that facilitates the healing process after an injury, results in relaxation and an increased sense of well-being, provides pain relief, and improves depression and anxiety. For those who want to try massage but are uncertain about a full-body massage, there are often opportunities to receive a shoulder and back massage that simply requires sitting on a special chair and does not involve taking off any clothes (other than a bulky jacket or sweater). These massages tend to be shorter in duration (e.g., 5–10 minutes) than a full-body massage that can last anywhere from 30 minutes to an hour and a half, but can still result in an overall sense of relaxation and tension reduction.

Meditation

Meditation is an ancient practice that may date as far back as the sixth and fifth centuries BCE. There are many different styles of meditation; thus, the term *meditation* often refers to a collection of disparate practices. Meditation can be practiced for the sake of the act itself or to achieve a specific outcome or to realize some benefit (e.g., inner peace, calm mind).

Generally speaking, meditation is practiced in order to train one's mind or to enter into a particular state of consciousness. Meditation is inextricably linked with religious practice and has connections to Buddhism, Taoism, Hinduism, Islam, and Christianity. In this context meditation is used to facilitate spiritual growth. In the 1950s and 1960s nonreligious forms of meditation were introduced to various countries throughout the world for the purposes of helping people improve themselves and for stress reduction.

Since that time, meditation has been scientifically studied to determine the range of physical and mental benefits of this particular practice. As with many of the other relaxation techniques, meditation has been shown to have beneficial effects in a variety of areas, including decrease in anxiety and depression, improved cognitive functioning, reduction in blood pressure, and lower production of stress hormones.

Although some may shy away from meditation due to its connection with various religious traditions, and others may find sitting in a *lotus* position while chanting not particularly appealing, meditation can take various forms and does not have to be connected with any religion of any kind. When practiced for the purpose of relaxation, the benefits for the mind and body are numerous, and thus it may be worth taking the time to learn how to meditate effectively.

Exercise

Exercise may seem like a strange activity to include in a book on relaxation, especially since it is included as a relaxation *technique*. Those who have exercised know that vigorous exercise increases heart rate and breathing rate and calls upon muscles to work hard. This hardly seems like an activity that can be relaxing. True. Usually the activity itself is not relaxing. It is what occurs when the exercise is concluded that makes exercise an effective relaxation strategy.

As will be discussed in more detail in later sections of this book, our body reacts predictably to increases in stress. The sympathetic nervous system, a branch of the autonomic nervous system, is designed specifically to make sure our bodies are ready to respond should we need to take action quickly (i.e., fight or flight). Engaging in physical activity activates this system as our brains and bodies recognize that proper energy is required in order to do what we're asking our bodies to do. Our heart rate increases to improve blood flow to our extremities and our breathing increases to further oxygenate our blood. This is surely not relaxing. However, when we stop exercising, another branch of the autonomic nervous system kicks in and slows everything down: this is what can make exercise relaxing. The parasympathetic nervous system functions to reverse the activating effects of the sympathetic nervous system. Thus, heart rate and breathing slows, among other things.

One of the things that is often recommended for those who struggle with anxiety is to engage in some form of physical activity (e.g., run around the block, do some push-ups or sit-ups). Anxiety alone can activate the sympathetic nervous system, and in the absence of the parasympathetic nervous system kicking in, the body will remain amped up and unable to slow down. This can have devastating medical consequences (see Chapter 2 for more information). Exercise, on the other hand, activates the sympathetic nervous system for a different reason, so when the physical activity is over, the parasympathetic nervous system gets activated and the body's systems slow down.

Finally, some regular exercisers and/or athletes may recognize feeling relaxed or at peace *in the midst of their activity*. When this happens, it usually occurs in the context of a repetitive activity taking place over some period of time. The repetitive nature of the activity, assuming the activity itself is not novel to the exerciser, allows the brain to disconnect from the activity at hand. Those who walk, run, bike, (either outside or on a machine), swim, or engage in any other repetitive activity often find they are able to daydream, think through the day's problems, or simply listen to music. They often characterize the experience as relaxing or peaceful in and of itself.

Of course, not everyone has such positive things to say about exercise. Indeed, exercise for the purpose of relaxation will not make sense for everyone. Thus, as with all other forms of relaxation, it is important to consider whether this is an ideal relaxation technique for you. Regardless, even if exercise is not relaxing, it is a highly recommended activity (assuming you are healthy enough for exercise) since the benefits of exercise on the mind and body are extraordinary.

None of the forms of relaxation mentioned above are guaranteed to result in relaxation for everyone, but they are often associated with feeling relaxed and thus worth trying. Certainly, some of the methods discussed above may sound quite appealing, whereas others might very well sound like they would be the last thing you would ever do. And, of course, there may be things you do that you know are relaxing for you but were not mentioned above. The important thing to take away from this section is that there are quite a few, relatively easy things you can do to relax, but the key is to figure out not only what works for you (i.e., helps you to actually relax) but also what you are *willing* to do. Relaxation techniques are not one-size-fits-all endeavors, so be choosy and remember that what works for someone you know may not work for you.

WHAT THE PROFESSIONALS RECOMMEND

Some of the methods of relaxation mentioned above are routinely recommended by professionals not only for relaxation but also for the other benefits they may offer (e.g., decrease in depressed mood, improved functioning of the body, improved memory). What follows below are forms of relaxation that were developed by professionals for the express purpose of inducing a relaxed state.

Deep Abdominal Breathing

Deep abdominal breathing is a relatively easy way to help manage stress and induce relaxation without having to get out of your chair. This relaxation technique is also referred to as diaphragmatic breathing, belly breathing, or deep breathing and is exactly what it sounds like—the diaphragm is inflated and the abdominal area or belly expands.

Many people do not do deep breathing correctly. Oftentimes what happens is people lift their shoulders and allow their chest to expand. While this is not harmful, it is generally not as efficient nor as effective as proper abdominal breathing. What ought to happen is the abdomen or "stomach" should expand when inhaling, and should shrink or contract when exhaling.

Engaging in this form of breathing allows more oxygen to be drawn into the lungs (this is, paradoxically, why people erroneously think their chest ought to expand when breathing deeply), which in turn pushes more oxygen into the bloodstream. Ultimately, this type of breathing is highly beneficial for muscles, which require oxygen for efficient and effective performance. Since the heart is also a muscle, the result of effective deep abdominal breathing is that the heart does not need to work as hard to push oxygen through the body because there is simply more oxygen already available.

If you remain unconvinced that your abdomen should be the area that expands when breathing deeply, consider individuals who engage in activities that get them to the point of being out of breath or requiring a lot of oxygen. Good examples of this are endurance athletes. Watch an athlete in the midst of their activity, especially when they are working particularly hard, and take note of how heavily they seem to be breathing. Then observe which part of their body expands each time they breathe. More often than not, you'll notice the abdomen expanding with each breath. Controversies in professional cycling aside, the men and women who race work extraordinarily hard and require massive amounts of oxygen in order to keep going despite the height of the mountain they climb or the miles they ride. Each breath they take shows up exactly where it should in their body in order to maximize the volume of oxygen inhaled: the abdomen. Watching a race like the Tour de France illustrates this quite well.

As noted above, deep abdominal breathing is a fairly simple technique; however, for those who are not used to breathing properly, abdominal breathing will take practice. It is recommended that you allow yourself up to two weeks of intentional practice before being able to rely on it as an effective relaxation technique. An effective way to practice and thus to know if you are breathing properly thereby getting the maximum benefit from each breath is to first either sit comfortably in a chair or lie on your back. Place your hands on your stomach so your two middle fingers just touch one another. When you inhale, your abdominal area should expand and your fingers should separate slightly (i.e., they will no longer be touching). When you exhale, your diaphragm will deflate, allowing your fingers to gently make contact again.

This inhale should be slow (e.g., for a count of 10) and through the nose, and the exhale should be for the same length of time and through the mouth. You can close your eyes if you wish. Once you feel confident in your ability to routinely breathe properly, you can engage in this type of breathing without anyone knowing you are using a relaxation technique. For example, if you have to give a speech and are feeling nervous, you can do several cycles (inhaling and exhaling is one cycle) of deep abdominal breathing in your chair or even at the podium before starting. Similarly, at the starting line of an athletic competition or right before a musical performance, deep abdominal breathing will not only fuel your body with much needed oxygen but will also interrupt the fight or flight response that gets activated and can interfere with performance when you're too anxious.

Deep abdominal breathing is highly recommended even if you don't need it as a relaxation technique. Engaging in this form of breathing will help the bodies of non-anxious people to function more effectively. For those who are prone to anxiety, this technique like so many others, when practiced properly and with regularity, will help to prevent stress-related diseases that are increasingly common in men and women. Additionally, you'll notice that other recommended relaxation techniques involve taking several deep breaths and/or incorporating deep breathing with the technique; therefore, learning how to do deep abdominal breathing will help you with other techniques discussed in this book.

Progressive Muscle Relaxation

Progressive muscle relaxation (PMR) is a method of relaxation adapted from Dr. Edmund Jacobson's progressive relaxation technique. Dr. Jacobson, a medical doctor who developed his technique in the 1920s and 1930s, recognized the connection between tension in the body and tension in the mind. He believed if human beings could reduce the tension in their bodies by relaxing their muscles, we would also experience a more relaxed state of mind. In addition to this supposition, he assumed that like many other skills and techniques, recognizing the difference between tension and relaxation can be learned through practice. He also noted that human beings cannot experience tension and relaxation simultaneously. That is, you cannot be stressed and relaxed at the same time. Learning how to relax the body (and the mind) therefore negates any tension we experience. We don't have to learn how to *not* be stressed. We simply have to learn how to be relaxed. Dr. Jacobson's progressive relaxation technique and its modern adaptation offer that opportunity.

To give you a sense of how much attention the progressive relaxation technique receives, an online search of this technique produced over 8,800,000 hits and a professional database search for scientific articles, book chapters, and books on various subjects related to this technique produced 1,200 results. Thus, this technique is discussed quite a bit among laypersons and garners a decent amount of attention by scientists who study the effectiveness of various relaxation techniques, including progressive relaxation. This technique is highly regarded as effective for relaxation.

Progressive relaxation requires a significant time commitment in comparison to deep abdominal breathing. Whereas deep abdominal breathing should be practiced 5–10 minutes a day and can be mastered in a couple of weeks, progressive relaxation should be practiced at least 20 minutes per day, and the original program developed by Dr. Jacobson involved more than 200 distinct relaxation exercises targeting different muscle groups. The program itself required several months to complete.

Despite the time commitment, the technique itself is simple in concept and practice. The idea is that we can achieve muscle relaxation by first tensing those muscles. For example, if you are aware of tightness in your muscles anywhere in your body, Dr. Jacobson's recommendation is to intentionally tense the muscles and then release them. By following his program, he said, the result would be a deep state of relaxation.

As noted above, the *PMR* technique is based on Dr. Jacobson's original work. Researchers and practitioners determined that a more simplified version of what Dr. Jacobson proposed was not only more practical but also just as effective as his original technique. Thus, instead of needing to devote months to complete hundreds of exercises, the contemporary version of this technique has been shortened to 15–20 muscle relaxation exercises and is discussed next.

The total time needed for each session is approximately 15–30 minutes depending on how well practiced you are and how long you take with each muscle exercise. You may also find that the more practiced you are, the less time you will need to achieve relaxation. This technique will be most effective for you if you are able to devote sufficient time to the technique, during which you know you will not be interrupted. It is recommended that you turn your cell phone off as well as other electronics that may interrupt your practice.

Be sure that wherever you choose to practice this technique the *location is quiet*. In addition to shutting off electronics, be sure family members, roommates, or anyone else will either not be around or will agree to not interrupt you. If there is background noise that you find difficult to shut out of your mind, it may be helpful to turn on something that generates white noise (e.g., a fan or machine that specifically generates white noise).

Ideally, you should practice this technique during a *regular or routine time*. In addition to practicing in the same location under the same circumstances, practicing at the same time will allow your body to be more amenable to relaxing. A concept call *state-dependent learning* suggests that when we learn something in a particular situation and/or state of mind, each time we practice we are much more likely to perform more effectively when we do what we have learned under the same circumstances. Thus, not unlike Pavlov's dog (the dog that drooled to the sound of Pavlov's bell because it had learned to expect food after hearing the bell), our bodies begin to recognize the repetitive signs of this technique and we will begin to relax prior to actually starting the technique itself.

Get into a comfortable position. All parts of your body should be fully supported, including your head. Thus, it is recommended for this technique that you assume a prone position by lying on a couch, bed, or the floor (assuming it is comfortable to do so). You can also sit in a chair that reclines and provides full body support. If you are feeling particularly tired, you may want to opt for sitting in a recliner so that you don't fall asleep. The goal here is to be relaxed but not to induce sleep. Also be sure the clothing you are wearing is not too tight and you remove all accessories (e.g., watches, jewelry, shoes) that may affect your ability to do each exercise or that may simply be a distraction.

Eliminate internal distractions by making sure you are as fully comfortable as possible. In addition to the fully supported position you assume as described above, be sure that you are not hungry or too full from having just eaten. You should be rested but not wired, your bladder should be empty, and you should commit to mentally putting aside your worries and concerns during the exercises. This last part can be challenging at first, but with practice it will become easier to accomplish.

Finally, approach this process with a *relaxed attitude*. As paradoxical as this may sound, do not try to make yourself relax. Rather, allow the relaxation to happen on its own by faithfully going through the exercises. Not everyone will achieve relaxation the first time through or even the first several times through, especially if you have a difficult time quieting your mind. That's okay. That's what practice is for. Relaxation will happen if you allow it to happen as a result of the process. Think about it another way: if you are *trying* to relax, you are expending mental energy to make something happen. The irony is your mind is actively working on something and therefore not at peace. Thus, relaxation will prove elusive.

There are professional recordings that can formally take you through a progressive relaxation routine. There is also an abundance of scripts available online or in books that can take you through the technique. A basic description of the process follows.

After you get yourself into a comfortable position under the conditions discussed above, it is a good idea to take several deep abdominal breaths as described in the previous section. There is some difference of opinion as to whether or not it makes sense to begin with the upper body or the lower body. The best progression is the one that produces the most effective results for you. As you practice this technique, you may want to experiment with the order of the muscle groups. The only thing that might suggest PMR should not be practiced at all is if you have injury to muscles that might be exacerbated by the intentional tensing of the injured muscles. It is possible, therefore, to perform a modified version of PMR by avoiding those muscle groups. As with other exercises like this, it is important to be sure your body is healthy enough for this type of activity by consulting with a medical professional.

A sample of the muscle groups and how to tense them include:

1. *Hands and lower arms*: allow arms to rest at your sides and make a tight fist with each hand and then release.
2. *Upper arms*: allow arms to rest at your sides and tense upper arm muscles and then release.
3. *Toes*: allow legs to rest on the floor or chair and curl toes then release.
4. *Feet/calves*: allow legs to rest on the floor or chair and point your toes tensing your feet and calves and then release.
5. *Legs*: extend both legs and raise them several inches off the floor or chair tensing your thigh muscles and then release.
6. *Stomach*: tense stomach muscles and then release.
7. *Buttocks*: pull them together and then release.
8. *Chest/shoulders*: press the palms of your hands together and push, and then release.
9. *Back*: push your back into the floor or chair and then release.
10. *Neck*: bring your chin to your chest and press down firmly, keeping the rest of your body relaxed, and then release.

11. *Jaw*: clench your teeth and then release.
12. *Eyes*: firmly clench eyelids shut and then release.
13. *Forehead*: raise your eyebrows as high as you can and then release.
14. Take a mental inventory of your body. If any area remains tense, repeat the exercise for that muscle group.

For each muscle group, focus on the tension in the muscles insofar as you know that they are tense but not strained or hurting. Beyond that, your mental energy during this technique should be focused on how relaxed each muscle group feels after completing each exercise. Notice the *before and after* tenseness feeling and how relaxed your entire body begins to feel. When practiced regularly, PMR can be a highly effective technique producing a calm mind and body.

Guided Relaxation and Imagery

Imagery is used for a variety of purposes, including enhancing performance, aiding in physical healing, pain management, and relaxation. Our focus, of course, will be on relaxation. Before diving in, however, it is worth discussing what imagery is and how it can be most effective regardless of its purpose.

Imagery is also referred to as *visualization*, *mental rehearsal*, and *mental practice*. The basic idea is that when using imagery you are picturing in your mind's eye a particular image or series of images. You can replay images you have previously experienced, create images you would like to experience, or conjure up something completely hypothetical that you don't intend to experience but intend to experience how the image makes you feel, for example, feeling at peace or relaxed.

Imagery is most effective when you can incorporate all of your senses into the movie playing out in your mind. For example, if you are imagining a scene on the beach, you will benefit from the imagery experience more fully if you not only picture the palm trees, the sand, and the water, but also *feel* the sand between your toes and the warmth of the sun on your skin. Additionally, you can imagine *smelling* the ocean breeze and the blooming flowers, while also *hearing* the breeze rustling the palm fronds while gentle waves roll onto the beach. If your scene involves food or anything else you might *taste*, it is useful to imagine that as well. The more senses you are able to incorporate, the better. This is not easy for everyone to do and can take a lot of practice. Some senses may be more difficult than others to include. If necessary, skip those senses and just use the ones that you are able to incorporate more easily.

When you are able to create images in your mind that are vivid and use as many senses as possible, it will seem even more real to your brain. That is, in fact, why imagery is so effective. Research with a variety of types of imagery has shown that particular areas of the brain are activated during imagery as if the person doing the imagery was *actually performing the task*. Thus, if your brain thinks you are actually on a beach listening to the waves roll onto shore and feeling the warm breeze on your skin, it will respond accordingly and relax.

Another factor that can improve the effectiveness of imagery is whether or not the images you "see" are from the outside looking in, like you're watching a movie, or from the inside looking out, like you are actually there experiencing it. The latter is known as "first person." This is a term with which some readers may be familiar especially those who play first person video games. If you're able to take the first person perspective in your imagery, it will feel more like you are actually experiencing the imagery and therefore the intended effects of the imagery (e.g., relaxation, improved performance) can be more pronounced.

As with PMR, there is an abundance of imagery scripts available online as well as professional recordings for sale. Imagery, however, tends to be more personal than PMR. In PMR, if you have an injured muscle group, or if you no longer have access to a muscle group due to amputation or congenital disease, you can skip that part of the exercise. Regardless, muscle groups are muscle groups. What makes one person's practice of PMR different from another's is how strongly and for how long a muscle group is tense. With imagery, however, a scene or series of scenes that would help one person feel relaxed might not look anything like what would be relaxing for another. Therefore, purchasing relaxation-oriented imagery CDs or MP3s may not be effective since they are taking a one size fits all approach.

In the brief example discussed above, you may have initially thought, *A beach scene? What's relaxing about that?* When flowers were mentioned, you may have started sneezing because you are highly sensitive to flower pollen. For some people, their scene would need to be devoid of people, whereas others might feel more relaxed being surrounded by friends and family or just your best friend. You get the idea. The scene that you would picture in your relaxation-based imagery is unique to you as is anyone else's. When possible it is helpful to create an imagery script that is tailored to you.

It used to be difficult to create your own relaxation and imagery tape. You needed recording equipment that most people did not have nor could easily get. Now, however, those who have computers simply need a recording program (some of which are freely available or included with software already on your computer) and a microphone. You can find a piece of music for the background that you like and that will facilitate relaxation, and then use a script that you create or modify one that already exists to best reflect your needs for relaxation.

If you do create your own script or modify one that already exists, be sure to keep or include several cycles of deep abdominal breathing. This will help slow your body and mind before you begin the imagery itself and you can therefore allow the relaxation to deepen as you imagine your peaceful and relaxing scene.

Biofeedback

Biofeedback is a technique that allows an individual to receive real-time information about how the body is responding. For example, the individual can *see* their heart rate increase/decrease, skin temperature rise/fall, or brain wave activity accelerate/slow down. The reason this type of unseen activity can be seen is that an instrument designed specifically to measure a particular physiological response is attached to the individual. For example, electromyography (EMG) either applies electrodes to the skin's surface or inserts fine electrodes directly into muscle tissue in order to measure the muscle's electrical activity. Using biofeedback for this purpose has allowed professionals to more effectively treat a variety of ailments including posttraumatic stress disorder (PTSD), headaches, and pain. A feedback thermometer, attached to a finger, measures changes in skin temperature, which results from changes in blood vessels. Noting changes in skin temperature can help individuals manage stress, headaches, pain, and anxiety. An electroencephalograph (EEG) is used to measure brain activity by detecting changes in the electrical activity occurring below the surface of the scalp's skin on which the sensors are applied. Many other instruments are used in biofeedback, but these are some common ones.

Feedback thermometers can be pretty simple, involving holding a small thermometer between your thumb and forefinger and noticing any changes that occur. As you might imagine, such a device is not terribly sensitive to small changes in skin temperature and is not as accurate as one that is used by a professional. The other two devices mentioned above tend not to be available to the general public. Thus, it is recommended that the most effective use of biofeedback will involve working with a well-trained professional who not only knows how to use the necessary equipment but can also help accurately interpret what the results mean. Ultimately, the purpose of biofeedback is to use the information generated by the apparatus being used so that the individual can purposefully manipulate their physiology to get the desired results. For example, sharp shooters or snipers learn how to control their breathing and heart rate so that they are not too aroused. Being able to predict when the heart will beat and how strongly allows the shooter to time the pull of the trigger to hit their target.

For the purpose of relaxation, monitoring brainwave activity can be highly effective. People who have difficulty relaxing are often dealing with a "racing mind," which will show up in brainwave activity. An individual using biofeedback to help with relaxation can see how active their brain is when they are feeling stressed or anxious. They can then engage in deep abdominal breathing, guided imagery, or cognitive behavioral therapy (or some combination). As they engage the part of their nervous system that slows body functions down, they will be able to observe changes in brainwave activity—thus they can "see" their brain start to relax.

Similarly, EMG can be used to give real-time feedback to the individual with respect to their degree of muscle tension. Individuals can be shown rather clearly what happens when their muscles are tense and when they are more relaxed. The EMG can be used to monitor problem muscle groups (e.g., neck and shoulders, lower back) that are known to be routinely tense. When engaging in a relaxation technique (e.g., deep abdominal breathing, PMR), the individual will witness changes in EMG data. When muscles are tense, there is more electrical activity, and when they are relaxed, electrical activity is diminished.

Biofeedback can be beneficial for anyone interested in learning about how particular systems in their body functions and what changes in these systems look like. It may, however, be especially useful for those who have difficulty trusting that their body is doing what it is supposed to do during relaxation. Biofeedback provides hard data showing the individual that their body is, in fact, transitioning to a more relaxed state. The number of sessions needed to demonstrate ongoing effectiveness will vary by individual. Ideally, however, after sufficient biofeedback sessions, the individual will be able to recognize their body's signs of relaxation without having to rely on biofeedback for evidence.

As noted above, it is recommended that individuals interested in using biofeedback work with a trained professional. A variety of professionals can receive training in biofeedback, and a number of professional organizations are designed to educate professionals and protect the public from those who may not be fully qualified to use biofeedback. In some states, nonphysicians may not be allowed to use certain types of biofeedback instruments. It is important, therefore, to do your homework and determine if the professional with whom you plan to work has ample training and credentialing, and is allowed by the state to practice biofeedback.

Cognitive Behavioral Therapy

Cognitive behavioral therapy (CBT) is a form of therapy used by many mental health professionals. This form of therapy targets how a person thinks and behaves in order to treat ongoing concerns or diagnosable mental illness. Often attending to a person's thinking or cognitions is the primary focus of this form of treatment. The idea is that if you can change how you think, your behaviors and your mood will also change.

CBT has been studied in the treatment of a variety of psychological disorders, including depression, many anxiety disorders, certain eating disorders, and substance use disorders. As with the other techniques discussed above, the focus here will be on how CBT can be used to facilitate relaxation. Often a component of CBT when used for this purpose is deep abdominal breathing and PMR.

When using CBT, a mental health professional will help identify what behaviors you want to change, which in the context of relaxation is likely to be behaviors related to feeling stressed, nervous, or anxious. For example, you may feel anxious when you have to give a public talk or speech and you end up shaking, sweating, and fumbling your words, or are unable to do the talk altogether. Others may notice that they have a hard time sitting still long enough to relax in front of the television or computer, or to read a book. Still others may report a general feeling of uneasiness or low level of anxiety that doesn't seem to ever go away. In these and other situations, the professional will help to determine exactly when and where the feelings and behaviors related to stress and anxiety occur, which will in turn inform the effective use of CBT for the individual's needs.

Being able to determine exactly when these behaviors and feelings occur can then help you identify your cognitions or thoughts before, during, and after feeling stressed or anxious. A major idea behind CBT is that our thoughts influence our feelings and behaviors, so if we're able to change our thoughts, then our feelings and behaviors can also change. So identifying thoughts that occur just before feeling stressed can help to pinpoint what type of thoughts are likely contributing to these unpleasant experiences. For example, just before giving a speech in class, a student might be thinking things like *I'm terrible at this*, *I'm going to make a fool out of myself*, or *Everyone will laugh at me*. You can probably guess that these types of thoughts tend not to inspire confidence in one's self and often contribute to feeling anxious. A professional using cognitive behavioral techniques will work with the individual to help them become aware of these thoughts when they occur and to come up with different thoughts that counteract the negative thoughts. Examples of this might be: *I've done this before and I have done just fine, Everyone makes mistakes, It's not that big of a deal. I will just keep going,* or *I've practiced this several times and I'm ready.*

It is also important to identify thoughts that may occur *during* the experience that is highly stressful. For some people, feeling stressed or anxious causes negative thoughts to increase in volume and frequency. Some people who seek the assistance of a licensed mental health professional may describe the experience in terms of having racing thoughts that they can't quite identify, or in other cases like there is a theater of voices either talking or yelling all at once. Regardless, the experience is highly unpleasant and can often encourage the person to avoid situations like this altogether. In the example in the previous paragraph, if the person giving the speech had this type of experience, it may be negative enough that they may try to avoid giving speeches altogether regardless of the consequences (e.g., receiving a failing grade). In these cases it is important for the individual not only to have more positive or constructive thoughts at the ready but also to have practiced skills that will allow them to slow down and calm down in the moment (i.e., deep abdominal breathing or a brief imagery script).

Finally, identifying thoughts that occur *after* the stressful or anxious event can help to determine what may happen that keeps the negative feelings going. It is also possible to identify when positive feelings arise after the event is over. Or, in the case of someone trying to fix the situation so they don't feel that way again, they have the opportunity to determine what thoughts and feelings they have about their solution. This part of the process helps to illuminate what may be reinforcing or punishing in terms of the way they may approach the same type of situation in the future. For example, if someone decides that their solution to feeling anxious about giving speeches is to not do speeches at all, they may feel relief and have thoughts related to that feeling that is likely to reinforce their choice to not ever give speeches in class again. Or if they gave a speech and had thoughts related to the speech being terrible and negative thoughts about themselves as a student or human being (e.g., *I'm stupid, I'm worthless,* etc.), that is likely to feel like punishment and will probably mean that the student will dread giving speeches and perhaps will try to avoid them in the future. In these circumstances a cognitive behavioral therapist would work with the individual to challenge these negative thoughts and counterproductive behaviors.

When people get caught up in a loop of negative thinking, their thoughts are often global (i.e., *This happens everywhere in my life.*), stable (i.e., *It will always be this way.*), and often internal (i.e., *It's all my fault.*). This cycle of thinking is usually linked to feelings of depression; however, depression and anxiety often coexist. So when someone is caught up in this type of thought process, it could very well contribute to not only feelings of depression because they start to feel hopeless but also feelings of anxiety about future situations they may have to face and about which they are clearly not optimistic. Thus, it is important for CBT professionals to challenge what are usually referred to as "irrational" thoughts or beliefs. Often this is done by examining the evidence for the person's thoughts and beliefs by asking things such as:

"Has it really *always* been this way?"
"Is it really *impossible* for you to be able to do things differently?"
"Is it true that there is *nothing* good in your life?"

In some cases individuals are quick to understand that they are thinking in terms of absolutes or using black-and-white and either/or thinking, which is not rational. They are able to identify errors in their thinking and recognize that what they are telling themselves is just not true. In other cases, however, the thinking may have been going on for so long, or the negative experiences are so plentiful that it is difficult for the individual to see that their thinking is flawed. In these cases it simply takes more time and patience for the individual to see that their thinking is irrational, and there is, in fact, evidence demonstrating how inaccurate their thoughts have been.

CBT is simple in the sense that the therapist is not making in-depth interpretations about the motives behind the individual's thoughts and behaviors nor are they asking the individual to try something that takes a high degree of education or intelligence to do. It is simple. When an individual is taught and practices the types of techniques described above, they are eventually able to use them on their own. The irony is that CBT techniques can be some of the most difficult techniques to use because they require an enormous amount of sustained and vigilant effort. Moreover, the process also requires individuals to recognize that they are, in fact, thinking something when they are feeling badly. It is relatively common for people to say, *I'm not thinking anything* when asked about what they were thinking before, during, or after a particular event. So prior to the steps discussed above and below, it is important to establish that the person *is* thinking something. This can be done by suggesting that the next time they feel stressed or anxious, they should turn their attention to what was going through their mind. This can take some time since for many people the negative thoughts in question are so automatic and long-standing that they have become something akin to background noise and the individual isn't aware of them at all. When encouraged to *think about their thinking* over time, individuals usually do identify specific thoughts and often have a reaction like *I had no idea I was thinking that*. At that point individuals usually become more aware of the depth and breadth of their negative thoughts.

So, in addition to identifying that negative thoughts are occurring in the first place, CBT techniques are effective when the individual is able to (1) recognize the negative thoughts *when* they occur, (2) recognize the thoughts *every single time* they occur (or as close to that as possible), and (3) use the CBT strategies learned *each time* the thought occurs. Multiply this process by the different types of negative thoughts people have and the different strategies needed to counteract these thoughts, and the individual may have to go through this process most moments of the day for many days or weeks on end. Once individuals are encouraged to become more aware of their thinking, a common response can be, *I had no idea how negative my thoughts were or how often I think them*. They then come to realize how enormous the task is to use CBT techniques to change their thinking. Part of the work then becomes helping the individual persist in their efforts and cope with how emotionally and physically tiring it feels to do this work.

Although it is not necessary for the individual to use CBT techniques every time their negative thoughts occur in order for the process to work, it is true that the more often they are able to use the techniques, the more quickly they will notice positive changes in their thoughts, feelings, and behaviors.

The techniques discussed in this section are recommended by professionals to help people cope with feelings of stress or anxiety and thereby to move into a more relaxed and peaceful state of being. Some of these techniques often require working with a professional in an ongoing way or for a few consultation sessions to learn how to use a particular technique. If you find that you are unable to relax on your own or that you are unable to sustain feelings of relaxation, consulting with a professional might be a good next step.

2

Why: The Importance of Relaxation in Our Lives

In the discussion of various relaxation techniques in Chapter 1, there was mention of benefits related to these techniques. There was also mention of how they can serve to prevent negative physical or emotional experiences or address these experiences after the fact. In the following sections, the effects of stress and anxiety on the mind and body as well as the mechanisms behind the benefits of being able to relax will be discussed. The final section will address the most severe form of stress one can experience: an alarming trend of literally working one's self to death.

PHYSIOLOGICAL RESPONSE TO STRESS AND ANXIETY

In the previous chapter, the autonomic nervous system and its branches were referenced: the sympathetic and parasympathetic nervous systems. Although you may be inclined to tune out at this point because you are uninterested in physiology or are afraid it might be too scientific, it is important for you to not skip this section for two reasons. First of all, understanding what happens in your body under prolonged experiences of stress and anxiety can also help you understand why the body breaks down, resulting in stress-related disorders or, in extreme cases, death. The second reason not to tune out is that although physiological processes can be highly technical, this section will discuss them in as straightforward a manner as possible. There is certainly a great deal more to how the various branches of our nervous system work; however, the focus of this section will not be on such details. Readers interested in having a more technical understanding of the body's response to stress should consult a textbook on human physiology.

Our nervous system really is pretty simple. It controls all actions in our bodies: the one's we do on purpose (voluntary actions) and the ones that happen all on their own (involuntary actions). Examples of voluntary actions include walking or reaching for something. You have to make those things happen. By contrast, involuntary actions include things like digestion, heart beat, and respiration. You don't have to command your body to do those things or make them happen. They happen all on their own—which is a good thing. In order for all of these actions to take place, the body has to communicate with the brain and vice versa. Understanding this process means understanding how the various branches of our nervous system work.

The nervous system involves nerves or fibers that transmit electrical stimulation throughout the brain and body. These electrical signals help to make sure the brain and body are in constant and effective communication with each other. The nervous system is subdivided into two branches: the central nervous system and the peripheral nervous system. The central nervous system includes the brain and the spinal cord—that's it. The peripheral nervous system includes everything else; that is, all the nerves that connect to your muscles, organs (except the brain), and glands commanding them to take action are part of the peripheral nervous system.

To give you a basic idea of how the two major branches of the nervous system work together, consider the example of your heart beating. In order for your heart to beat properly (or at all), the heart itself has to be able to communicate with the part of the brain responsible for instructing it to beat (i.e., the medulla oblongata—a structure in the brain stem). When the brain sends a signal to the heart to beat (i.e., pump blood), the signal travels to the spinal cord and then out to the peripheral nervous system, where the message to circulate blood reaches the heart. The heart successfully beats and sends a signal back through the peripheral nervous system entering the central nervous system through the spinal cord and up to the brain. This signal from the heart lets the brain know not only that the heart got the brain's instructions but also that it successfully carried out the command and pumped blood. The entire process happens far more quickly than it took you to read the description of the process. Depending on what part of the body the impulse, or signal, is traveling to and for what purpose, the speed of the impulse can exceed 200 miles per hour. That's *faster* than a NASCAR on the straightaway of the Daytona 500 but 3 million times *slower* than the speed of the electrical impulse that travels to anything plugged into an outlet.

Now, in order to understand how and why our internal systems may operate more slowly or quickly at some times than at others, it is important to discuss the further subdivisions of the peripheral nervous system (remember this system includes nerves everywhere in the body *except* the brain and spinal cord). The peripheral nervous system is subdivided into the somatic and autonomic nervous systems. The somatic nervous system includes nerves that involve voluntary movement of the skeletal system (e.g., walking). The autonomic nervous system involves nerves that regulate involuntary functions such as heart rate, secretion of hormones, and breathing. The autonomic nervous system will be the focus of the rest of this section.

As noted previously, the autonomic nervous system includes the sympathetic and parasympathetic nervous systems. In the most basic language, the sympathetic nervous system speeds things up and the parasympathetic nervous system slows things down. Of course it's not quite that simple, but for our purposes this description will suffice. Many of you may be familiar with the concept of *fight or flight*—that applies here. The sympathetic nervous system controls the fight-or-flight response. The idea is that when we detect a threat to either the body or the mind, the sympathetic nervous system is activated and prepares our body to take aggressive or protective action: fight back or run away. Either of these responses is highly adaptive when the danger we detect is threatening our physical survival. That is, if we don't defend ourselves or get out of harm's way, we could die.

The sympathetic nervous system is able to help us in this way by calling into action the parts of our body and its systems that will help us to either fight or run away. For example, fighting or running requires that we are able to effectively use our arms and/or legs. Thus, during the fight-or-flight response, blood flow increases due to accelerated heart rate and blood pressure, and is directed out to our extremities. Similarly, we require more oxygen, so our breathing rate increases and the passageways into our lungs (bronchi) dilate, creating a larger opening for the air we inhale. Our pupils also dilate, which allows more light to reach our retinas. This provides more detail of our visual environment, which is important for accurately identifying the threat. Additionally, our bodies stop digesting and our immune system is lowered because the brain recognizes that these and other nonessential functions will not help in a dangerous situation.

The parasympathetic nervous system, on the other hand, reverses these processes: blood flow is circulated more evenly throughout the body, our heart rate and breathing slow, and our pupils constrict back to normal along with the bronchi of the lungs. The other systems in our bodies such as digestion and immunity also resume normal functioning. Things slow down or are resumed, and our body is brought back to a state of rest, or at least a reduced state of readiness to take action.

In the fight-or-flight response, our brain and body work together to mobilize all of our resources so that we get out of the threatening situation unscathed or at least alive. This is what happens when you almost get hit by a car and you feel your heart beating rapidly and you are breathing so fast you might hyperventilate. This is what happens when you see a dog charging at you and you don't know whether it is friendly or not. However, this is also what happens when the threat is psychological. Psychological threats are things that threaten our emotional well-being. These types of things are usually labeled *stressful* events. The brain recognizes these types of experiences as threats, just like the charging dog or the near-miss with the car. Therefore, the brain does not distinguish between the *I could actually die* type of threat and the *This just feels really awful* type of threat. This means that the psychological threats activate the same system as physical threats.

All of us experience stress throughout our lives. Stress can be the result of negative or positive events. For example, it is usually stressful when you get fired from your job or fail a test. But it is also stressful to get a job you want, ace a test, or even win the lottery. Stress is anything that results in a change in your environment regardless of whether you're happy for the change or mad about it. Usually we experience stress negatively the more we believe we do not have control over the stressful situation. Change can be construed as a psychological threat because we now have to adapt to something different and the question then becomes whether or not we'll be able to. You might be thinking at this point that some people thrive on change whereas others crumble. Exactly. We all experience changes in our lives (i.e., stress) differently. Ultimately it isn't the stress itself, but our reaction to or perception of the stressful event that can cause problems for us. Those who are more inclined to believe there is nothing they can do about the situation to make it better are likely to suffer more than those who believe they can influence the situation to make it precisely what they want it to be.

As noted above, any event the brain recognizes as a threat (physical or psychological) will result in the activation of the sympathetic nervous system. The problem with psychological threats is that there is nothing to physically fight against or to literally run away from. The threat itself lays in our perception of the situation, not the situation itself. Nonetheless, the brain takes action and sends signals to the rest of the body to be sure it is physically mobilized to take its own action. When the threat is one that might physically harm us, we take action via the fight-or-flight response. When the threat is over (we vanquished or escaped it), the brain recognizes this and the parasympathetic nervous system is activated to bring our entire system to homeostasis or balance. When the threat is psychological, this will not happen. Not unless you take action in another way. This means you have to do something to purposefully activate the parasympathetic nervous system rather than relying on your brain and body to manage things on their own. When the threat is psychological, unless you convince it otherwise, the brain will continue to register danger and keep your body mobilized. That means your heart rate will stay elevated, your breathing will remain more rapid than at rest, your digestion will not be allowed to re-regulate, and your immune system will remain suppressed. This is not good for you psychologically or physically. Over time your body can adapt to high levels of stress in an unhealthy way.

The general adaptation syndrome (GAS) was identified by Hans Selye over the course of his decades of work on the effects of stress. He proposed that GAS has three phases: alarm, resistance, and exhaustion. In the alarm phase the stressful event occurs and you experience an *alarm reaction*, which is your sympathetic nervous system kicking. During the *alarm* phase your body is notified of the threat and it mobilizes its resources so it can take action. During the second phase, *resistance*, you fight against the stressor using the physiological resources at your disposal. Part of this physiological process is the flooding of stress hormones throughout your body such as cortisol and adrenaline. The final phase, *exhaustion*, is reached if the stress persists. If you are unable to get away from the stress or eliminate it, the resources made available to you will be used up and any reserves you have will be depleted. Under these conditions you are more susceptible to getting ill, and if pushed too far, your body may start to shut down, ultimately resulting in severe illness or death.

In the following two sections, the physical and psychological effects of a chronically activated sympathetic nervous system will be discussed. When the threat is psychological in nature, you can take action to prevent stress-related illness and disease. You can engage in any of the relaxation techniques discussed in Chapter 1.

PHYSICAL HEALTH EFFECTS OF CHRONIC STRESS AND ANXIETY

The fight-or-flight response serves an adaptive function. Without it our species and all others with the capacity to respond similarly would not have survived. As you probably imagined or may have already known, when we are in the fight-or-flight mode, our body has to work quite a bit harder than it does when it is at rest. This is okay. We're built to be able to withstand this type of exertion; however, we are not built to be able to withstand activation of the fight-or-flight response over a prolonged period of time. Over time our body will start to wear out or shut down physically, psychologically, or both. In this section we'll look at the physical effects of chronic stress and anxiety. The following section will address the psychological effects.

There are numerous illnesses and diseases that are often a direct result of chronic stress or are made worse by experiencing too much stress. How much is too much and how long is chronic cannot be pinpointed because each of us responds differently. Some bodies can withstand more than others. Regardless, it's not advised to try to find your limit. Preventing as many of the negatives effects of stress and anxiety as possible is, however, highly recommended. It is also important to note that a diagnosis or ruling out of any of the conditions described below should be done by a qualified medical professional. Moreover, whether or not the presence of any of these disease processes is the result of stress or something more serious should also be determined by a trained medical professional. Below is a description of several stress-related conditions, but is not intended to be exhaustive.

The stress-related illness with which you may be most familiar is *heart disease*. As discussed in the previous section, when we're in the midst of the fight-or-flight response, our heart is working a lot harder than it normally does. Over a long enough period of time, this can result in hypertension or high blood pressure. This can, in turn, lead to more serious heart-related conditions like heart attack. A heart that is already weakened by previous events or age may not be able to withstand much heart-related excitement. Sometimes a single, acutely stressful event can result in a heart attack.

Gastrointestinal (GI) problems can also result from stress. For a long time many people believed that ulcers were the result of stress. What we know now is that stress does not cause ulcers, but it does make them worse. Problems in the GI system that can be caused by stress include chronic heartburn (a.k.a. gastro-esophageal reflux disease, or GERD) and irritable bowel syndrome (IBS). Heartburn is not about the heart, but is related to acid from the stomach entering the esophagus. The result is a burning sensation in the chest area. IBS involves abdominal pain and cramping along with changes in bowel movements (e.g., constipation, diarrhea). None of these experiences are pleasant and in many cases can be managed or prevented by managing one's level of stress.

Another stress-related malady that most readers have probably experienced is headaches. Headaches can include typical headaches that are unpleasant but not debilitating to migraines that can be accompanied by nausea or vomiting. The pain associated with headaches is experienced in the head or neck and is often easily dispatched with over-the-counter pain medications or relaxation exercises. Chronic headaches, of course, are unpleasant and may begin to impact one's psychological health as well. Therefore, a change in lifestyle may be in order rather than trying to quell the pain of each headache.

Asthma is a condition that affects millions of people of all ages. Asthma is the inflammation of the bronchi (airways) in the lungs. When the bronchi are inflamed, the openings narrow and thus there is less room for oxygen to get into the lungs. The result is wheezing, coughing, tightness in the chest, and shortness of breath. Asthma can be treated effectively with medication alone. Some forms of asthma require medication that has a long-term effect (prevents asthma attacks) whereas other medications are used in the midst of an asthma attack. While stress has not been shown to cause asthma, it can make asthma worse; thus, in addition to prescription medication, asthma sufferers may also benefit from managing stress via the use of relaxation techniques.

Another disease that can be exacerbated by high levels of stress is diabetes. Diabetes involves high levels of blood glucose (blood sugar) due to problems with insulin. If diabetes is not properly managed, it can result in myriad problems including vision problems, heart disease and stroke, amputations, and kidney disease. A fact sheet published by the Center for Disease Control (CDC) in 2014 estimated that over 9 percent of the population of the United States, or 29.1 million people, have diabetes. The CDC also indicated that between the years 2009 and 2012, 71 percent of adults aged 18 years or older who reported that they had diabetes also had high blood pressure (hypertension). Hypertension can be the result of things beyond a person's control (e.g., genetics, result of a disease process), but it can also result from experiencing a high degree of stress. Regardless, learning a variety of relaxation techniques can help manage this particular complication of diabetes.

Alzheimer's disease is a form of dementia that is believed to affect one in nine people in the United States according to the 2014 Alzheimer's Association Report. Alzheimer's is the result of the widespread death of nerve cells in the brain and overall loss of brain tissue. The brain starts dying and therefore cannot work properly. This is made apparent by the emergence of symptoms such as memory loss, confusion, difficulty with problem solving, and changes in personality. In 2006 a group of researchers out of the University of California, Irvine, found that stress hormones contribute to development of the characteristic problems in the brain associated with Alzheimer's. Since there is, as of yet, no cure for this disease, it is recommended that stress for individuals diagnosed with Alzheimer's be kept at a minimum and relaxation techniques used to help manage existing levels of stress.

Although there are other illnesses and diseases thought to be negatively impacted by stress, it is important to note that stress has also been linked overall to an accelerated aging process and premature death. Scientists interested in studying the effects of stress on how we age compared mothers who were experiencing high levels of stress due to being the caretakers of a chronically ill child to women who were not such caretakers. These researchers discovered evidence that stress in this case seemed to accelerate the aging process by approximately 9–17 years. Similarly, another group of researchers examined the effects of stress related to a group of elderly men and women who were taking care of their chronically ill spouse. When compared to another group of elderly men and women who were not taking care of a chronically ill spouse, the death rate was 63 percent higher in the caretaker group.

Stress management is vitally important to maintain one's overall physical health and to potentially prevent or slow down debilitating diseases and even premature death. Thus, reducing the effects of stress may help to slow signs of aging and may help you to live longer. Given the potential benefits that are available to maintaining a less stressful life, it is worth trying out a few of the relaxation techniques described in Chapter 1, or adding some additional techniques to the one's you already use.

MENTAL HEALTH EFFECTS OF CHRONIC STRESS AND ANXIETY

Just as stress can negatively impact our physical health, it can also negatively impact our mental health. In some cases, stress can be the cause of some psychiatric conditions.

There are a few psychiatric diagnoses that specifically include the experience of stress as a criterion of the diagnosis. The *Diagnostic and Statistical Manual of Mental Disorders* (DSM) recently reorganized how disorders are classified. The new category for stress-related disorders is *Trauma- and Stressor-Related Disorders*. The disorders included in this category are: reactive attachment disorder, disinhibited social engagement disorder, post-traumatic stress disorder, acute stress disorder, and adjustment disorders.

The first two disorders, reactive attachment disorder and disinhibited social engagement disorder, are disorders of childhood and are believed to be the result of a child not being provided adequate care. A child with reactive attachment disorder does not show the typical response to caregivers when stressed. They will rarely or very occasionally seek out a caregiver for comfort, and when they do receive comfort, it does not appear as if they are benefitting from the comfort. The explanation for this is that they were not provided stable care during their critical early childhood years and are therefore unlikely to seek comfort or respond to comfort when stressed.

Whereas children diagnosed with reactive attachment disorder are characterized by a tendency to withdraw from caregivers, children diagnosed with disinhibited social engagement disorder tend to engage inappropriately with adults, which is determined in part by cultural expectations. A child diagnosed with this disorder may readily interact verbally or physically with adults in a way that suggests a familiarity with the adult that does not exist. For example, the child may initiate hugging a stranger, or the child may willingly go with an unfamiliar adult without hesitation. Both disorders are rarely seen in clinical settings but demonstrate how the stress of inadequate care during childhood years can be significantly problematic.

Posttraumatic stress disorder, or PTSD, has become a relatively well-known disorder in part because of the publicized difficulties many men and women serving in the armed forces have as a result of active duty. Despite a greater societal recognition of the disorder, it is still a relatively rare phenomenon. The projected lifetime risk for developing PTSD in the United States by age 75 is just under 9 percent. It is true, however, that prevalence rates are likely higher in occupations where exposure to traumatic events is much higher (e.g., veterans, first responders). It is important to note that exposure to a traumatic event, no matter how serious the event is, does not in and of itself guarantee that the individual who experiences the event will develop PTSD. It is not known precisely why some people can be exposed to death or near-death experiences or other forms of violence and not develop PTSD whereas others do develop symptoms of the disorder.

The diagnosis of PTSD includes an extensive list of symptoms. These include intrusion of the traumatic experience through flashbacks, vivid dreams or memories, or signs of psychological or physical distress after experiencing something that reminds them of the trauma; avoiding anything associated with the traumatic event (e.g., people, places, events);

changes in thoughts or mood connected to the trauma (e.g., belief that they're to blame or that they're bad, social withdrawal, inability to experience positive feelings); and changes in arousal or reactivity to things connected to the trauma (e.g., exaggerated startle response, angry outbursts, self-destructive behaviors). The emergence of these symptoms can take place immediately following the traumatic event or they may not appear until years after the trauma. A diagnosis of PTSD, however, does not occur until symptoms have been present for at least one month. Prior to that time, most people who will eventually be diagnosed with PTSD meet the criteria for acute stress disorder, which has similar symptoms to PTSD, but the duration of symptoms is from three days to one month. Thus, it is possible for someone to experience what looks like PTSD, but their symptoms last only for several days to a few weeks. In that case, acute stress disorder is the appropriate diagnosis.

The final group of disorders in the *Trauma- and Stressor-Related Disorders* category is adjustment disorders. The primary symptom of this set of disorders is the development of emotional or behavioral problems in response to an identifiable stressful event that appear within three months of the event. The distress experienced is out of proportion to the event itself. This means, for example, that if a feeling of sadness or anger is expected with a particular event (e.g., loss of a job, divorce), the experience and expression of those feelings is much bigger than what would be expected. Additionally, these symptoms impair the person's ability to function in school, at work, or in social situations. Overall, this means that the stressful event impacts the person to such an extent that they are not able to function as they normally would in everyday life.

Two additional mental health disorders that are significantly affected by stress are depression and anxiety. Depression is formally diagnosed as *major depressive disorder* and anxiety encompasses 10 different anxiety disorders including *social anxiety*, *panic disorder*, *agoraphobia*, and *generalized anxiety disorder*.

Depression, or major depressive disorder, is one of several *depressive disorders*. Major depressive disorder is different than *feeling down* or *having the blues*. Many people will have periods in their life during which they feel sad or down. In instances like these, it is possible to experience a shift in mood by engaging in enjoyable experiences (e.g., going to the movies, hanging out with friends) or even by having someone try to cheer you up. Because this type of experience is fairly common, it can be difficult for the average person to understand why a clinically depressed person can't just "snap out of it" or respond positively to the things that "should" cheer them up when they feel down.

Major depressive disorder involves what are called *depressive episodes*. These episodes last a minimum of two weeks but can sometimes last for months. They involve several symptoms including having a depressed mood, feeling a loss of interest or pleasure, and in some cases both. Other symptoms that can be a part of a depressive episode include difficulty sleeping or sleeping too much, eating too much or not eating enough, noticeably low energy, difficulty with decision making or stringing thoughts together, preoccupation with death including suicidal thoughts or actions, feelings of worthlessness, and restlessness or being slowed down to the extent that others notice. When someone experiences a combination of these symptoms, it is important for the person to receive professional help from a trained mental health professional. Although stress is not necessarily a cause of major depressive disorder, it can be. Stress can also be a contributing factor and can make the symptoms of depression more pronounced.

Social anxiety is characterized by having significant fear of any socially oriented situation in which the individual might be evaluated or judged. This might include meeting others for the first time, eating in front of others, or giving a performance. The overall fear in these situations is that the person will do something that might be embarrassing or humiliating, or that might cause them to be rejected by others. The types of events that often contribute to social anxiety would be considered to be stressful by most people; however, those with social anxiety will become debilitated by the intensity of their reaction to these events.

Panic disorder involves having *panic attacks*. Panic attacks are intense experiences of fear during which the person may feel chest pain, have heart palpitations, sweat, shake, feel nauseous, and fear that they are dying. While some people in everyday life might experience anxiety or fear and characterize their experience as a panic attack, often what they really mean is that they're *really* scared or anxious. A true panic attack is a terrifying experience. Individuals who have panic attacks fear having additional attacks and may go to great lengths to avoid situations in which they might have another one. Moreover, the fear of having another panic attack can in and of itself trigger an attack. Additional stress in the life of someone who has panic disorder may mean that they will experience more panic attacks than usual or experience more severe panic attacks.

The diagnosis of agoraphobia is done when a person has an intense fear of situations in which they do not think they will be able to escape or will be able to get help if needed. Situations that might provoke this fear include using public transportation, being in an enclosed space, being in an open space, being in a crowd, or being outside of one's home alone.

Some readers may think *I have this fear sometimes* and it's not that bad. However, some important features of agoraphobia that make it different than the fear someone without this disorder might experience are that the fear of the situation is so intense the individual avoids the situation altogether or endures it with significant distress, sometimes to the point of having panic attacks (in that case, both agoraphobia and panic disorder are diagnosed). Additionally, the fear is in excess of what would be expected of the situation (i.e., some fear may be expected, but at a certain point it is far beyond what would be expected). Just like the disorders mentioned above, everyday stress can make the symptoms of agoraphobia more intense.

Finally, generalized anxiety disorder (GAD) involves worrying excessively about a variety of activities or events. The worry is persistent and occurs more often than not for at least six months. As with the other diagnoses, GAD is a relatively uncommon phenomenon, but it is twice as likely to be diagnosed in women as in men. Additionally, the middle adulthood years are when the diagnosis is most likely to be made. This is a time when adults are establishing themselves more firmly in their careers and they are often caring for their own children as well as aging parents. Thus, stressors are likely to be higher in number during this time period. Although the symptoms of GAD are not as intense as the symptoms of the other anxiety disorders discussed above, the symptoms are enduring and don't have particular parameters that might help the individual avoid their symptoms. They simply experience their symptoms in most situations most of the time, which can lead to stress-related illnesses and other concerns.

A factor related to both depression and anxiety is something called *learned helplessness* and can precede the onset of either type of disorder. Learned helplessness is a behavior in which someone consistently experiences a situation that they try to fix or get out of. The situation itself is quite painful physically and/or psychologically. Despite the person's best efforts, the situation remains unchanged and they cannot get out of it. Over time this can lead to feeling like no matter what the person does, nothing will change, so they stop trying. Thus, they learn that they are helpless to do anything about this situation. This experience has been directly connected to clinical depression and anxiety. This also explains why some people seem like they have given up or reject any help offered to them—they have and they will because their experience tells them that nothing will work so it is not worth trying.

It is fair to say that each psychiatric diagnosis listed in the *DSM* could be covered in this section since all of them can be affected by one's overall level of stress. The ones selected are conditions familiar to most readers or are disorders where stress is a specific component of the diagnosis. Regardless, if you think about stress and how managing stress takes energy, it is easy to see that since we have a finite amount of energy to manage the experiences of our lives, when we run out of energy, it becomes harder to cope with life's challenges. Thus, dealing with stressful life events takes energy away from other pursuits including trying to cope with or recover from mental illness. In this way, managing one's overall stress becomes critical for one's overall health.

INCREASE IN STRESS LEADS TO UNHEALTHY BEHAVIORS

When we're stressed we usually try to do whatever it takes to feel less stressed. Some people naturally gravitate toward or have learned to use relaxation techniques like the ones already discussed in Chapter 1. Others may turn to behaviors that seem to help reduce stress immediately but ultimately do not have that effect and may eventually create more problems than the person had to start with. The maladaptive behaviors that seem to be the most powerful and therefore the most difficult to get rid of are the behaviors that make you feel better quickly. Usually what comes along with such fast-acting relief is that the feel-good effects tend not to last very long, leaving you faced with wanting or needing more relief more often. You may even need to engage in the behavior more intensely or more frequently than you did initially just to get the same sense of relief. If this sounds like drug abuse and addiction, then it won't surprise you at all to see that substance abuse and addiction are discussed below. Other behaviors can also have the same type of effect and will be similarly discussed.

Nicotine use, consumption of alcohol, and cannabis (a.k.a. marijuana) use are discussed here as it is not uncommon for people to turn to these substances to try to manage their stress. These three are also grouped together because they are legal drugs depending on your age and the state in which you live. (As of this printing, Colorado and Washington are the only states in which cannabis can be used for medicinal and recreational purposes. An additional eight states have legalized the medical use of cannabis.)

All three substances are referred to as *psychoactive* drugs, which means they can affect one's mood. The reason these substances have such an effect on mood is that they are chemicals that are introduced into our system and eventually make their way to the brain, where they interfere with the normal functioning of our brain's natural chemicals. This in turn can influence a variety of functions and experiences including mood.

When people use nicotine they often report that feelings of anxiety or frustration are reduced and their subjective experience is that they feel better when they smoke. The reason for this is that nicotine affects the neurotransmitter called dopamine. Dopamine is a powerful chemical that is involved in the pleasure centers of the brain. When dopamine is released, we can feel calmer and have an overall sense of feeling good. Nicotine is a chemical that among other things triggers the release of dopamine. Since it does not take long for nicotine to reach the brain when it is smoked (it only takes a matter of seconds), the good feelings that come with the release of dopamine happen quickly after you start smoking. This efficient and fast-acting mechanism is in part the reason why quitting smoking is one of the most difficult addictions to kick.

Although most people who smoke note that they do so to relax, the irony is that physiologically the body is under *more* stress when nicotine is introduced into the body's system. Since nicotine is a stimulant, there will be an increase in heart rate and blood pressure, and blood vessels constrict, which means less oxygen is getting to the brain. Lastly and perhaps most importantly, smoking does not actually fix the problem that caused the stress to begin with. So not only is the body under more stress from smoking (despite the psychological effects of dopamine release), the thing that originally caused the stress to begin with is still there.

When it comes to alcohol, the neurotransmitter that seems to be affected the most is called serotonin. This brain chemical is important for mood regulation. Serotonin levels can get out of balance for a variety of reasons and heavy drinking is one of them. Whereas nicotine is a stimulant, alcohol is a depressant. This means that when you drink alcohol, the effect is a slowing down of your internal processes—your brain activity and the workings of the entire nervous system slow down. Due to this calming effect, alcohol is often used by some people as a relaxation technique. It is not that uncommon for adults of drinking age to talk about having a drink after work to relax or unwind. It is true that alcohol can have this effect; however, when this particular substance is relied upon for relaxation, the result is usually that the individual will need to increase their dose of alcohol to get the same calming effects. When that happens, the person is in danger of developing dependence on the substance and becoming addicted to it, which over time can devastate the brain and body. Oftentimes when people are treated for alcohol addiction, it is revealed that they have been self-medicating, which means that they have been using alcohol to help them cope with ongoing stress or anxiety.

As with nicotine, more problems and stress are created as a result of using alcohol to ineffectively cope with stress.

Although cannabis has important medical uses (e.g., pain management, treatment of nausea, and stimulation of appetite), it is still possible to use cannabis in ways that can cause more harm than good. In addition to nicotine and alcohol, cannabis is a substance that is included in the list of *Substance Related and Addictive Disorders* of the DSM. When under the influence of cannabis, individuals can experience symptoms such as problems with movement and coordination, anxiety, and impaired judgment. It is also possible to experience euphoria and a sense that time is slowing down. Individuals who use cannabis for nonprescribed reasons often say that they are using it to help them cope with a particular problem. Similar to nicotine and alcohol, the use of cannabis can make the original problem worse. Moreover, when cannabis is misused, it can lead to neglect of work, school, and/or family obligations, which undoubtedly will cause more stress.

Other substances that have psychoactive properties include some prescription medications (e.g., OxyContin, benzodiazepines) and illegal substances (e.g., cocaine, heroin). The problems inherent with illegal substances is likely apparent; however, it may seem strange that prescription medications can cause problems when they are intended to treat them. Prescription medications can be addictive for the same reasons that the illegal substances are. In addition to treating symptoms of the diagnosis that lead to the prescription in the first place, these prescription medications may seem to temporarily *solve* ongoing stressors by creating an intense sense of well-being, euphoria, or numbness. If any of these are welcomed feelings and seem to help the person cope with life stressors, it will be difficult for the individual to stop taking the medication even when there is no longer a medical reason to.

One final substance that is garnering increasing attention from scientists in terms of its potential addictive properties is food. Not all foods have the same type of feel-good effects described above, but some do—that is they affect the same areas of the brain as some drugs. The idea that you can become addicted to some foods (like food high in sugar) is controversial. An interesting study was conducted by undergraduate students at Connecticut College who allowed rats to run a maze and in one condition receive a reward of either Oreos or rice cakes. In another condition the rats were rewarded with either a shot of cocaine or saline (salt water). What the students found was that the rats that had the food choice spent as much time on the side of the maze that had the Oreos as the rats who received a shot of cocaine. It would be tempting to conclude that Oreos have the same effects as cocaine and are therefore as potentially addictive —which the student researchers appropriately did *not* conclude. Despite the researcher's conclusions, *Time* magazine published an article on newsfeed.time.com with the headline "Oreos May Be as Addictive as Cocaine." Scientifically the only way to determine if, in fact, Oreos are as addictive as cocaine would be to give the rats a direct choice between the two, which did not happen in this study.

Regardless of the strength of the response in the brain (i.e., as strong as something like cocaine), scientists have determined that certain foods (e.g., fatty foods, foods high in sugar, simple carbs) have *feel good* effects on the brain. If we are experiencing stress or are feeling bad for some other reason, it is not surprising to know that we turn to foods like this because they literally make us feel better. The problem is, like with the substances discussed above, the feeling does not last long, which means we need more of these types of foods to keep feeling good. Overtime, depending on how much we eat and what types of food we are eating, we can develop other problems linked to eating these types of foods such as diabetes, hypertension, and heart disease. Additionally, many people report feeling physically and emotionally bad after eating foods high in sugar and/or fat. This in and of itself can contribute to additional stress. Moreover, depending on what is going on in a person's life, what their genetics are, and whether the food is used as a means to manipulate one's mood, these things in aggregate may put some people at a greater risk for developing an eating disorder. Eating disorders are very dangerous and as a class of disorders have the highest mortality rate of any psychiatric illness.

Finally, when people experience high levels of stress, their ability to tolerate more stress or frustration is limited. Instead of turning to the behaviors discussed above, what may happen is that the individual may "lash out" verbally or physically. In some cases, lashing out in these ways may be more likely because they are under the influence of a particular substance (e.g., alcohol). Verbal outbursts can consist of simply yelling out of frustration or cursing at someone or calling them names to express the degree to which they've had it. Physical displays of frustration can be directed toward inanimate objects (e.g., walls, windows, and chairs), pets, or people. It is possible that when engaged in this type of behavior, the individual is not only inappropriately expressing their emotions, they are compounding the situation by committing a crime: vandalizing or destroying someone's property or abusing an animal or a person. Regardless of whether the verbal or physical outburst rises to the level of being a criminal act, this type of behavior is almost guaranteed to create more problems than were there to begin with, thereby increasing the degree to which the person feels stressed.

KARŌSHI AND KARO-JISATSU

Karōshi is a Japanese word that translates to mean *death from overwork*. In an article published in 2009, Atsuko Kanai wrote about the deadly phenomenon occurring in Japan. He noted that dying from working very long hours has been acknowledged since the 1980s and that it has gotten worse over the years. In his article he argued that the extensive hours that these workers endure is not by choice but by virtue of the fact that they believed they had to as required by their employer. Similarly, *karo-jisatsu* is a phenomenon that refers to suicide due to depression related to being overworked.

Although death due to working too hard was identified in the early 1980s, changes weren't made in how the Japanese Ministry of Health, Labor and Welfare addressed this phenomenon until 1995 and then again in 2002. In 1998, the ministry changed their standards for what classified as a mental disorder. As a result karo-jisatsu became a legitimate and recognized problem. In his article, Atsuko Kanai explained karo-jisatsu and karōshi in terms of the employment conditions and in terms of the economic climate of Japan. He argued that rights as they applied to employees needed to be reconsidered and changed so that working conditions were no longer deadly.

It may be difficult to believe that someone could literally work themselves to death, but when the body is pushed to the point of extreme exhaustion without adequate opportunity for rest and recovery, it can begin to shut down (i.e., GAS). If that couples with the sense that the situation is beyond someone's control (i.e., learned helplessness) and there is the absence of enough social support, karōshi can occur. Deaths attributed to karōshi are classified as being the result of heart attack or stroke related to stress. Prior to either of these occurring, some workers may have become so distressed by their working life that they became depressed and believed that life was no longer worth living under those conditions and they may have committed suicide (karo-jisatsu). Regardless, it is clear that work-related stress to this degree is devastating and preventable.

3

How: The Positive and Negative Effects of Relaxation

As discussed in Chapter 2, experiencing stress affects both the mind and the body primarily in negative ways. The effects of relaxation will be the focus in the sections that follow. Although experiencing relaxation is generally a good thing, the ways in which relaxation may not have the expected benefits will also be discussed.

HOW YOUR BODY RESPONDS TO RELAXATION

The section "Physiological Response to Stress and Anxiety" in Chapter 2 focused on the sympathetic nervous system—one of two branches of the autonomic nervous system. The other branch of the autonomic nervous system is the parasympathetic nervous system. As a reminder, the sympathetic nervous system prepares your body to take action (i.e., fight or flight), whereas the parasympathetic nervous system helps your body recover from the alert status. When the parasympathetic nervous system is activated, our previously accelerated heart beat begins to slow down, our rapid breathing becomes more protracted, and our body begins to cool down. The fight-or-flight mechanism is turned off and energy is redistributed throughout the body rather than being directed to the extremities. As noted earlier, when the body is chronically activated via the sympathetic nervous system, the body and mind can suffer negative and potentially debilitating effects. By contrast, when the parasympathetic nervous system is activated, both the body and the mind benefit, and as researchers have recently discovered, these benefits can occur at the genetic level.

Each of us has over 20,000 genes. Researchers studying how genes work and what happens if they are manipulated have discovered that genes can be essentially turned on and turned off as a part of the normal developmental and aging process; however, this flip of the genetic switch can also be the result of pathological influences. This mechanism has been found to influence something as benign as eye color and something as serious as cancer.

As we grow in our mother's womb and eventually experience the world around us, certain genes are turned on whereas others are turned off. Much of this is expected and happens at certain, predictable periods in our development. Researchers, however, have studied what happens when something goes wrong or when we're exposed to something like chemical toxins or environmental pollutants. The results of such studies indicate that exposure to harmful toxins interacts with genes. The result can be that some genes are turned on or activated when they shouldn't be and others are turned off or deactivated. Both can result in disease processes. The good news is that researchers have also discovered that exposure to things that are beneficial to us can activate or deactivate genes in a way that *enhances* our health. Relaxation is one of those beneficial experiences. Thus, relaxation can affect our genetic functioning.

The Harvard Medical School reported the results of a study involving a group of people who had engaged in a form of relaxation (e.g., yoga, meditation) over a long period of time and compared them to another group of people who were considered novices (i.e., those who had not regularly used a form of relaxation). Blood samples were taken from both groups just prior to, immediately after, and 15 minutes after a relaxation session. The results of these blood tests confirmed that both groups showed a positive gene response to the relaxation session. However, the group comprised of people who were already long-term practitioners of relaxation showed the greatest benefit. The more consistently one engages in a form of relaxation, the greater the chances one's gene functioning will improve.

Our genetics, of course, influence every aspect of our minds and bodies. One of the effects associated with genes and relaxation has to do with inflammation. Inflammation can negatively affect heart health, gastrointestinal functioning, and the regulation of our body's blood sugar. As noted above, activating the relaxation response (i.e., the parasympathetic nervous system) has the time-limited effect of changing whether or not some genes are turned on or off. With respect to inflammation, getting the body to a relaxed state can turn off the genes that would normally activate chronic inflammation. The genes that are activated or turned on via relaxation activities seem to have an effect at the level of energy usage, blood sugar regulation, all the way down to the cellular level with the functioning of mitochondria. These findings are provocative in the sense that many of us have believed that we cannot change our genetics. Genetic researchers studying the effects of relaxation have shown that while we cannot change the genetics we have, we may be able to change how they function.

The study of the effects of relaxation on genetic functioning is relatively new in comparison to what is known about the benefits that stress management techniques, including relaxation, can have on cardiovascular disease and high blood pressure. In fact, stress itself seems to be a more significant risk factor for heart attacks than something typically associated with heart attack: hypertension. Thus, since stress has such a negative effect, it would stand to reason that deactivating the stress response and activating the relaxation response would have positive effects. Although researchers caution that more studies are needed to fully understand the effects of relaxation and other stress management strategies, results to date show that reducing stress in combination with eating well and engaging in exercise reduces the risk for cardiac problems.

Connected to heart health is blood pressure. High blood pressure has been reliably connected to cardiovascular disease; however, what reliably predicts high blood pressure is stress. High blood pressure causes the heart to beat faster and with more force, which ultimately weakens the heart. Additionally, high blood pressure can cause damage to the walls of arteries, which negatively affects blood flow. Engaging in some form of relaxation (e.g., deep abdominal breathing) can temporarily reduce blood pressure, whereas long-term practice of relaxation techniques can lead to longer-term benefits. Thus, relaxation can be a protective factor for the heart and overall cardiovascular health. As is the case with other medical issues, consultation with a licensed medical provider is necessary to determine if a more medically oriented intervention (e.g., medication) is required. If that is recommended, it certainly does not necessarily preclude someone from using relaxation strategies, but it may mean that certain strategies (e.g., exercise) may need to be delayed or modified until one's system can adequately handle such exertion.

Although the cardiovascular system may be the most well-known system affected by prolonged stress, other systems can also be negatively affected. The gut, or organs of the gastrointestinal system, can respond to stress by producing things like pain throughout the gastrointestinal system, exacerbating ulcers, and contributing to irritable bowel syndrome (IBS). Research demonstrating the positive effects of relaxation on how our gastrointestinal system works has thus far found potential benefit only for those experiencing IBS. Interventions such as mindfulness training, meditation, and cognitive behavioral therapy have resulted in symptom reduction. Thus, IBS is not cured as a result of engaging in some form of relaxation; however, it is possible to experience some relief from the physical and emotional distress that accompanies this syndrome.

Other processes or diseases that may be impacted by engaging in relaxation include overall immune system functioning, cancer, and asthma. Research has been conducted in these areas with promising results. Researchers caution that much more needs to be examined before a conclusion can be drawn one way or another. It is possible, however, that the evidence found in the area of stress management and genes can help to explain why engaging in relaxation strategies over the long term can boost immune system functioning since inflammation is a type of immune system response. Research in the area of stress management and cancer suggests that the benefits gained have more to do with associated experiences with cancer such as fatigue, sleep problems, overall mood, and anxiety.

One final effect of relaxation on how the body functions is sleep. Persistent difficulties falling or staying asleep is called *insomnia*. Estimates of the prevalence rate of insomnia reported by the National Center for Sleep Disorders Research at the National Institutes of Health indicate that as many as 40 percent of adults have dealt with insomnia-related symptoms over the course of a year and as many as 15 percent report that they suffer from chronic insomnia. Sleep is vital to the optimal functioning of mind and body; therefore, preventing or treating insomnia and other sleep disturbances is paramount. Although there are numerous causes of sleep-related problems, overall tension and the inability to relax are significant factors. Practicing relaxation techniques prior to going to sleep can not only help you fall asleep but can also help to reduce anxiety that might precede sleeping related to the fear of not being able to fall asleep. Those who are well rested have more energy, are less likely to overeat, have healthier-looking skin, and have a reduced risk of heart attack. Those who get fewer hours of sleep over the long haul have been found to have shorter life spans. So relaxation itself will not make you live longer, but it can help with getting enough sleep if you find that you don't get enough and that just might make you live longer.

Many of the relaxation techniques mentioned in Chapter 1 are effective for activating the parasympathetic nervous system, thereby helping to reduce tension and feeling more relaxed. These include deep abdominal breathing, meditation, progressive muscle relaxation, and imagery. Other techniques will, of course, aid in your pursuit of feeling more relaxed overall but may not be practical right before bed (e.g., exercising). Therefore, it is important to try techniques that seem to work for you and that you can easily incorporate into your sleep routine.

Although not all research conducted to date has provided definitive proof that relaxation will prevent or cure serious illnesses and diseases, what has been found suggests that relaxation by and large can have beneficial effects on several different areas of the body.

HOW YOUR MIND RESPONDS TO RELAXATION

In addition to slowing the body down physiologically, relaxation can have a similar effect on the mind. A common complaint of those who experience stress and/or anxiety is having *racing thoughts*. Oftentimes the thoughts that are racing through one's head in these situations are also negative. So not only is there a multitude of thoughts flying through one's mind like lightning, but these thoughts are also tinged with things like self-defeat, helplessness, and hopelessness. None of this fosters a state of relaxation and in fact can directly contribute to tension throughout the body. What can accompany this flurry of thoughts is confusion and difficulty acting or making decisions.

Taking action or making decisions, especially ones that are beneficial to your well-being, requires a rational mind. Sure emotion can be involved in the decision-making process, but being able to think clearly about what the concern or dilemma is along with all possible solutions and their associated consequences requires the ability to think fluidly, clearly, and rationally. Have you ever noticed someone panicking when they can't decide what to do, especially if they feel pressure to act quickly? This type of panic (not to be confused with panic disorder discussed in Chapter 2) is the result of the inability to mentally slow down and systematically work through the decision-making process. You may have, in fact, told someone in a situation like this to *calm down* or *slow down*. Although saying something like that does not usually evoke a state of relaxation in someone in this state, the recommendation is not far off the mark. The person needs to find a way to calm their mind, which is, however, not always easy to do.

Cognitive behavioral therapy can assist with the negative tone that accompanies rapid-fire thinking. Gentle confrontation of the veracity of the nature of someone's thinking can help them slow their mind. What can happen when thoughts turn negative is that we can start thinking catastrophically—or in terms of the worst case scenario. This can elicit the physical fight-or-flight response and can activate the mind to hurry up and come up with a solution. Inevitably, however, each solution that is offered up is just as quickly shot down as not being good enough or perfect enough to prevent the presumed catastrophe. This then leads to more pressure to find something better as quickly as possible. Cognitive behavioral therapy can help someone in this thinking spiral to slow down by selecting one element of the thought process going on at the time to discuss and evaluate. It may seem as though this type of analysis has the potential to contribute to even more stress; however, the opposite tends to be true when done with someone trained in this type of therapy. If, for example, someone is concerned that they may not pass an exam, it is not uncommon for them, if they struggle with catastrophic thinking, to get from failing an exam to homelessness. That may seem ridiculous to some readers; however, if you believe that doing well on exams in high school is critical to getting into a good college, which is critical to getting a good job, you can begin to see how someone might then think that if they don't pass or get a good grade on this exam, everything else will fall apart—to the extreme.

Cognitive behavioral therapy can help someone rationally evaluate things like the chances of actually failing the exam, and if they do, what consequences are realistic. In the event that some element of their catastrophic thinking is accurate (e.g., *Not getting good enough grades will mean I can't get into the college I want to.*), the therapist can help them deconstruct the assumption that they won't get into any college or that they won't be able to get a good job, and so on. Our brain is an amazing organ, but what it is capable of can backfire. The brain, for example, cannot tell the difference between reality and dreams especially when it comes to the emotional experience of the dream. Similarly, if we imagine a scenario occurring, like the one briefly described above, and we imagine it happening enough times, the brain will start to believe that it *will* happen and will interpret this as being dangerous and worthy of the fight-or-flight response. This is in part why there seems to be evidence for the *self-fulfilling prophecy* in many situations like this. It's not that you can make bad things happen with your mind alone, but if you believe they *will* happen, you will respond as if there is a catastrophe and inadvertently make happen what you were desperate to prevent to begin with.

In addition to cognitive behavioral therapy, including a relaxation technique designed to slow down the body itself may be necessary. If the sympathetic nervous system has been activated to such a degree that the person seems to be breathing rapidly and shallowly and perhaps even shaking, calming the body down is essential. While the mind can calm the body and the reverse is also true, it is important to recognize for yourself if your tense, overstimulated body is causing your mind to race, or if your thoughts are coming so quickly that your body thinks there is danger and is mobilizing to take action. Since the body and mind work in tandem, calming your mind without also attending to the body may be futile.

Relaxing the mind can also help someone manage the symptoms of depression and anxiety. The racing thoughts discussed above, especially those that are predominantly negative in nature, over time can wear a person down such that their mood can take a dramatic turn downward. The downward spiral that often takes place involves negative thoughts about one's self and the world around them and hope that the future will be better. Engaging in relaxation is not necessarily a cure or specific treatment for depression; however, it is likely to help give the person respite from the persistent negative thoughts. Relaxing the mind may even allow someone to take a different perspective such that they are able to question the accuracy of their negative thoughts, thus interrupting the downward spiral. When this occurs, treatment techniques such as cognitive behavioral therapy or supportive psychotherapy are more likely to be effective.

The racing mind can either be a symptom of anxiety or can contribute to the development of the symptoms noted in the preceding paragraph. Relaxation itself can be an effective treatment for anxiety; however, it is often the case that other techniques are needed for more effective treatment and full recovery. Regardless, including some form of relaxation designed to help both the mind and the body let go of tension can benefit the anxious person in the same way it can help the depressed person: their racing thoughts can slow enough so that they can process their ideas more slowly and deliberately. This further allows space for the individual to question to what degree their anxious thoughts and feelings are warranted. That is, they may recognize that when their thoughts are allowed to race ahead, unchecked, their mind ends up in the type of catastrophic thinking mentioned earlier.

Another way to think about the various ways relaxation can affect the mind is that you are giving your mind a vacation of sorts. It is a gift you can give yourself almost anytime and almost anywhere. By taking time out of your daily life to slow down, breathe deeply, and allow the thoughts associated with your day to simply float out of your mind as soon as they enter, you are teaching your mind to let go. You are telling it that whatever thoughts are swirling around can wait. If they are really that important, they will find way to return but at that moment your mind is on vacation from wrestling with, fighting with, and processing those thoughts.

You may even find that once you let those thoughts go, they don't return because they weren't as important as you thought they were.

EFFECTS OF RELAXATION ON LIFE EXPECTANCY

When adults who have lived to the age of 90 and beyond are asked what they did to live such a long life, many of us stop to listen because we want to know what we can do to live a long time like they have. However, it is likely the case that not only do we want to live longer but we also want that time to be healthy and joyful rather than painful and distressing. In response to the question, some older adults will say things like they do not take life too seriously, or they make sure they have a scotch and soda before bedtime. Others will quip that the secret to living a long life is to maintain a filthy sense of humor. What seems to be a unifying factor when unscientifically examining what it is about these folks that have allowed them to live long and vibrant lives is that they seem happy with themselves and with how they have lived their lives. They seem to have little regret. Although this is not a commentary on relaxation per se, it is plausible that by living lives that suit them, they experienced much less stress than those of us chasing the dreams and promises of an ideal lifestyle not defined by us for ourselves, but defined by others and imposed on us.

There is little doubt that living a life you do not find enjoyable or rewarding in a meaningful way is stressful. We have already discussed in this chapter how stress can negatively impact your overall health and lead to potentially deadly diseases. Thus, it would stand to reason that if chronic stress can contribute to the development and maintenance of serious disease processes that could be fatal, then ongoing practice of relaxation techniques would prevent these disease processes and give you a greater chance of living longer. Recent scientific efforts suggest that this seems to be the case. It's not that relaxation in itself will *make* you live longer, but it will allow your mind and body to function in more healthy ways contributing to a longer and more healthy life.

A highly technical study conducted by Nobel Laureate Elizabeth Blackburn examined a facet of chromosomes called *telomeres*. Telomeres are a kind of cap that covers the ends of our chromosomes. These caps have some length to them, which serves to more effectively protect our chromosomes; however, when these caps become shorter, the death rate of our bodies' cells accelerates. Cell death leads to aging, so the faster cells die, the faster we age. Blackburn found that those of us who endure higher levels of stress than our low-stress counterparts have shorter telomeres. She specifically demonstrated this in a study of mothers caring for children who had a chronic illness. Moms who reported the highest levels of stress were found to have much more rapidly aging cells than the least stressed moms. Another study conducted by Blackburn and a colleague demonstrated that it is possible to lengthen our telomeres, thereby protecting our cells from the aging process. When we engage in healthy lifestyle habits (e.g., stress management, healthy diet, moderate exercise), these microscopic caps lengthen. They further discovered that the more beneficial changes participants made, the greater the increase in the length of these caps.

A less direct way that practicing relaxation can improve your life expectancy is via the avoidance of coping strategies that are unhealthy or damaging. The following section will discuss some of the things we do in an attempt to relax or unwind that do more harm than good. When we engage in harmful coping habits such as overeating, smoking, or abusing alcohol, we set ourselves up for myriad mental and physical health-related problems that are associated with shorter lives. Moreover, when we engage in these types of coping strategies, we tend not to have as enjoyable a life than if we were to cope with stress and discomfort more effectively.

A more recent area of study as it relates to stress and thus indirectly relates to relaxation is how our *perception* of the stress response (e.g., increased heart rate, sweating) contributes to unhealthy and damaging physical responses. Health psychologist Kelly McGonigal conducted a TED Talk in which she reversed course on her previous decade-long view of stress. She noted that until recently she viewed stress just like the rest of us: stress is bad and unhealthy and can kill you. While this is not patently untrue, she revealed that recent research has identified an exceedingly important caveat to the experience of stress. We have known for some time that learning to view stress more positively can have a positive effect on your mental health. Researchers have now determined that a shift in perspective regarding stress can also have important physiological benefits. McGonigal shared with her audience that people can experience an enormous amount of stress (based on self-report) and if they viewed their stress response as helpful, their blood vessels stayed relaxed and open, rather than constricting, just as if they were experiencing joy or courage. She revealed that it wasn't that these participants were in a relaxed state. They were, in fact, experiencing the stress response. Their hearts were beating faster but not harder. Because their blood vessels remained relaxed and open blood flowed more easily, it allowed better flow of oxygen throughout their bodies. By consistently interpreting your stress response in the context of your body preparing you for the challenge you are about to face, you can reduce what is physiologically harmful about the stress response and allow your body to work *for* you.

What we know about how relaxation may help us to live longer and healthier lives is not nearly as comprehensive as what we know about how the damaging effects of chronic stress can affect us. What has been discovered, however, provides hope that relaxation may prevent or slow down some processes that contribute to aging and perhaps a premature death.

THINGS WE DO TO RELAX THAT MAY HARM US

Consider what you do currently in your life when you want to relax. How many of those things are found in this book (see Chapter 1)? How many of the things you do are you likely to find in another type of book, such as a hypothetical book entitled *What Not to Do to Relax*?

The most obvious strategies people use to try to relax that are also likely to do more harm than good are drugs (prescription and nonprescription) and alcohol. Before you skip past this section because you do not want to be preached at one more time, understand that the intent of including this is not to suggest that some drugs or alcohol are *never* okay, but they have the potential to do great harm. When they are used for the purpose of eliciting a relaxation response, the likelihood of becoming dependent on that particular chemical can increase. It is not uncommon for those who end up in treatment for alcohol or drug dependence to learn that they had been self-medicating, which means that they were using a nonprescription substance to treat an ongoing problem.

For many adults unwinding or relaxing after a long, difficult day can involve having an alcoholic drink. Drinking in moderation is not harmful for most people, and depending on what is being ingested, it can have positive effects on one's health. Drinking alcohol is a problem, however, when it becomes necessary to have in order to feel relaxed. Some people report that their minds stop racing when they have enough to drink or that they are so mentally overstimulated that they want to feel numb. While this can seem like a welcome solution to a distressing problem, the reality is the amount of alcohol needed to achieve this desired effect will increase. Over a long enough period of time, the body will become dependent on having alcohol in the system and the person will no longer require it to relax; they will require it in order to not feel ill. The potential for dependency and becoming an alcoholic is high when this occurs. And oftentimes, important interpersonal relationships will also suffer. So the short-term solution of using alcohol in order to eliminate or quiet a distressful state of mind puts you at an increased risk for a longer-term and devastating set of problems.

Drugs have a similar process. As noted above, the term *drugs* is intended to refer to both prescription medications and nonprescription substances. Not all drugs are prescribed or used for the purpose of getting relaxed, but those that are used for that purpose often have addictive properties. The drugs that act more quickly and leave your system more quickly will be more addictive than those that take longer to produce an effect and to leave your system. While there are certain types of medications prescribed for the treatment of tension and anxiety that are non-addictive, there are other types that are highly addictive. When prescribed a medication for this purpose, it is important to talk candidly with your physician about whether or not the medication they are prescribing has an addiction potential. It is also important to let them know if you have a history of addiction to any substance since they may either choose to prescribe something else or closely monitor the dosage you take.

Nonprescription drugs are often illegal and therefore have that added layer of harm; however, above a certain age, nicotine is legal and in some states marijuana is legal with or without a prescription (although as of the writing of this book, marijuana is illegal in all states when it comes to federal laws). When it comes to nicotine specifically being used as a relaxation strategy or stress reliever, the irony is that nicotine is a stimulant. It is designed to activate your sympathetic nervous system, not the parasympathetic side of things. This irony can be explained through a few things that are usually involved with smoking cigarettes. The sensation of feeling better can certainly come when it has been quite some time in between cigarettes. If a smoker starts to feel a craving or it has been long enough that withdrawal symptoms start to occur, then the reintroduction of nicotine in the system can not only make someone feel better but can also feel like a sense of relief, which is often associated with relaxation or at least less stress. Moreover, when you think about the act of smoking a cigarette itself, long-time smokers are able to take very deep breaths and exhale slowly and completely. This is, of course, a recommended relaxation strategy—without the cigarette, of course. The act of breathing deeply and rhythmically will undoubtedly help to facilitate a relaxed state. Finally, as is the case with most substances including those already discussed, there is often a ritual associated with the use of chemicals. The ritual can be as simple as always smoking at the same time every day or around certain events, and as complex as including particular paraphernalia assembled and used in a precise way along with when and where use of the substance occurs. Rituals like these create a sense of familiarity and the idea that what is coming next is known and planned for. Rituals are used routinely in sport to help athletes reduce anxiety around performance, so the use of a ritual with the use of a substance can have a similar effect.

Finally, an often used strategy intended to produce a calming effect involves consuming another type of substance: food. Most readers will be familiar with the concept of *comfort food*. The idea behind these foods is that they taste good because they are usually high in calories, fat, and carbohydrates. Moreover, they impact the pleasure centers of the brain, and they are often associated with a pleasant time in one's life. Mac-n-cheese, for example, is a common comfort food for the reasons listed, and the pleasant time usually evoked is childhood, when most of us had very few cares. Whatever the particular food is, it is a safe bet that all readers will be able to identify foods or meals they consider comfort food. Another phenomenon associated with the misuse of food is *stress eating*. Foods similar to comfort foods are the targets of consumption when we feel stressed. It is unlikely to see someone engaged in stress eating reach for a bowl of carrot sticks or a bunch of celery. More often than not, the foods of choice will again be those that are high in carbohydrates, fat, and calories. Neither comfort food nor stress eating in and of itself is a bad thing. The problem comes when we start to rely on these types of foods to feel better emotionally over a long period of time. If we are under constant stress, regardless of the source(s) of the stress, we will find that we are usually eating comfort foods. These are the foods that when overconsumed are associated with numerous health problems such as diabetes and heart disease.

To be fair, any strategy listed in this book could be included in this section provided the strategy is overused and engaged in with such singular focus that all other pursuits and interests are ignored. Anything that dominates and consumes our attention and energy will more likely than not become a problem for us even when it started out as a viable and reasonable solution. Thus, when you decide on a relaxation strategy, whether it is one from this section or from Chapter 1, it is a good idea to determine why you have chosen that particular strategy and what you expect it will do for you. Then consider if there is any way it could harm you. Keep reevaluating your strategies. What seemed like a good idea to begin with may clearly become a liability in the future.

WHEN RECOMMENDED TYPES OF RELAXATION CAN BACKFIRE

There really are very few downsides to learning how to relax your mind and body. In fact, for a long time it was believed that in order to effectively cope with clinical levels of anxiety, people needed to learn how to relax when they felt anxious. It has recently been determined that for many people this is an ineffective strategy for dealing with anxiety. Before discussing this, however, there are a few other, more obvious reasons why relaxation is not always ideal.

First of all, relaxation does not equal sleeping. Sure, in order to fall asleep it is essential that the mind and body are both calm and relaxed; however, if the overall goal is relaxation and not sleep, it is important to be sure your mind and body can distinguish between the two. For example, going through a relaxation routine that will allow you to get up in front of an audience and give a speech or perform in one way or another works best if you don't end up dozing off. If you are asleep you might not wake up in time, or you may be too groggy to effectively do what you needed to do, and all that would likely cause more stress.

Related to this is something called the Yerkes-Dodson Inverted-U. This idea suggests that in order to perform at your best, there is an optimal level of arousal. Typically the optimal level of arousal is "moderate" and found in between being too aroused and being under-aroused. When this is graphed, the relationship between performance and arousal level looks like an upside-down U. Being too aroused (i.e., over-aroused) usually means that you are anxious to a level that is interfering with your ability to think clearly and attend to whatever is required of you, and if a physical performance is involved, your body may be too tense to work at its best. By contrast, being under-aroused doesn't necessarily mean you are asleep but it can. It also means that your mind and body are not ready to take action (i.e., they both need to be awake enough to perform). The next time you watch a sporting event, take note of what happens just prior to the start of the competition. What are the athletes doing? Are they interacting with others? Are some off on their own? Right before the start of a game or match, it is not uncommon to see, especially in team sports, a huddle of sorts designed to *amp up* or arouse the team. There's often yelling, chanting, physical contact (e.g., hitting, head-butting, back slapping, etc.), and at times something that looks an awful lot like a mosh pit. Whether they know it or not, most of these athletes are intentionally raising their arousal level. In these instances, they know that in order to get onto the field of play and perform at their best, their bodies have to be ready. Again, whether they know it or not, they are activating their body's fight-or-flight response. There are stories of athletes and other performers who sleep or are in some other state of deep relaxation right before a competition, but this tends not to be a good idea for most performers. In fact, recently Tim Howard, goalkeeper of the U.S. National Soccer Team, was interviewed about playing in the 2014 FIFA World Cup. He stated that before competition he feels "anxious" and that he likes that feeling because it lets him know that he is about to enter into competition, that he is about to do something important. Sport psychologists agree with this approach and suggest that allowing yourself to feel aroused or even a bit anxious is a cue to your mind and body that both need to be, and are, ready to take action.

There is one additional caveat to this relationship between performance and anxiety that has to do with how difficult the task is. When the task is perceived to be an easy one (from the perspective of the performer), arousal should be higher than normal in order to perform well, whereas if the task is perceived to be a difficult one, arousal should be lower than would be expected under normal competition experiences. For most people, a game like tic-tac-toe or even hangman is easy. It does not require a lot of effort. The stakes are often low, so it probably doesn't really matter whether you win or lose. But imagine if the outcome *did* matter. This game is so easy it would be tempting to go into a high-stakes competition of hangman feeling overconfident and under-aroused. When this happens, mental energy is low and therefore concentration on the game tends not be as focused as it should be. Mistakes are more easily made and defeat can more easily occur. This phenomenon can explain why in some sport competitions a highly favored team loses to a much lower ranked and less skilled team. The better team may have entered into the competition thinking it will be so easy that they do not need to try that hard. The reality is they may need to hike up their arousal level so that they do not make sloppy mistakes or unforced errors.

Difficult tasks, on the other hand, require a lower level of arousal simply because they are not well learned or well understood yet. Think back to when you first learned how to ride a bike or some other skill that you now find really easy. Now, most of us can hop on our bikes without a second thought and pedal away; however, when we were first learning how to balance and pedal and steer and watch for cars all at the same time, we really needed to not be distracted by *anything* else. We needed to be relatively calm and focused. If we got upset (i.e., angry/frustrated or sad/crying), we would make more mistakes, which would only serve to intensify the level of arousal. Now, because it is an easy task, some of us may even turn to a bike ride to achieve a sense of calm and relaxation.

These ideas all have scientific support; however, like all things in this book, it is important to remain connected to your own mind and body. It may be tempting to increase or decrease your arousal level based on what others are doing, but if what they need in order to perform at their best is not what you need, you may find yourself benched or tongue tied before you know it. If the pre-competition mosh pit is what you need, join in. If what you need is to turn inward and listen to your favorite music to get your mind and body ready, then do that.

As noted at the start of this section, those who are experiencing clinical levels of anxiety (i.e., something that can be diagnosed as an anxiety disorder) need to experience their anxiety in order to learn how to manage and cope with it. Thus, for individuals experiencing this type of anxiety, using relaxation techniques can backfire or at least lead to a more protracted recovery process.

Conventional wisdom along with a hefty dose of scientific research previously suggested that in order to treat anxiety, especially the type that can be predictable (e.g., specific phobias, social phobia), it was important to learn how to relax. The process would involve first teaching someone with high anxiety a relaxation technique. Often the technique would include deep abdominal breathing and imagery. After learning the technique, the individual would be exposed to something *similar* to the thing that causes them a great deal of anxiety, but in this case the anxiety should not be too high. For example, if someone had a phobia of spiders, instead of exposing the person to a spider right off the bat, they might be shown a drawing of a spider or even just the word *spider*. The individual would rate their level of anxiety and then would be instructed to use their relaxation technique to reduce their anxiety level. This process would continue until the individual could be around an actual spider but be relaxed, or at least have the capacity to reduce their anxiety. This is an effective form of treatment and is not necessarily a terrible way to go; however, current research suggests that including the step of learning relaxation can slow down the treatment process and can also backfire by not allowing the person to learn that anxiety and/or the thing that caused the anxiety is, in fact, tolerable. Current researchers suggest that by using relaxation people inadvertently learn that anxiety is something to be avoided and perhaps even feared.

As noted above, there are instances where some anxiety is advantageous. At minimum, however, anxiety is not something that we need to run away from. Anxiety can be instructive. It can tell us when something is not right, which can lead us to identify the problem and subsequently identify solutions. It can also tell us when we are ready to embark on something important. Anxiety, therefore, can be a signal of sorts that what is about to happen is important and we need our mind and body to be ready for it.

An additional note about how relaxation techniques can backfire involves the possibility of overdoing it when it comes to exercise.

Regular, moderate exercise has numerous physical and mental health benefits. It has been associated with reducing one's risk for cancer, dementia, and heart disease, and it has been found to improve overall mood, decrease anxiety, and improve memory. Given all of these benefits it is tempting to assume that the more you exercise the better you will feel. Up to a point this is true; however, for each of us there is a tipping point beyond which regular, moderate exercise can turn into an exercise regime that is intense and occurs each day no matter what. Various terms have been given to this phenomenon: exercise dependence, exercise addiction, over-exercise, exercise abuse, and so on. Although not a formally diagnosable condition, this type of approach to exercise can be a signal that something more serious is going on (e.g., an eating disorder) or it can lead to severe physical and mental problems. Individuals who engage in too much exercise to the point that it is no longer good for them will usually exercise despite being injured, they will become angry or irritable when they cannot exercise or are delayed in their exercise routine, and they may choose exercise over engaging in interpersonal relationships, which usually means their relationships will suffer.

Finally, there is a phenomenon called *relaxation-induced anxiety*. This experience is not diagnosable; however, it can certainly cause distress for some people. For those who experience this paradoxical phenomenon, trying to relax can cause them to worry about what they will think about when they become relaxed. They may be distressed by the unknown quality of the experience or because the thoughts they know they will have when they calm their mind are in and of themselves distressing. Therefore, the thought of relaxing and allowing those thoughts to surface can cause tension. Some people are afraid of what others will think of them when they are relaxed. They have concern that they might be perceived as lazy, or as being out of control, or even that others will think they are not relaxing in the right way. It is not uncommon for those who experience diagnosable levels of anxiety to perceive relaxation activities as a waste of time or as being unproductive with the underlying concern that this is precisely what others will think if they knew the person was trying to relax.

As noted in the beginning of this section, relaxation is usually beneficial. It is important, however, to be aware of the ways in which relaxation can backfire so that you can recognize it if it happens to you. Then you can try something different or if necessary ask someone to help you find a more effective strategy.

4

Who: Psychologists' Theories about Relaxation

This chapter will discuss three theories on the importance of relaxation and the benefits it can have for those who regularly or even sporadically engage in it. The theory developed by Dr. Herbert Benson, which he called the Relaxation Response, will be explored first followed by the Relaxation Response Resiliency Program (3RP), which is based on Dr. Benson's work with the Relaxation Response. Finally, the Attentional Behavioral Cognitive (ABC) Relaxation Theory developed by Dr. Jonathan Smith will be examined.

RELAXATION RESPONSE

Originally published in 1975, *The Relaxation Response* by Herbert Benson, MD, was a guide to aid the multitude of people who struggle with stress-related illnesses learn how to care for themselves through relaxation. Back in the 1960s and 1970s when Dr. Benson studied the Relaxation Response, the idea that someone could *intentionally* bring about a state of relaxation (i.e., lower one's heart rate, calm one's mind) was revolutionary. He was scientifically swimming upstream against a current characterized by the idea that the mind and body were separate and medical intervention to the body was the only thing that could treat, heal, and cure anything that ailed you. Dr. Benson theorized and eventually supported the idea that human beings were quite capable of treating themselves for many things that caused them problems. He went as far as to say that as much as 90 percent of the things that bring someone to a physician's office can be treated via self-care. He was not dismissing the importance of medication, surgery, or any number of other medical interventions, but he believed they were overused to the detriment of patients' overall health.

Back in the 1960s and 1970s heart disease was recognized as a leading cause of death in the United States. In one of his books, Dr. Benson discusses the "Hidden Epidemic" of hypertension, which puts people at risk for heart disease and stroke. Fifty years later this epidemic is no longer hidden but we still have not eradicated it despite knowing what we can do about it. Identifying the reasons that our culture or each of us individually has not eliminated something that is easily identified and easily treated is not the purpose of this section nor of this book; however, if you know you experience hypertension due to stress and you have not been able to consistently use the proven strategies covered in this book, it might be a question worth answering for your own health. Eliciting the Relaxation Response was and still is offered as an effective treatment of hypertension.

Benson suggested that there were four causes of hypertension: poor diet, not enough exercise, the nature of one's family, and environmental stress. At the time, he acknowledged that the degree to which each of these factors might be more or less influential in the development of hypertension was unknown. Today, this is still unknown but mostly because whether or not the nature of one's family has more of an impact than environmental stress or lack of exercise will depend largely on the person. Who are *you*? How well do you tolerate stress in general? How well do you tolerate a particular type of stress? What else is going on in your life that might affect how you manage stress? We also now know that a fifth factor can be added to this list: sleep. Lack of sleep is associated with myriad diseases and can greatly influence your ability to manage stress. So you may be a stellar manager of stress, but if you are not well rested, your stress management skills and your health will likely suffer.

Over 50 years ago, Dr. Benson discussed the fact that the environment around us changes rapidly. One can certainly argue that however fast things were changing in the 1960s and 1970s, things are changing at an even faster pace in the twenty-first century. Regardless, he noted that the changes that occur in our environment contribute to our overall level of stress. Stress itself does not necessarily have to be a bad thing or based on a bad event, although that is what people usually think of when they think about what is stressful in their lives. Examples that can counter this notion are things like winning a lot of money in the lottery, getting married, getting promoted, or having a baby. Most people would opine that these are positive or good events; however, they are stressful events because they reflect a change in your situation. Any change requires that we have to adapt. For most of us, that adaptation is initiated with the fight-or-flight response. As discussed already in Chapter 2, our minds recognize that something is different in the environment, so our body is then put on alert to take action. But, of course, actually fighting or running away in most stressful situations does not make sense. Dr. Benson noted that the repeated and inappropriate activation of this physiological survival mechanism means that we are not very good at adapting as quickly as the environment demands. Therefore, we experience feeling stressed and many of us end up with stress-related illnesses.

When he really examined this phenomenon and the idea that human beings could intentionally alter their physiology, he was met with a great deal of skepticism by his colleagues since, as noted at the beginning of this section, most scientists and physicians were of the opinion that the mind and body were separate. That notion may seem absurd to the student and thinker in the current century. Vast amounts of data on the mind-body connection have been amassed since the time Dr. Benson posited his theory; however, at the time it was believed that the only way to cure an ailment of the body was to treat the body itself with medication, surgery, and so on. In this day and age there are still some scientists and physicians who have held on to this notion; however, more and more professionals trained to help human beings as they navigate their lives recognize the power of the mind and its potential to affect the body for better and for worse. Dr. Benson, a pioneer in this respect, recognized that repeated stress can result in a negative and harmful mind-body interaction, while repeated engagement of the Relaxation Response can result in a positive and beneficial mind-body interaction. As evidence for his assertion that not only are the mind and body connected but that we can intentionally change our physiology through our minds, he drew from the scholarly work of B. F. Skinner and Neil Miller, and the ancient practices of yoga and meditation.

B. F. Skinner is most notably recognized for his training of pigeons, rats, and other animals to behave in certain ways based on reward and punishment. This process is knowns as *operant conditioning* and is guided by the notion that when a behavior is rewarded or reinforced, it is more likely to be performed again, whereas when a behavior is punished, it is more likely to be avoided and not performed again. Behavior doesn't operate quite that neatly; however, Skinner was able to successfully demonstrate that he could reliably train a pigeon to peck the right key or set of keys in its cage based on reinforcement and punishment. These principles were believed to generalize to human behavior and have been demonstrated to do so. Although Skinner was not examining how our bodies work internally, he was able to demonstrate that voluntary movements (e.g., pecking, sniffing, walking) can be intentionally manipulated and controlled. Benson next turned to Neil Miller's work on biofeedback, which more directly speaks to the mind-body connection implied in the Relaxation Response.

Miller's work highlighted the fact that in addition to voluntary mechanisms of the body, involuntary mechanisms can also be changed or controlled. He first demonstrated this by showing that through reinforcement and punishment an animal could control the amount of blood flow to its ear. Blood flow, heart rate, how much blood goes to a particular region of the body, and so on are involuntary functions. That means you cannot simply say to yourself, *Blood, I command you to flow to my brain* or *Heart, I demand that you beat faster*. Miller's early work in biofeedback suggested that something like that is possible to learn, however. As discussed in Chapter 1, biofeedback involves continual measurement of a particular physiological mechanism (e.g., skin temperature, heart rate). When an individual is instructed to engage in a particular behavior such as a relaxation technique, they will be able to watch changes occur in their physiology. Changes can also occur when the individual is instructed, for example, to think anxious thoughts. They can then observe the engagement of the sympathetic branch of the autonomic nervous system (i.e., the fight-or-flight response) via an increase in heart rate, breathing, or skin temperature. Miller's work in biofeedback and the work of others in the decades that followed effectively proved that Benson's ideas were based in science and the Relaxation Response intervention was a legitimate and viable treatment of stress-related symptoms and illness.

Outside of scientific pursuits are practices that have been used for hundreds or thousands of years. Yoga is an ancient practice associated with Buddhism. The primary tenet of this practice is to allow the practitioner of yoga to develop control over his or her mind. Some contemporary practices of yoga focus more on the exercise element that may facilitate weight loss or fitness, which can certainly occur; however, its roots are in helping human beings connect more deeply with themselves. Scientists who were curious about the benefits of yoga and the claims that were made by its practitioners determined that it was possible through yoga to reduce how much oxygen the body consumed or to slow the rate by which the body used fuel (i.e., metabolism). These findings further support the notion of the mind-body connection and the control we can have over our bodies' involuntary functions. Similarly, monks in Japan who regularly practiced meditation were studied. The results were similar to that of the yogis. Scientists reported that the use of oxygen and the rate of fuel consumption in Zen monks was equivalent to that found after several hours of sleep.

Dr. Benson systematically studied practitioners of Transcendental Meditation and continued to uncover the nature of the connection between mind and body and the benefits of the practice itself. He was able to determine that although there was some overlap between meditation and sleep, as alluded to in the preceding paragraph, meditation and sleep are two separate states of consciousness and neither can be a substitute for the other. In addition to this work, other researchers were examining the effects of other techniques such as autogenic training, relaxation hypnosis, and progressive relaxation. All were found to have some effect on the autonomic nervous system such that they activated elements of the parasympathetic nervous system: slowed breathing, slowed heart rate, decrease in blood pressure, reduced muscle tension, and so on. Dr. Benson along with these other researchers was able to scientifically support what regular practitioners of these various art forms have known for centuries: the mind and body are connected, and when the mind is at peace, so is the body.

Thus, in order to help individuals calm their minds and bodies Dr. Benson developed what he called the "Relaxation Response" and detailed a recommended procedure. He further noted through his decades of working with patients and using the technique himself that there are two essential ingredients:

1. Engaging in some type of repetitive behavior, which can include the recitation of a particular sound, word, phrase, or prayer, or it can be a physical movement.
2. *Passively disregarding* intrusive thoughts about everyday life that will enter your mind and redirecting your attention to whatever you are doing for #1.

With respect to the first ingredient, when we think of being relaxed or trying to get to a relaxed state, we usually think that we need to be motionless. For many people this will be quite effective and therefore the use of a repetitive sound (e.g., vocalizing *ohm*), word (e.g., saying the word *calm* or *peace*), phrase (e.g., saying *I am at peace*), or prayer will make sense. Others who engage in physical activity that has a repetitive element to it (e.g., riding a bike, running/jogging, swimming) will find that focusing one's attention on the repetitive movement can elicit a sense of relaxation. A runner, for example, can pay attention to the cadence of their steps or their breaths. Dr. Benson suggests that one can say *left, right, left, right* with each step or *in, out, in, out* with each breath. An alternative can be to simply count one's steps or breaths. The idea is to calm your mind by giving it something monotonous to do that does not require effort.

As for the second element, Dr. Benson acknowledged that extraneous thoughts about the day or problems we have yet to solve will inevitably enter our minds while we try to relax. As noted above, he suggests a passive approach to dealing with such intrusions. Rather than trying to *not think* about these things (which tends not to work very well), we should instead literally or figuratively shrug our shoulders and redirect our attention to whatever we have chosen for our repetitive task. This approach has resurfaced in recent years when it comes to helping people deal with anxious thoughts. It used to be that the instruction was to make the thought go away by countering it with another thought (e.g., instead of thinking *I'm going to fail*, think *I've worked hard and will do my very best*). Although this works for some people, many either don't believe the alternative thought and thus experience a resurgence of the original thought or have found that there may be some truth to the original thought, which means that making it go away because it is wrong or not helpful will not be effective.

What is recommended more frequently now in this type of situation is what Dr. Benson instructed several decades ago. When you notice that the thought is there, you don't have to do anything with it other than to *hear* it and allow it to keep moving. It entered your mind, so allow it to keep right on going rather than holding it there by finding a way to make it go away. Let it go away on its own. The added benefit with the Relaxation Response is that there is something that you can simply redirect your attention to (i.e., the repetitive thought or action). This is not in an effort to make the intrusive thoughts go away, but to simply get back to what you were doing in the first place: allowing you mind and body to find a place of calm.

As with any other relaxation technique, part of this process involves finding a comfortable position for your body if you are not exercising. Dr. Benson recommends closing your eyes (again only for the non-exercisers) and relaxing each muscle group. This, of course, can be done via the progressive muscle relaxation technique discussed in Chapter 1. While he also suggests that breathing should be normal, it is certainly useful to determine whether or not you are breathing with your abdomen (see Chapter 1 for a description of deep abdominal breathing). Along with each breath Dr. Benson instructs that your sound, word, phrase, or prayer should be uttered on the exhale.

He suggests that 10–20 minutes is a sufficient length of time to elicit the Relaxation Response and that this routine should be practiced once or twice a day. Finally, before getting up to go about your day, he recommends that you allow your normal thoughts to return and allow yourself a few minutes to reorient yourself to your surroundings.

Just like any other skill, eliciting Benson's Relaxation Response technique requires practice. It is possible that initial relaxation sessions may yield no effect or may even leave you frustrated (and paradoxically more tense) because you were unable to relax. In this case it is important to remember that your body will *learn* to relax; you just have to help it along by giving it time. When you regularly attempt to engage in the Relaxation Response and follow a routine such as practicing at the same time every day, in the same place, and using the same repetitive behavior, your mind and body will both learn to associate each of those things with feeling more relaxed. These things become signals of what is to come. When that connection is made, many people notice that as soon as they sit down in their relaxation chair or put on more comfortable clothes, they immediately start to feel more relaxed—before the process officially begins. He also notes that, especially when someone is using his technique in an effort to address a medical issue (e.g., hypertension), it should always be done in conjunction with a consulting physician.

Practicing the Relaxation Response also involves not only what the actual process will entail but when and where it will occur. You may find that what you thought were the ideal time and location turn out to be problematic because you actually do not have enough time or the location is too busy. Part of practicing will be experimenting with the timing and location. Benson noted that he was told by practitioners that they benefitted by using the Relaxation Response on the subway or in the hallway outside a classroom. Others reported that they closed their office doors at work or used a closed bedroom at home. The reality is that the Relaxation Response can be practiced effectively anywhere at any time. You just have to find the right combination for you, and keep practicing.

RELAXATION RESPONSE RESILIENCY PROGRAM

The Relaxation Response Resiliency Program (3RP) is an eight-week treatment program based on Benson's work on the Relaxation Response and the decades of research that have been conducted since then. The developers of 3RP noted that this program also has its roots in cognitive behavioral therapy (CBT) and positive psychology.

Once Dr. Benson established the effectiveness of Relaxation Response training, the procedure was formally incorporated into a rehabilitation program for cardiac patients. Subsequent to this use of the Relaxation Response, other researchers used this type of training with cancer patients, women with premenstrual syndrome, and those who simply elected to take part in a work-based stress management program. In aggregate, the results of these studies indicated that Relaxation Response training has been found to be effective for helping people sleep, manage pain, rely less on medication, and lower hypertension.

Since his initial work with cardiac patients, Benson and his colleagues developed two programs designed to include not only Relaxation Response training but also other modes of treatment and prevention to help patients who were dealing with serious medication concerns. The first program, the Cardiac Wellness Program, is completed in 13 weeks and is designed to reduce cardiac risk factors. Individuals who take part in the program engage in supervised exercise, receive nutrition counseling, practice eliciting the Relaxation Response, and receive training on how to reduce stress. Results of this program indicated that those who completed the program were less likely to be hospitalized after completion of the program compared to similar patients who did not complete the program. Moreover, the researchers of the Cardiac Wellness Program reported that those who completed the program had a mortality rate lower than that of a similar group of cardiac patients who simply received the standard of care for cardiac rehabilitation.

The second program, the Medical Symptom Reduction Program, was developed for patients with chronic illnesses that may be made worse by experiencing stress. The focus of this program is not only on stress reduction but on reducing one's maladaptive responses to stress. This is a 12-week program that helps participants develop and maintain healthy behaviors. It also incorporates CBT techniques intended to address patients' ways of thinking that may promote or detract them from engaging in healthy behaviors. Results of studying these participants showed reductions in symptoms that can be associated with stress, including symptoms related to depression and anxiety as well as medical symptoms like chest pain, nausea, headaches, and back pain.

These precursors to 3RP clearly suggested that seriously ill patients could benefit from learning the Relaxation Response and other health-facilitating behaviors. They benefitted both mentally and physically by learning how to reduce their physiological reactivity to stress. The idea behind 3RP is to build on these preexisting successful programs while focusing on the construct of *resiliency*. Being resilient refers to the ability to positively adapt to situations that cause suffering and to the extent possible to return to the state you were in prior to this distress. Thus, the Relaxation Response *Resiliency* Program is focused on teaching skills to help prevent and cope with situations that contribute to one's level of stress. An additional construct to which the developers of 3RP point as being important in developing resiliency is *allostasis*. Allostasis refers to the degree to which the brain can keep the body's systems stable despite the demands of the environment. For example, when you experience something that would normally cause discomfort or anxiety, the question is how effectively is your brain able to respond to the activation of the sympathetic nervous system by calming the body down? The process the brain uses to identify when the body's systems are over- or under-activated and then send the necessary signals to the body to regain stability is allostasis. When we are consistently under a great deal of stress, the brain is required to work harder to bring your body back to baseline functioning. This reflects something called a high allostatic load, which can increase the chances that you will more easily become ill.

To combat this, medical professionals and researchers recommend developing skills that can reduce your allostatic load and take the pressure off your brain and body from having to manage excessive stressors. Learning how to reliably elicit the Relaxation Response is one such skill that contributes to your resiliency or your ability to bounce back from highly stressful situations. Another way to think about this is in terms of someone who is physically fit compared to someone who is not. All other things being equal, if both individuals are asked to run a mile as fast as they can, who do you think would recover more quickly from the run? That is, whose rate of breathing and heart rate will resume baseline (per mile running) functioning? The physically fit person has conditioned their body to cope with such a demand by training and remaining physically fit. Thus, in this way, they have developed resiliency and their body is able to more effectively cope with that type of physical demand and will more easily return to normal functioning. Relaxation Response training can have the same effect when it comes to environmental stress. Your mind and body will react to something that is demanding of it, especially if it is perceived to be a threat. The question is, how quickly will your body get back to baseline functioning? How quickly will your mind recognize that the situation is not threatening and signal the body that it "stand down" and deactivate the fight-or-flight response? The more quickly your mind and body make this happen, the more resilient you are, and the healthier you will be. This is the theory on which 3RP was designed.

As noted earlier, 3RP is an eight-week program. Participants meet for one and a half hours each week of the program and focus on managing chronic stress, specifically as this management targets participants' resiliency. The developers of the program noted that their interventions are designed to address five elements of resiliency that were previously identified by other researchers. These five components are thought to be specific skills that can be learned and are as follows:

1. Managing responses to fearful situations so that we can continue to function well despite feeling fear
2. Using healthy social supports in order to receive help from and provide help to others
3. Learning new, more adaptive, ways of thinking about negative experiences
4. Experiencing optimism and positive feelings such that the experience feels rewarding and motivating
5. Developing a sense of purpose and meaning with an accompanying sense of the direction in which one wants to live one's life.

Learning to manage fear in response to stressful situations involves developing the capacity to regularly elicit the Relaxation Response. It is recommended that each person identify the strategy that is most effective for themselves not only in terms of the physiological effects of the strategy but also so that the individual is open to experiencing the other facets of the program. Thus, the program is not just about learning a particular Relaxation Response strategy, but it is also about identifying and coping with stress, and it focuses on growth and life enhancement.

In terms of managing stress itself, participants are taught not only how to identify stressful situations when they arise but also how to view these situations such that they do not automatically elicit a strong stress response. Our experience of stress is bound not only by what the stressful event is but also by what we think about the event itself. For example, taking a school-based exam is likely to evoke stress in most people; however, not everyone is debilitated by such an event. One explanation for that is how each of us views or appraises such an event. If one person considers an exam to be just one element of their overall grade, that person will probably not experience the exam as stressful as someone who believes the exam will make or break not only their grade but their entire future. Thus, 3RP helps participants learn what the warning signs of stress are for them (these will be different from person to person), how to effectively get support from others, and what they can do specifically to think and feel better about the situation.

The third element, growth/life enhancement, introduces a focus on that which makes life worth living. Participants are encouraged to examine how they can more effectively relate to others in terms of not only how they can elicit support from others when they are experiencing stress but also how they can interact more effectively with people on a daily basis. Additional areas of focus for this growth-oriented component include recognizing the ways in which they are developing skills to cope effectively, identifying ways that spirituality is important to them, and identifying what they appreciate about life. Proponents of 3RP suggest that experiencing stressors themselves can help foster each of these elements. Thus, the point is not to eliminate stress altogether, but to recognize that stressors and our accompanying methods of coping with them can be instructive. They can tell us what we like and don't like about how our lives are spent, which people in our lives are healthy for us, and how a sense of spirituality can help engender a sense of peace and well-being.

The program developers indicate that although 3RP is highly structured, it still has the capacity to be individualized based on the needs and skills of each participant. They note that the structured nature allows it be implemented in a group setting but can also be easily adapted to individual work. Each week of the program involves covering a new topic area related to areas such as the nature of stress, the Relaxation Response, and resiliency. Each session begins with an appraisal of how each participant has been doing with respect to their stress levels as well as their work on their previous week's goals. Each session also introduces a new strategy designed to elicit the Relaxation Response. The purpose of this is to expose participants to a wide variety of techniques from which they can choose the one(s) that seem to be the most effective for them. Each session concludes with goal setting completed in collaboration with program facilitators. In between each session participants are tasked with keeping track of their efforts at eliciting the Relaxation Response and any changes they notice in their overall stress experience. As noted above, although structured, the program is individualistic in that it incorporates self-reflection and analysis to determine what is working and what is not. Program facilitators undoubtedly provided their own observations regarding how effectively each participant seems to be learning and implementing new skills. This type of feedback can be invaluable as it is often difficult to accurately self-assess one's own progress.

Some researchers have extended the use of this program and studied it with specific ailments. One study that has been completed examined the effectiveness of 3RP with patients coping with pain related to chronic temporomandibular disorder (TMD)—pain involving the muscles of the mouth. Participants in this study received standard medical care for their conditions as well as taking part in 3RP. Researchers indicated that this version of 3RP focused on pain management specifically and included psychoeducational material about pain. Overall the results indicated that not only did the patients like the program but as a group reported a reduction in the intensity of their pain, how often they experienced pain, how long the pain lasted, and that they were able to tolerate their pain better than before the program.

An additional study that was conducted based on the work of this program was completed in an online format. The purpose of the study was to determine whether or not it is possible and effective to implement a stress management program, usually conducted in person, in a virtual format. In addition to online contact with the program facilitator, participants interacted with a virtual environment that they were able to alter on a limited basis to make the experience more personalized. The results indicated that participants liked the virtual format and perhaps more importantly self-reported a decrease in overall stress. On formal questionnaires participants also showed reductions in symptoms related to depression and anxiety and the overall number of reported mental health-related symptoms. The findings of this study have provocative implications. Many people spend much of their lives using electronic mediums; we now shop online, communicate online, and take college courses online. Health care is somewhat behind the curve when it comes to delivering services via technology; however, there is an increased desire from professionals and needs from patients to be able to provide and receive health-care services from a distance. There are certainly disadvantages to not meeting in person with a medical or mental health provider; however, in cases where travel is impossible (e.g., due to weather or an impairment) or burdensome (e.g., a patient who moves several hours away but who wants to continue to work with their established health-care providers), intervention via technology can be a viable solution.

Although the core of 3RP is based on decades of study demonstrating not only the Relaxation Response itself but the beneficial effects it can have on the mind and body, 3RP developers indicated that additional research is required to establish this specific program's effectiveness with a broad array of physical and psychological ailments. More studies are also needed to determine whether or not services provided via technology are as effective as those provided in person; however, the virtual world stress management program seems to suggest that technologically based services can be effective.

ATTENTIONAL BEHAVIORAL COGNITIVE RELAXATION THEORY

Attentional Behavioral Cognitive (ABC) Relaxation Theory was developed by Jonathan Smith, who studied relaxation, its effects, and what happens when it is practiced for many years. Although he presents his theory as extending and expanding on previous work in the area of relaxation, he acknowledged that his work was influenced by that of Albert Ellis, pioneer and powerhouse behind cognitive behavioral strategies that are often used in CBT.

Smith defines relaxation as "sustained, passive, simple focus." He believes that relaxation is not meant to be approached with a detailed rigid plan that must be pursued no matter what. Rather it is a decision one makes and a process one allows to unfold, however it unfolds, for each of us; the process, the benefits, and the strategies used will be unique to each practitioner of relaxation. There is no one way to do it, or no single timeframe by which one will experience the benefits; relaxation is not something you do, it is something you allow to happen. Related to this is a concept Smith calls the "paradox of passivity." Generally speaking, this means that the harder we try to achieve relaxation, the more elusive it will become. Therefore, taking a more passive approach (i.e., not trying to make relaxation happen but simply allowing it to happen on its own) means that not only you are more likely to feel relaxed but also the benefits that come from relaxation will move beyond the relaxation process itself (e.g., my mind is at peace, my body feels heavy and warm) and will positively affect your overall experience with everyday life.

Smith acknowledges the important work conducted by Benson and others in the area of the Relaxation Response; however, Smith suggests that these previous ideas may not provide the best explanation of what relaxation is nor of what it can do for people. He indicates that although the Relaxation Response can be beneficial, what it is incapable of doing is answering larger life-oriented questions that point to whether or not we will continue practicing relaxation techniques, why some of us feel anxiety when we try to relax, and why we struggle with structuring our lives to support relaxation-oriented activities. Additionally, he indicates that once someone has achieved the ultimate benefit of the Relaxation Response—which as a reminder is a reduction in physiological arousal—there would seemingly be no further need of pursuing relaxation strategies. Smith points to the fact that those who continue to incorporate relaxation into their way of living experience benefits beyond mere changes in physiology. Those who practice relaxation over the course of their lifetimes report experiencing ongoing change and growth, suggesting that relaxation is more than just the activation of the parasympathetic nervous system.

Smith has engaged in a systematic examination of what relaxation is, how people experience it, what people think of it, and the myriad ways people seem to benefit from it. As a result, he has developed a theory of relaxation that extends and expands on prior theory and research. His findings suggest that relaxation is not merely a tool to get you from point A to point B: from tense to relaxed. It is something that can be incorporated into your daily life, and that has the potential to change how you view yourself and the world around you. As such, he concluded that relaxation is not unidimensional but is something that must be understood and examined in terms of multiple dimensions.

His studies began with asking a variety of people a simple question: "How do you feel when you are relaxed?" The responses he received suggested to him that there is a serious disconnect between what helping professionals are taught about relaxation and the experience of being relaxed, and what the average person experiences. Smith indicated that far too often people are told what they ought to expect as a result of experiencing relaxation. These expectations come from well-meaning people who believe that what is known to happen in research or through one's own experience is what ought to happen with everyone else. Thus, the implication is that if you are not experiencing what you are *supposed* to be experiencing, then you're doing it wrong. This, he said, is relaxation dogma that can impede not only our understanding of relaxation but also of other people's willingness to engage in it. Smith's theory, therefore, is an attempt to allow for the wide variety of experiences that people have when they engage in relaxation as well as their unique beliefs about it and attitudes toward the process. To help account for these individual experiences, Smith proposed three central constructs to the theory: "R-States," "R-Beliefs," and "R-Attitudes." He posited that the combination of all three can determine whether or not one's unique relaxation experience will be effective.

R-States refers to "relaxation states." Smith contends that the psychological experience of relaxation is as important as, if not more important than, being able to quantify the physiological changes that take place beneath the skin. Moreover, he points to the fact that when you ask someone how they feel when they are relaxed, they do not typically talk about brain wave activity, blood flow, or skin temperature. They often say things like *I feel calm* or *I feel content* or some variation thereof. In his work to find a way to measure R-States, Smith developed several questionnaires that have helped to identify nine different R-States: sleepiness, disengagement, physical relaxation, mental quiet, mental relaxation, strength and awareness, joy, love and thankfulness, and prayerfulness.

An important facet of the ABC Relaxation Theory is the idea of letting go or withdrawal. *Sleepiness* reflects this in that it embodies dozing off and drowsiness, which Smith characterizes as a way of disconnecting from the world. Indeed, outside of the context of relaxation, some individuals welcome sleep because during that time they do not have to contend with their daily lives. *Disengagement* is a more explicit nod to relaxation being a way of withdrawing from the world around you. He noted that those who describe their relaxation experience in terms of disengagement are typically referring to loss of sensation in the body, feeling far away, feeling indifferent, disconnected from one's physical surroundings, and temporarily forgetting about time and place. This may sound scary to some, but the idea is not that these are permanent experiences, just what relaxation can feel like in the moment. *Physical relaxation* can refer to the experience of Benson's Relaxation Response. Smith noted that descriptors of this particular state include things like "heavy," "mellow," "sedate," and "limp." *Mental quiet* refers to what is happening in one's mind. This specifically refers to cognition, or mental processes, and the fact that in this state a person is quiet; that is, the experience of someone in this state is that they are not thinking anything. *Mental relaxation* is less about the absence of cognitive experiences and more about the idea that what is happening in the mind is peaceful or soothing. The *strength and awareness* R-State suggests a somewhat paradoxical state in comparison to relaxation. This state reflects the experience of feeling energized or focused. Smith suggests that the strength and awareness component and its seemingly energized state of being likely reflects a reduction in overall tension, allowing someone to feel less distracted and thus more focused and more aware. The *joy* state identified in Smith's studies explains the relaxation experience more so than the other states. Smith suggested that this state is characterized by the person seeing things positively and having positive emotional experiences. He further postulated that a reduction in physical and mental tension facilitates a type of clarity that allows more joyful experiences into our awareness. The last R-State is *prayerfullness*. While this state certainly refers to what some people feel like in the act of prayer, the state itself is not exclusive to traditional religious experiences. He indicated that prayerfullness can also reflect experiences such as thankfulness and spirituality.

Smith noted that the nine R-States can in and of themselves feel reinforcing. That is, you may engage in relaxation for the purpose of experiencing one or more of these states; however, as with the rest of his analysis of the process of relaxation, he suggests that there is more to the R-States than pure reward. Not only do we benefit from the experience that comes with being in a particular state, but the various R-States can also help us focus better, help us to be more passive when our tendency is to be always active, facilitate us getting from one state to another, activate a particular skill or experience (e.g., creativity), and may allow us to develop an understanding of why the practice of relaxation is personally beneficial.

Early in his work, Smith suggested that the R-States beginning with reduced stress or *sleepiness* progress in order until the practitioner reaches a state of *prayerfulness*. He later noted that the idea of a sequence of states through which practitioners will predictably progress is arbitrary and that theoretically any sequence of states is possible. However, he eventually concluded that there were two potential paths, one of which he called the "path of Disengagement" and the other the "path of Joy"—both of which ultimately lead to prayerfulness. Given Smith's overall perspective that the relaxation process is idiosyncratic to each of us in that we approach it differently than the next person and that what we get out of it will also be unique, it would seem that describing particular paths through which we may progress seems antithetical to his approach.

R-Beliefs refers to "relaxation beliefs" or what you think about relaxation. *R-Attitudes* refers to "relaxation attitudes" or how you approach the relaxation process. Although not quite this simple, generally speaking those who have negative beliefs about and attitudes toward relaxation (e.g., it won't work and I don't have time) are unlikely to reap much benefit, whereas those who have positive beliefs about and attitudes toward the process are likely to experience enduring and potentially life-changing benefits.

Smith catalogued common types of thinking that can interfere with one's ability to benefit from the relaxation process. These reflect Smith's R-Attitudes. Readers familiar with the work of Albert Ellis will recognize him as the source of much of this list. The list is extensive and will not be included in its entirety here, but includes thinking in terms of absolutes that do not allow for a middle ground, thinking that you know how something will turn out before it even happens, turning things you want to have happen into things that *have* to or *must* happen, turning simple frustration when things do not turn out as planned into catastrophe, blaming other people or the environment for your stress, assuming that if one strategy did not work then none will, and thinking that your experience with stress is unlike anyone else's and therefore nothing and no one can help. As you can see, the types of thinking illustrated are not likely to facilitate relaxation. Some of them might prevent you from trying to relax in the first place, and if you do try a relaxation strategy, you may only do so begrudgingly almost guaranteeing that you will not benefit from the process.

R-Beliefs by contrast aid the relaxation process in terms of making it more meaningful not only in the moment but also with respect to long-term benefits. Smith noted that beliefs about relaxation give meaning to the various experience of relaxation one might have. For example, if you believe that relaxation will benefit you and that you will feel differently than before you began the process, you are less likely to be bothered or concerned by your body feeling heavy or by feeling drowsy, or at peace. Smith also posited that R-Beliefs can range from being concrete and specific to the relaxation process to more abstract, reflecting a shift in one's belief about how one lives one's life. For example when engaged in a particular technique, a specific R-Belief might be *I have so much work to do. I'll think about that later. Right now I'm focused on my breathing*, whereas a more abstract R-Belief could be *I will live one day at a time*.

Smith identified eight distinct R-Beliefs: optimism, acceptance, honesty, taking it easy, love, inner wisdom, god, and deeper perspective. These beliefs can be combined in any number of ways. Thus, it is not that someone may experience one belief or another at any given time, but that one can experience more than one of these in each moment or over the course of one's life. He also indicated that the beliefs that one has can be directly related to the various R-States that he proposed. For example, if you have the R-Belief of *taking it easy* then relaxation will likely lead to an R-State such as *mental quiet* or *mental relaxation*.

An additional construct referred to as *N-States* is included to describe experiences during the relaxation process that might be sources of distress or distraction. In the example above, the thought *I have so much work to do* would be considered an N-State because it would undoubtedly be either a distraction from the process and/or a source of distress. At this point the relaxer has a decision to make. He or she could leave the relaxation process to attend to the work, or counter this state with an R-Belief like *I'll think about that later. Right now I'm focused on my breathing*. Smith categorized plausible N-States in terms of how someone might appraise the relaxation process and negative or distressing consequences of engaging in "passive simple focus."

The N-States that reflect relaxation appraisal include difficulty in letting go of active and purposeful effort; fear of losing control; concern about becoming lazy; unfamiliarity with what R-States might feel like, which might feel threatening; and previous relaxation experiences that were ineffective or distressful, and the experience of relaxation may remind individuals of some other experience that has nothing to do with relaxation itself. The second category of N-States involving concern about passive simple focus includes developing sensitivity to sensations that individuals were previously unaware of; remaining detached or disengaged after the relaxation process has ended; making negative thoughts or experiences that were previously forgotten or ignored a part of one's awareness; having temporary loss of contact with reality; breathing too shallow and rapid or too slow, leading to distressing changes in physiology; and experiencing changes in the activity level of various parts of their brain (e.g., those that used to be less active are more active and vice versa).

Over the course of several years identifying and refining the various elements of ABC Relaxation Theory, Smith and colleagues have not only developed psychometrically sound questionnaires designed to measure the veracity of this theory but have also provided evidence that who you are and what method you choose as a relaxation tool have a direct impact on what you will ultimately experience as a result of the process. Who you are and what you believe may, for example, influence you to choose progressive muscle relaxation, leading to a state of physical relaxation, whereas someone else with different beliefs might elect to engage in meditation, leading to a state of disengagement or mental quiet. Additional research seems to have yielded inconsequential differences between genders and various cultures. Thus, it does not seem to matter whether or not you are male or female or in what culture you live when it comes to the benefits of relaxation. What has been found, however, is that three R-States that research participants seem to desire the most—mental relaxation, strength and awareness, and joy—are also reliably associated with reductions in physical, mental, and emotional tension. These three R-States have also been consistently linked to the R-Beliefs of optimism, inner wisdom, and acceptance. Smith therefore concluded that this combination of R-States and R-Beliefs contributes what he called "adaptive relaxation," which facilitates one's overall health.

Beginners or veterans of relaxation practices can benefit from adaptive relaxation. We can all self-assess and determine whether or not we experience this combination of R-States and R-Beliefs. If not, we can adjust our approach and techniques in order to develop these aspects of the process. We can also determine for ourselves, however, that if we are already experiencing an overall improvement in health, it may not make sense to tinker with what we are doing just to align ourselves with this research finding. Indeed, Smith acknowledges that further research by others is necessary to identify which aspects of his theory continue to receive empirical support and are therefore worth putting into practice and which elements may need to be changed or eliminated from the theory. Regardless, paying attention to one's own process is the best evidence for whether or not you are getting what you want out of your relaxation method(s) of choice.

Relaxation is not a destination. That is to say, once you've practiced a technique or two and found yourself in a relaxed state, you are not cured of your stress and tension. Incorporating relaxation techniques in your everyday life will help you stave off the harmful effects of ongoing tension and may even cause you to consider whether or not you want to continue the activities that consistently contribute to your overall level of stress. Moreover, just because a particular strategy worked now does not mean it will continue to work in future. Our life circumstances change (which in and of itself can be stressful), and our ability to do certain things can be compromised (which can also be stressful); thus, it is important to continually engage in self-awareness such that you take stock of your level of stress, if your strategies are working, why they aren't working, and what you may need to do differently.

Smith reminds professionals that in helping clients facilitate their own relaxation process and identify that which might interfere with clients' effective practice of relaxation, professionals need to listen to the existing beliefs and attitudes of the clients. He recommends that professionals should help clients become the best relaxation practitioners they can be based on who they are, rather than trying to help clients become the type of relaxation practitioner the professionals think they *ought* to be.

5

When: Relaxation throughout the Life Cycle

The positive and negative aspects of relaxation as well as the various techniques discussed in the previous chapters are, theoretically, universal when it comes to age. That is, what can help someone relax as an adult can also help a child, an adolescent, or an older adult. There are, however, factors that might affect the use of relaxation in these various age groups. Keeping these factors in mind can make the use of relaxation more effective and more enjoyable at any age.

GENERAL PRINCIPLES ACROSS THE LIFE SPAN

Recent research in the area of understanding the ways in which neural processing in the brain is implicated in the experience of anxiety has helped to explain how anxiety for particular objects or situations may develop. Many readers may be familiar with the idea of *classical conditioning*—this is the theory that involves Pavlov's dogs. This particular theory says that we have the ability to make connections between two or more experiences and learn that they go together. In his original work, Pavlov discovered by accident that his dogs learned particular cues that always occurred just before they were fed. Pavlov had not intended to study how dogs learned; however, the fact that the dogs had learned to anticipate when they were about to be fed intrigued him, which lead him to devise the study in which he rang a bell and then fed the dogs their food. The dogs learned the connection between the bell and the upcoming food and began salivating (drooling) before they even saw the food coming. This theory explains why your dog might get excited when you grab your car keys or your running shoes—your dog has learned that car keys are equated with going for a ride and the running shoes equal getting outside and going for a run or walk. Your dog is not really excited about the keys or shoes themselves; they are excited about what they *know* is coming next. Human beings are no different when it comes to this type of learning. One example of classical conditioning that many people can relate to is the connection between lightning and thunder. We know what follows lightning: thunder. The lightning itself is not so scary (i.e., of course, if you or someone or something important to you has not been hit by lightning), but the thunder is what we brace ourselves for. For some of us a flash of lightning may cause us to hide under a blanket or grab the arm of the person next to us.

Scientists who study how the brain actually works have been able to develop complex models illustrating how something originally innocuous like lightening can produce a fear response. These researchers have extended Pavlov's original work by showing that it is not so much what the dog or human being is experiencing as it is what is happening in the brain that makes this type of learning occur. A well-known case study that illustrates this type of learning and how fear can be produced in children is the case study of "Little Albert." Little Albert was a very young child, around nine months of age, when an experiment in which he took part was conducted. In 1920 a well-known behavioral psychologist John Watson and his graduate student set out to demonstrate the notion that through the application of the principles of classical conditioning, they could create a fear response to an object in a child who originally did not fear that object. In this case Little Albert was allowed to play with a white rat. He was comfortable with the rat until Watson made a very loud noise behind Little Albert, which caused him to cry. Watson made the loud noise each time Albert reached for the rat until the point at which all Watson had to do was put the rat in front of Little Albert, and he would cry without the loud noise. Little Albert learned to fear the rat. The association was so strong that two to three weeks later Little Albert showed intense distress when similar objects were put in the same room with him.

Both Pavlov's and Watson's experiments demonstrate how relatively easy it is for us to make connections between things that previously had no connection, and therefore how easy it may be for us to develop a fear response or anxiety to something that might not inherently cause such a reaction. For some of us these learned connections cause some distress but not enough to be debilitating—they may even be something we seek out. For example, those who watch horror movies can anticipate when something scary is about to happen. We have learned to associate the actual scary scene with the preceding dialog, music, mannerisms of the actors, or some other cues. So we hide our eyes right before we think such scenes are about to take place. Of course, we keep watching this type of movie despite knowing we are going to be scared. Some experiences, however, are much more significant and can interfere with one's ability to function in everyday life.

An example of such an event might be a car accident. Those who have been in a car accident, no matter how minor or severe the accident was, understand how scary something like that can be. For some people the terrifying experience of the accident has become inextricably linked with cars. In this case, they may not be able to ride, let alone simply sit, in a car without experiencing significant distress to the point that they avoid them at all costs. For others, this result gets *generalized* beyond cars, and they experience this intense fear when confronted with riding in any motorized vehicle. This type of fear will likely significantly impair this person's ability to do what they need to do in their daily lives. Still others walk away from the accident shaken but able to use motorized transportation of any kind without much, if any, distress. Of course, this wide range of responses has the attention of neuroscientists and behavioral scientists who have attempted to try to figure out why some people develop a debilitating fear or phobia of something whereas others, having experienced the same situation, walk away psychologically unscathed.

Explanations of these divergent responses can get technical and complex; however, current research suggests that some of us are simply genetically predisposed to develop phobias or other forms of clinical anxiety. We may have extensive family histories (assuming a biological connection between family members) suggesting that we inherited anxiety from our biological ancestors. Indeed, scientists who study the brain have identified certain neurological pathways in the brain (i.e., the route via which particular information is transmitted from one part of the brain to another) that can be more sensitive in some people. This means that when something that *could* produce fear or anxiety is experienced, those with more sensitive pathways in the brain not only are much more likely to experience anxiety in the moment but also experience the anxiety persisting long after the situation has come and gone. There are also certain structures in the brain (i.e., millions of neurons grouped together to form a functional structure than can be identified in the brain) that process various emotions, including fear. The amygdala is a structure that is known to process fear in addition to aggression. When the amygdala is not functioning properly, it is possible to experience an exaggerated fear response or, alternatively, no fear at all.

Other research has revealed that in both children and adults there is a difference in how a threatening situation is processed depending on whether one already has clinical anxiety or not. Scientists have found that those with anxiety are more likely to pay closer attention to the threatening situation, whereas those without clinical anxiety are able to pay attention to something different. This suggests a particular bias in terms of what information is processed, but it also points to the self-sustaining nature of anxiety. If we are experiencing something threatening that causes us anxiety and we continue to pay attention to the threat, we are likely to continue to feel anxious, which causes us to pay further attention to the threat, and so on. This is a cycle that many get caught up in and is very difficult to break. Related to these findings is the discovery that not only do anxious people pay more attention to the thing that caused the anxiety to begin with, they are also much more likely to recall this event and experience residual anxiety related to it. This does not mean that such individuals intend to remember such events or wallow in their anxiety; rather it simply does not take much for the memory of the situation to be activated and the accompanying anxiety to be reexperienced—sometimes just as intensely as the original experience. Developing this type of understanding of how anxiety is processed has direct implications for prevention and treatment of anxiety disorders in individuals of all ages.

Research over the last several decades has allowed us to understand more precisely the role genetics and the brain can play in the development of things like anxiety. We have also learned more about how to more accurately identify those who may be susceptible to developing anxiety. In addition, we have honed our ability to intervene more quickly and effectively in an anxious or feared situation to help the person calm both their physical and psychological systems. Although these advances can benefit anyone dealing with anxiety of any severity, they may be particularly important as we help children manage the stressors they may experience so that they have the skills to help them cope with any situation that might cause distress throughout their lives. Giving children such tools early on may also help keep some children from developing what is believed to be the most common psychiatric condition among this developmental period: anxiety disorders.

The sections that follow explore particular challenges that we may experience depending on where we are in our life spans. This book thus far has taken a somewhat generic approach in the sense that much of what has been covered is what is typically recommended to help people relax or deal with stress and anxiety. Generally speaking these things are readily applied to the experiences of most adults. Although some of what has been covered can also be applied to individuals of other ages, it is important to address the challenges that are unique to children, adolescents, and older adults. Moreover, given the challenges that may be exclusive to a particular age range, it is also the case that the interventions need to be tailored to the developmental level, knowledge base, and abilities of the person in question.

RELAXATION IN CHILDREN

It often seems that children do not have much to worry about—especially from the perspective of adults. Many of us who are decades removed from childhood look back on that time with wistfulness and longing. We recall a time when we did not have any responsibilities or obligations. We do not remember experiencing any distress, and if we do, we may dismiss that childhood experience as being nothing or not that bad. Of course for some of us, our retrospective perspectives on this time might be spot-on. Others may be minimizing what were just as intense and debilitating experiences as if we had experienced them as an adult. The reality, of course, is that each child is different in terms of what stressors they are exposed to as well as how they handle them. Moreover, the reality is children of nearly every age can experience a multitude of pressures. Without recognizing these pressures and how to cope with them, children are susceptible to the long-term negative effects of anxiety.

When children reach school age, whether the traditional entry into school during kindergarten or earlier as a preschooler, they begin to be challenged in ways not previously experienced. Once around a regular group of children and when in a performance-based environment, children are faced with learning how to fit in and find a peer group as well as dealing with the expectations that accompany an academic setting. Depending on how these things go and how the adults in their life also respond, children may be more or less anxious about being sure they have the *right* friends and about earning the *right* grades. Of course, this implies that all anxiety is simply acquired through various life experiences. The reality is that for some children there may be genetic or biological underpinnings that nearly guarantee a child will become anxious under the right circumstances. Many parents may describe their child as *always* having been an anxious child. And some adults can look back on their lives and have similar recollections—that they *can't remember a time I wasn't anxious*. Not all anxiety experiences rise to the level of a clinical, diagnosable anxiety disorder; however, clinical anxiety is the most common form of psychiatric problem in children, affecting around 20 percent. Some of these children will experience anxiety only during certain situations in childhood. They may effectively grow out of their anxiety as their brains, bodies, and psychological functioning mature. For others, anxiety may persist into adulthood, which can give rise to additional difficulties, including depression and substance abuse. Thus, identifying children who may be susceptible to anxiety is important in order to teach them skills that can help them manage, if not prevent, anxiety when experiencing stressful situations.

When considering the experiences of children, it is useful to acknowledge that children are born with varying degrees of being comfortable in the world. The three most basic types of temperament are *easy*, *slow to warm*, and *difficult*. Easy babies are characterized by the ease with which they transition from one situation to the next or one person to the next. All children struggle with being around strangers or strange situations at certain periods during childhood; however, easy babies are simply not as bothered by these changes as the other two types. On the other extreme are the difficult babies. It is important to note that these children are not being difficult for the sake of being difficult or to make others' lives difficult. Their little brains and bodies are simply not as able to easily adapt to new situations and people. In fact, for difficult babies these experiences are quite distressing and they require much more comforting and soothing, sometimes with little effect. In between these two extremes are the slow-to-warm babies who have a moderate degree of difficulty adjusting to changes in the world around them. They may show signs of distress but it is not as intense as that of difficult babies, and they are more easily soothed. Recent research has suggested that these early temperaments can predict what we're like in adulthood. Easy babies are much more likely to be laid back adults whereas difficult babies are much more likely to be adults who experience more stress and may be more anxious than their peers.

Of course, which temperament one is born with does not fully explain worry and anxiety. Although these temperaments imply differential neurological functioning (i.e., babies with different temperaments have brains that work differently), we can certainly inherit a predisposition to anxiety that may not immediately show up. It may take a certain type or quantity of stressful experiences for such a predisposition to reveal itself. Additionally, as noted in the introduction, we can learn to become afraid of things we experience. A child may enter a situation that is often stressful for many children blissfully unaware of this fact. Once that child sees the stress and worry covering the faces of their childhood peers, they may learn that they are *supposed* to worry about starting school for the first time, or reading from a book in front of a group of people, and so on. We can also learn to fear certain situations from our parents or other adults. An intense fear response to a spider by a parent, for example, can result in a shared fear of spiders in the child despite the fact that the child has never had a bad experience with spiders before.

A knee-jerk reaction to responding to children who are experiencing distress of any kind is to make it better as quickly as possible. Most of us do not want to see our children suffer if we can help it. We kiss boo-boos and apply Band-Aids, give hugs, and take them to the doctor if they are sick and we do not know what to do. This knee-jerk reaction is usually quite helpful. It makes the child feel better and depending on the situation may prevent an injury or illness from getting much worse. Taking away the pain and distress associated with anxiety in children, however, can often backfire. When we see our children feeling anxious, our impulse is to remove them from the situation that is causing them distress; however, the result of this type of help is that the anxiety will not only persist but will likely get worse. It can also mean that the child is unable to develop normally especially if the feared situation is school.

School phobia is not an uncommon form of anxiety in children. There are a variety of reasons why a child might experience anxiety about school. They may be uncomfortable around their peers and fear being judged by them, they may have been bullied, or they may have gotten sick at school one day and are afraid to go back for fear they will get sick there again. The list is potentially endless. When a child expresses distress about going to school or even refuses to go because they are afraid, their tears and the scared look in their eyes are likely to mean that most adults will want to protect them from that experience. Of course, it is important to discern if there is a fear-causing situation that can be reasonably addressed by the parents or school personnel. If this is the case, once the issue is resolved, the child may have no qualms about returning. For example, if a child is getting bullied by a particular peer, discussing this with school personnel and ensuring that this is addressed appropriately can reassure a child that not only will they be left alone by the offending child but that others are looking out for them and can help them solve things that are problematic. In other situations, like presenting something to the class, it will be important for the child to understand that they do have to go to school and participate in class just like everyone else. The alternative is that if the child is allowed to not participate, they have learned that they were right to be afraid of such a thing, which means that anxiety for this particular situation (and anything similar) has been reinforced. School counselors can be consulted to talk with the child about what makes the experience feel so fearful and about basic strategies they can use that can help them manage the feared situation. In cases where the child is not able to engage appropriately in class or refuses to attend school, a consultation with a psychologist specializing in childhood anxiety is recommended. This type of practitioner will work not only with the child to teach them effective coping skills but also with the parents on how to manage getting their child to school and, if needed, on strategies for homework completion.

Experts in the field of anxiety strongly recommend that interventions are tailored to the developmental level of the individual—which is particularly important when it comes to children and adolescents. They suggest that since children vary in terms of their cognitive, social, emotional, and behavioral development, it is crucial that this is taken into account in order to maximize effectiveness when crafting an intervention or series of interventions. For example, a five-year-old cannot cognitively process information the same way a 10-year-old can. Five-year-olds consistently misunderstand and misperceive information in their environments more so than a 10-year-old would simply because their brains are not as fully developed. Additionally, practitioners and researchers in this area note that behavior that may be expected of one age group would be developmentally inappropriate at another. An emotional outburst expressed out of frustration would be expected from a child in elementary school, but not from a preteen or teenager. Thus, the same behaviors are not developmentally created equal. Largely, the interventions that exist to help children and adolescents manage fearful situations have been found to not be developmentally tailored. That is, they are not designed with varying developmental tasks and capabilities in mind. An example of this is traditional cognitive behavioral therapy. While this is generally a highly effective strategy for managing stress and anxiety, it is a set of interventions that are best suited for those who are advanced in their cognitive development. Most young children, for example, cannot think about thinking, understand how their thinking might affect themselves in the future, or reflect on consequences of various behaviors.

Interventions for children regardless of what is causing the distress are generally similar to that which is applied to any age group. This idea is to help them slow down their body's physiology so that among other things their heart rate and breathing slow down. Additionally, the intent is to intervene with negative and anxious thoughts that may further fuel the anxiety itself. Recent research indicates that although traditional instruction on relaxation techniques produces expected results in children, techniques that use metaphor are preferred by children while producing the same results. Those who interact in any capacity with children know how difficult it can be to capture and sustain a child's attention. Thus, a dry, clinical script for relaxation may not work simply because the child may not be interested. Interpreting these principles through metaphor can keep a child's attention long enough so that they benefit from the intervention.

One particular study found that instructing children on how to tense and relax major parts of their body was just as effective as asking them to pretend like they were a turtle going into its shell; however, the children generally preferred the turtle exercise than the more traditional one. Another intervention for kids uses a cat to help children understand how a cat can feel scared, what it looks like when a cat is scared, and how the cat can be helped to feel less scared. This workbook, the Coping Cat Workbook, challenges children to relate to the cat and identify when they have felt scared like the cat and what it looks and feels like when they are scared. This can help children by reassuring them they are not the only ones who can feel scared (the therapist is also instructed to share scary experiences they had) and can help them understand what fear feels and looks like so they can identify it when it is happening. They are also, of course, also taught coping techniques that they practice with a therapist and then at home to help them manage their fears and worries. Another technique used with children is a variation on the deep abdominal breathing intervention that can be quite effective in inducing relaxation. It is effectively the same technique but is referred to as "balloon breathing." The child is told to imagine that as they inhale a breath, it is like they are blowing up a balloon in their belly, and when they exhale, the balloon deflates. This is an imagery that kids can relate to and that can effectively teach them how to breathe properly for this technique.

Because children still require a good deal of care and attention from parents and other adults, their participation in helping a child identify, understand, and cope with their distressing feelings is critical. As noted earlier, a good example of this can involve school refusal. Without a well-developed understanding about what is happening with their child and the most effective ways to help their child deal with the situation so they can manage similar life situations, the parents may be in danger of falling into the instinctual desire to shield their child from the situation that is causing the anxiety. Similarly, school personnel, coaches, extended family, and other important adults who have regular contact with an anxious child are often enlisted to help implement strategies or at least support the strategies implemented by others. Consistency for an anxious child can not only help them feel more safe and secure but also shows them that everyone else is in agreement with how to best handle whatever is going on. This means that if compliance is an issue, there is less of a chance of ongoing resistance. If the child knows that not everyone has the same expectations of them (e.g., attending school, completing homework) the child can use this to their advantage by enlisting the help of those who are likely to be more sympathetic to the child's desires such as not reading in front of the class. The result of this, of course, is that their chances of being able to effectively cope with fearful situations drops dramatically.

It is important when intervening with children to take into consideration what their particular developmental level is in the context of their abilities to process information, interact with others, and regulate their emotions and behaviors. This does not mean that a softer approach should be taken with children in the sense that they do not need to be challenged to manage stressful situations; they simply need to be challenged appropriately given their developmental level and to be subsequently taught techniques that they can realistically understand and implement. The same can be said of adolescents who are decidedly more advanced in all developmental spheres than the childhood versions of themselves; however, their brains are still not fully developed, which means their concerns need also to be understood in the context of who they are and what they are realistically capable of. The unique challenges adolescents face are addressed in the next section.

RELAXATION IN ADOLESCENTS

Many of us well beyond our adolescent years can look back and remember what was difficult, tumultuous, and even stressful about those years. Dealing with the dramatic changes that come with puberty, trying to figure out who we are and what we believe in while simultaneously navigating dating relationships, are just a few of the things that cause consternation among pre-teens and teenagers.

Although there is slight variation depending on what resource is consulted, the age range for adolescence is considered to be 10–18 years. Childhood years are marked by significant and dramatic changes in physical development in terms of learning how to use one's body to move through the world. We start out with very little ability to move our bodies *on purpose*, but the connection between the brain and the body develops quickly and we learn how to reach for what we want and to become mobile via crawling, then walking, then running. We learn basic self-care, and of course, we are learning how to form words and to understand the world around us. By the time adolescence rolls around, it is not that everything is completely mastered by then, but the major tasks decidedly shift from learning what our bodies are capable of to learning how and why our bodies are going through rapid changes. Our brain functioning also goes through dramatic changes, making it difficult for us to manage emotions and make sense of what is going on around us, despite the fact that we are more cognitively advanced than those much younger than us. As adolescents we also have to learn how to manage the changing relationships with our parents as we try to assert our independence in a more adult-like way, as well as trying to be more adult in our relationships with peers, which, of course, includes entering into dating relationships and all the complications that can come with that.

The less tumultuous changes include the ability to process information in a much more advanced capacity. We are able to think abstractly and can contemplate events that have not yet occurred and reason through ethical situations. Additionally, we have the capacity to determine what we think about our abilities to think and reason—which is known as metacognition (thinking about thinking). Our fluid sense of identity starts to become more solid. We typically have accumulated enough experiences that we are able to say with some degree of certainty what we like and do not like about people, cultural trends, activities in which we can participate, and so on. That is not to say that we have got it all figured out by adolescence, but we are usually on a path that will get us there more so than when we were children. All of this is to say that what is going on in adolescence is different than what is going on in childhood or any other developmental period. It is not necessarily better or worse, just different, which means that understanding an adolescent's concerns and intervening to address them are necessarily going to be different.

An example of this might involve the fact that a child might be concerned about making friends whereas an adolescent might develop a greater concern for whether or not they will be successful in attracting the person they hope to date. Certainly adolescents are also concerned about their friendships, but it is developmentally expected that they will be somewhat, if not more, concerned about dating relationships. What also starts to emerge more definitively is an adolescent's personality. As noted in the previous section, infants are born with a particular temperament that is usually the precursor to the adult personality; however, infants and children are much less complex when it comes to nuances in personality and what makes one person unique compared to another. Adolescents are much more differentiated from one another in their social, emotional, cognitive, and behavioral abilities, which means it will start to become more clear with whom they fit and are more comfortable and those with whom they just do not seem to get along. This can be comforting in the sense of finding a group that is a good fit, but it can also be distressing if one does not fit with the group they want to, or if they feel like they do not fit in anywhere.

Generally speaking, the types of things that are likely to worry an adolescent include exams, fitting in, feeling harassed, getting a job, having a baby (both males and females), moving away from home, driving and being stuck in traffic, and taking on new responsibilities. Rebelliousness emerges (or becomes stronger) during this developmental period as adolescents try to take more control of their lives. Of course, each adolescent is different and this is not an exhaustive list; however, these are the types of things experienced during adolescence that can differentiate this developmental period from childhood and even adulthood.

When adolescents get stressed, they are likely to feel a variety of symptoms, some of which they may not recognize as being related to stress and others they may simply not want to admit to. Symptoms can include an overall sense of feeling sick, headaches and sore muscles, gastrointestinal problems (i.e., constipation, diarrhea, and indigestion), difficulty sleeping, inability to concentrate, anger, feeling tired most of the time, or a loss of interest in sex. Although some adolescents have the type of relationship with their parents that they are willing to talk about these things with them, many adolescents do not. Thus, it is certainly important for adolescents to be aware that these symptoms can be an indication that they are experiencing stress and need to intervene on their own behalf to reduce their overall tension and feel more relaxed. Parents, on the other hand, may need to simply be vigilant for lingering changes in their adolescent. Irritability and fatigue, for example, can certainly be caused by any number of things; however, if symptoms like these or any others that are noticed seem to linger, then it is worth talking with your adolescent about what may be going on with them and, if needed, bring them to a physician or psychologist to talk about their concerns.

As noted in the previous section, experts strongly recommend taking a developmental approach to working with stressed and anxious individuals. This means that one size does not necessarily fit all when it comes to helping human beings relax. The approach taken with a kindergartener should necessarily be different than that taken with a sophomore in high school. The principles that underlie relaxation strategies are the same but the delivery and/or instructions may vary. Adolescents, for example, are developing a greater sense of real autonomy. While younger children certainly engage in autonomous behaviors like picking out clothes and dressing themselves or making themselves a sandwich, adolescents are taking on employment, driving a car, and considering what they want to do with their lives when they move away from home. Despite the fact that many adolescents *can't wait* until they can make all of the decisions about their lives and no longer have to be accountable to their parents, it does not take long for them to feel the weight of this responsibility and become stressed or anxious about how they will handle it all.

Capitalizing on this desire to be more independent and in control of their own lives can be beneficial when designing stress management and relaxation strategies. Adolescents can feel much of the time that their lives and bodies are spinning out of control; however, teaching pre-teens and teens that they have control over more than they think can in and of itself help to reduce tension. Although many systems in our bodies work on their own without any conscious input from us (e.g., we do not have to tell our heart to beat or our lungs to breathe), they are responsive to things that we do. This means that we can influence these systems to function more like we want them to. Our hearts and lungs will keep beating and filling with air without us giving it any thought, but we can slow our heart rate and breathing if either one occurs too rapidly. We can manipulate our muscles so that they become tight or loose. And we can make changes in our behavior—especially that which might be contributing to overall stress.

Some adolescents might respond quite well to simply talking with them about the nature of their stress and how their mind and body are responding to what is contributing to their overall tension, and teaching them skills they can use to calm the mind and body. Others, however, might reject outright any discussion or recommendations simply because they are coming from someone else and it may feel to them like this is another situation in which an adult is telling them what to do. In this case, motivational interviewing can be effective. The simplest way to describe this is that motivational interviewing involves understanding a person's motivations and helping them understand what in their life is hindering or facilitating those things. For example, an adolescent might be motivated to have more responsibility but they are having difficulty convincing their parents to give that to them; however, when they are overwhelmed or frustrated or don't get what they want, they tend to have emotional outbursts and end up yelling at their parents and storming off to their room. If it is reasonable to expect that additional responsibilities are appropriate, then a discussion about the ways in which they are currently handling stress and frustration and how they do not get what they want as a result might be beneficial. At that point, it is possible that an adolescent might ask what they should do instead—which is, of course, an open door to talking with them about stress management and relaxation strategies. If they do not ask, then they can be asked if they want to try something different that might be more effective.

Another example that is likely to be of importance to many adolescents is the ability to perform well in whatever activity they find valuable. For some this may be in the realm of academics and for others it may be outside of school-based achievement and focused on music, acting, painting, and other fine arts, or sports. Regardless, during this developmental period, adolescents start to determine what they enjoy and what they are good at—and they tend to seek out those experiences. So if their performance starts to suffer in a way that does not make sense to them, it is possible that stress and anxiety might be the interfering factors. An athlete, for example, might find that while in competition she has difficulty maintaining her focus. She may realize that she is worried about performing up to the standards that her coach and others expect of her. Alternatively, there may be other things going on in her life outside of sport but that are causing her distress, and she is preoccupied about these things even while competing. Or a student who has excelled in math since he was in elementary school may find that the pressure to place high in local and national math competitions has become overwhelming. Although he still enjoys solving challenging mathematical problems, he does not enjoy the tension he feels prior to and during a competition. As a result his performance has suffered and others are wondering *what's wrong* with him.

Both the athlete and the mathematician would benefit from talking with someone about how they are doing overall and what they think is happening in these performance situations. A part of that discussion might also include whether or not they want to continue competing in the way they are currently (especially for the mathematician). Both would likely benefit from identifying exactly what they are thinking and how they are feeling when their performance starts to suffer. They can then be taught strategies that can range from deep abdominal breathing prior to the competition (and at any point during the competition when feasible) coupled with cognitive strategies to counteract the negative or distracting thoughts they have that are pulling them from what they are trying to accomplish at that moment.

Certainly there are no guarantees that an adolescent will cooperate or see the value in what is being discussed; however, at minimum it may get them thinking that there might be another way, and they may, on their own, research how to handle stress or how to get what they want. The point is that adolescents often need and want to feel like they are in control.

Stress, tension, and anxiety can very much make any of us feel like we are out of control. For an adolescent this can be particularly distressing and might even exacerbate the stress they are already feeling. Helping them to see that developing these skills can not only help them gain control over their thoughts, behaviors, and body, but can also help them ultimately get what they want out of life, making them feel more confident, autonomous, and well prepared to deal with life's challenges and ultimately feel more relaxed.

RELAXATION IN OLDER ADULTS

In this culture it is a common refrain, especially of those in the workforce, to say something like *I can't wait until I retire*. The implication is that retirement brings few, if any, worries and the ability to do whatever you want whenever you want. There are simply fewer commitments and obligations. Certainly for some retirees this is exactly what their postwork years feel like. For others, this time is filled with as much, if not more, stress as when they were working 40 plus hours per week. Additionally, there are some who are unable to formally retire at all because they cannot afford to do so. Understanding common stressors for older adults can be important for prevention as well as identification and treatment of stress that may turn into something more severe such as depression or anxiety.

As adolescents are attempting to assert their independence, many older adults begin to lose theirs. Tight finances can mean that an older adult is no longer able to afford a fully independent lifestyle. Moreover, failing health can mean it is not safe for them to do so. The result of these significant changes can mean that they have to live with family or in an assisted living situation. Although there are many benefits to living with family or in an assisted living facility, when an older adult has enjoyed, if not prized, their independence, the inability to maintain this despite their best efforts can be experienced as a significant loss—not unlike the death of a cherished loved one. When this occurs it is important as much as possible not to minimize this loss. Since our ability to move about as we would like to—to get up and go whenever and wherever—is something many of us take for granted, it is easy to overlook how pivotal our independence is in our lives.

Related to this is the decline or loss of physical functioning. For some older adults the changes in physical functioning may be gradual, whereas for others it may be quite abrupt resulting from a fall, stroke, or something equally debilitating. Regardless of the reason for the loss in functioning, this can be devastating, not only for the loss of independence that may accompany these changes but also purely for the loss itself. For those who have valued being particularly active in their lives whether for their health or for leisure, the inability to do what they had previously been able to do can be difficult to cope with. Some older adults will, of course, regain functioning. Others may regain limited functioning and others may have lost a particular ability altogether. As with the loss of independence, the loss of physical functioning can be quite difficult to cope with. Runners who can no longer race, active grandparents who can no longer keep up with their grandchildren, or gardeners who can no longer get down on their hands and knees and dig in the dirt may find it significantly challenging to cope with either never being able to do these things again or having to do them differently than they have before.

In addition to the two types of losses already discussed, there is also the loss of loved ones due to death. The most significant loss for most older adults is the death of a spouse or partner. Older adults who have stayed committed to their partner for decades are likely to experience this death quite acutely. In some cases this loss is so painful that the surviving partner may effectively will themselves to death. In some couples the death of one is followed by the death of the other within weeks or months. Of course, individuals whose relationships are newer than a lifetime love affair can still experience significant distress from this loss. The length of the relationship is not necessarily an indicator of the degree of pain felt. Factors such as how much time is spent together on a daily basis, how much the surviving partner may have relied on the other, and how fondly the surviving partner felt about their partner are likely better indicators of how this loss might affect them. In addition to this type of loss is the loss of one's peer group. It is not uncommon for older adults to deal with the death of multiple people they know in the span of a few years or less. This can lead to bereavement overload, which means that one loss cannot be fully grieved and coped with before the next loss occurs. Of course, anyone at any age can experience this for various reasons; however, bereavement overload tends to be something that older adults are likely to confront the older they get.

There are certainly a multitude of situations and experiences that can be stressful for someone as they age; however, the final one that is often significant is retirement itself. As noted in the opening paragraph of this section, retirement is not necessarily something that can occur for everyone, nor is it necessarily something that everyone looks forward to. Retirement often means that finances will not be as plentiful as they were when they were working. Just over half of all households with people of working age have any retirement savings at all, which means that fewer than 50 percent of these households have no savings at all. Among those close to retirement age, the average savings is around $12,000. Thus, many people simply cannot afford to retire.

Those who can retire with a comfortable income due to savings, pensions, or other sources of income may still feel a loss. Those who have identified closely with their career or job may have difficulty letting it go. Additionally, for many, one's friend group and social support comes from fellow employees. Retirement may mean that even if they do not have to let go of those connections altogether they certainly will not have the same degree of contact as they used to. Thus, retirement, while offering freedom and flexibility to fill one's days with whatever one wants, can mean that not only will our days look differently without work but our social lives will too.

Regardless of the stressor itself, symptoms of stress in older adults may often be revealed through physical symptoms. An older adult who consistently complains of aches and pains may be letting others know that they are under stress even if they do not know it themselves. Older adults may also have changes in the ability to fall asleep or stay asleep, and they may experience a change in weight. There are certainly a variety of things that can explain such changes—some of which may be a sign of stress in and of itself such as depression. Older adults may become more irritable or have rapidly shifting moods, which may mean that they become socially withdrawn either because others do not want to be around them anymore or vice versa.

Despite the numerous sources of stress, some of which may be the result of something that will not change, it is possible to help an older adult cope with what is going on in their lives. This can mean not only that will they be able to effectively deal with what is currently causing them distress but also that they will have the skills they need to cope with future stressors. This can also mean that the remainder of their lives can be lived as vitally and as enjoyably as possible.

Just like with children and adolescents, it is important to consider the particular age period of the individual when crafting a relaxation intervention for an older adult. This may often mean that the individual in question has physical limitations that preclude some forms of relaxation (e.g., exercise or progressive muscle relaxation) or cognitive decline (e.g., dementia) that may make more complex interventions more challenging to understand. Generally speaking, however, helping an older adult learn how to relax their mind and body uses the same principles as for any other age and can be just as effective.

Exercise can be a particularly effective relaxation and stress-relieving strategy; however, as already noted, certain exercises may not be appropriate.

It is important to be sure a physician or other licensed medical provider has cleared the individual for physical activity. Additionally, it is important to know if there are any limitations. For example, an older adult may be encouraged to walk or jog but only at a slow pace, or only on flat, even surfaces and with someone else. Others may be encouraged to engage in anaerobic exercise such as weight lifting but may be precluded from working particular muscle groups or may be limited in terms of how heavy the weight can get. Assuming that the individual is cleared for physical activity, there are so many possibilities that it will be important to devise a plan that involves a form of exercise the individual likes and is willing to do. Regardless of the health benefits of a particular exercise, if they are strongly opposed to doing it, it makes sense to save that form of exercise for a later time and focus on what they are willing to do. For some older adults the type of exercise is not as important as the social aspect of it. Therefore, identifying classes they can take or groups they can join that are designed for older adults can be particularly advantageous.

Another technique that will require medical clearance is muscle relaxation. Typically this form of relaxation requires tensing and subsequently relaxing particular muscle groups. Injured or particularly weak muscle groups may need to be avoided or manipulated with significant caution. It is unlikely, however, that an older adult who has even limited mobility cannot benefit from this technique. The focus of tensing and then relaxing muscle groups may need to remain on the face, upper body, or lower extremities depending only on the physical health of the older adult.

Music is one of the oldest expressions of human creativity that exists. Music often defines who we are and with whom we identify. It can challenge or drive cultural norms and evoke myriad emotions. Listening to calming music in particular can help reduce tension, fear, and anxiety. Beyond music designed to induce a sense of calm is listening to music from one's childhood or adolescent years. This is the music with which many adults continue to identify. Even fast-paced or hard-pounding music can help someone relax or feel joy if it is their favorite music and/or if it evokes fond memories. There have been examples of older adults with dementia who seem completely cut-off from the world but who, when headphones are placed on their head and music played, seem to come alive and clearly respond to the music. As with any other intervention, when possible, find out what kind of music is preferred. If listening to favorite music does not seem to help facilitate relaxation, then it may make sense to compile music designed specifically for relaxation (e.g., compilations produced for massage therapists).

Imagery paired with relaxation or on its own may also be effective. Teaching an older adult how to engage in effective imagery can help them re-create fond memories and relaxing times or fabricate a new experience that is soothing and pleasant. Imagery combined with relaxation training such as deep abdominal breathing can help calm their mind and body. The mind is given something pleasant to process, which can also result in a more relaxed body on its own, but as already noted, combining this with a specific relaxation technique will almost guarantee a decrease in overall tension. Just as with all other interventions, working with the individual closely on this intervention is critical. It is possible to give someone a script for them to imagine; however, imagery tends to be more effective when the script is crafted with significant input from the person doing the imagery. This is particularly the case for imagery based on an actual experience. The way in which another person can be most helpful is to help ensure that the script is detailed enough and incorporates as many sensations as possible.

Older adults are often confronted by stressors unique to that particular time in life. Just as at any other age, older adults may vary widely in their ability to cope with whatever stressors they experience. Of course, even if someone is able to cope effectively *so far*, it is possible for them to become overwhelmed by a particular situation (e.g., loss of a partner) or the quick succession of multiple stressors such that they do not know what to do. It is important to identify when an older adult is over-taxed regardless of the reason why or the perspective that others may have that *it's not that big of a deal*. If they are stressed about something, it is necessary for them to learn how to directly cope with it rather than to try to minimize it or pretend like it is not happening. Helping an older adult reengage with activities that they have historically enjoyed can be enough to reduce stress and boost their mood. If, however, their mood seems to worsen or their physical functioning seems to decline for no particular reason, it will be important for them to be evaluated by a licensed medical and/or mental health provider. They may need a more formal intervention before traditional relaxation techniques can be effective.

6

Where: Relaxation around the World

In Chapter 1 various techniques and activities were discussed that can help someone relax and de-stress. Although the items included in that section were not intended to be an exhaustive list of what can be done, they were certainly identified as activities that are relatively common in the United States. What follows in this section is a sampling of the types of activities, techniques, and treatments practiced around the world. Some of these will be familiar to readers whereas others will be quite foreign. Regardless, they are activities born out of rich histories and cultural traditions. Many of them have science to suggest they can be effective in helping manage stress, whereas others seem to have more anecdotal evidence (i.e., people who do the activity say it is enjoyable or relaxing). As with the earlier section on various forms of relaxation, this is not intended to be a fully inclusive list. Traditions that were thought to effectively represent the particular culture in question were selected; however, many other activities were not. For example in Malaysia a popular de-stressing technique is to stick your feet in a pool of water and allow hundreds of tiny fish to nibble at your feet and get rid of dead skin, and in Kashmir it is common to use leeches to rid the body of poisons. What follows are no less traditional in terms of cultural origins; however, most, if not all, of the practices that are described can be done in the United States—if not with a little modification.

CHINA: ACUPUNCTURE AND ACUPRESSURE

Traditional Chinese medicine includes practices that are more than 2,000 years old. These practices include medicinal use of herbs; massage; qigong, a form of exercise; and acupuncture. Many of these forms of treatment are often included in Western applications of *holistic* medicine. Acupuncture and acupressure operate on similar principles but use different methods to achieve similar results.

Acupuncture comes from the Latin words *acus,* which means needle, and *punctura,* which means to puncture. Acupuncture uses very fine needles that puncture the skin for the purpose of addressing the imbalance of *qi* throughout the body. Qi, which is also known as *chi* or *ki,* refers to energy and is usually translated to mean natural energy or energy flow.

The needles themselves are usually made of stainless steel and are either disposable (which means they are thrown away after one use) or reusable provided they are sterilized between uses. Shorter needles are favored for acupuncture points around the face whereas longer needles are used for areas of the body that have ticker tissue. Prior to the needles puncturing the skin, the areas of the body receiving treatment are sterilized with alcohol. Once the needle punctures the skin, they may be moved around via spinning or flicking. Although many who have undergone acupuncture report that there is some pain, it is generally short lived, and some recipients report feeling little to no pain from the insertion of the needles. The degree of pain felt can be explained in part by one's own level of pain tolerance but also by the degree of expertise of the acupuncturist. Acupuncture has been used to treat a wide variety of issues, including chronic pain, headaches, allergies, nausea and vomiting, depression, cancer, addiction, and epilepsy.

The word *acupressure* is derived from the Latin roots of *acus* meaning needle and *pressura* meaning pressure. As noted above, the principles on which acupressure is performed are the same as used for acupuncture: to address the imbalance of *qi*. The primary difference is the use of pressure rather than puncture. Additionally, despite the Latin root meaning needle, acupressure does not use needles to exert the pressure but uses fingers to simulate the acupressure points. Acupressure is often incorporated into various forms of massage and has been applied to help reduce pain, nausea, and vomiting.

Both of these forms of traditional Chinese medicine are safe when performed by trained and professional practitioners and, in the case of acupuncture, when the needles are sterile. In terms of their effectiveness to treat a range of ailments, empirical studies suggest there is not enough evidence to support a claim that these two practices are effective in treating the various illness and issues associated with them. For example, although there is some evidence that acupuncture can address lower back pain, scientific results indicate that the therapeutic effects (i.e., what the recipients said about their pain reduction) were small and that most of the benefit felt was determined to be caused by environmental and social factors. This means that something like acupuncture being performed in a calming and pleasing environment by a pleasant and professional practitioner may more fully explain the reduction in pain than the procedure itself.

Acupressure has also received scientific attention. One product in particular has been studied to determine if it really helps to relieve symptoms related to motion sickness. An acupressure wristband is what it sounds like. It is a band of stretchable cloth worn around the wrist. The wristband itself is snug, but it has inside of it a small, hard disk that is positioned precisely over the acupressure point on the wrist known in Chinese medicine to affect nausea. The theory is that by having this pressure applied while experiencing a boat, plane, or car ride, motion sickness will be prevented. Results of various studies show promise for this type of product, but scientists caution that more research is needed before this type of treatment can be supported as effective.

Traditional Chinese medicine has grown in popularity in the United States. The use of herbal supplements has been in practice for many people in this country for many years. Studios offering qigong exercise are plentiful, and practitioners offering acupuncture and/or acupressure are not difficult to find. Although the needles used in acupuncture are a far cry from those used to inject medicine or draw blood, those who are wary of needles or have a clinical needle phobia might want to consider acupressure as an alternative. One can receive this form of treatment as part of a traditional massage or as a standalone procedure. Either way, for those looking for an alternative treatment of ailments that affect overall well-being, acupuncture and acupressure are safe and readily available alternatives to try.

FINLAND: SAUNA

Many people in the United States have heard of *sauna* and may have even enjoyed one on occasion. A sauna is either a wooden room located in the interior of a building or can be a small, standalone hut. The room is heated to a high temperature usually between 170 and 230 degrees Fahrenheit. The heat source includes large rocks on which water is poured to produce steam. Saunas are usually, but not always, sex specific, and depending on the location of the sauna and/or the cultural expectations, one would sit in the sauna completely naked, naked underneath a towel wrapped around oneself, or wearing a bathing suit or other suitable attire. In Finland you can expect that enjoying a sauna means you will be in the room with other people you may or may not know and the expectation or tradition is that everyone is naked. In terms of the co-mingling of the sexes, there are no hard and fast rules for this, but those who grow up in a sauna culture seem to instinctually *just know* when it is okay to enter the sauna when others of the opposite sex are in there, or when one is old enough to stop using the sauna with one's parents, and so on. In the United States, however, public saunas are almost guaranteed to be separated by sex.

The high temperatures in a sauna means that skin temperature will rise rapidly after just a few minutes. The body's primary cooling mechanism, sweating, results in the production of several cups of sweat after a short period of time. Generally speaking, it is not recommended to stay in a sauna for more than 20 minutes for those in good health. Individuals who may not be well for whatever reason or who may have ingested a substance (e.g., alcohol or some medications) that may interfere with one's body to produce sweat are admonished to not use a sauna. There is scarce evidence that using a sauna has health benefits that extend beyond feeling a reduction in stress and overall sense of relaxation. Indeed sitting in this type of heat helps to lower blood pressure and slow one's pulse, which for the average healthy person is entirely safe. For those with heart or other circulatory problems, however, using a sauna can be dangerous. The Finns' penchant for enjoying such an effective relaxation strategy helps to explain why Finland is consistently ranked at or near the top in the list of the happiest countries.

The sauna, or *sauvasauna* as it is called in Finnish, is such a long-standing cultural tradition that nearly every home in Finland has a sauna built into it and most Finns use the sauna weekly. As noted above, enjoying a sauna involves sitting in a hot wooden room while occasionally producing steam by pouring water on the heat source. In Finnish this type of steam has its own word: *loyly*. This word is used exclusively in the context of steam producing in a sauna rather than steam produced by any other means. Additionally, a traditional Finnish sauna experience often also involves the use of a small bundle of leafy branches usually from a birch tree. This bundle is called *vihta* or *vasta*, depending on what part of Finland one is from, and is used to gently beat one's skin with the branches. The result is to stimulate the skin and relax the muscles. This practice has also been shown to help reduce the irritation from mosquito bites.

After warming one's body and using the *vihta* to stimulate the skin, it is customary to cool one's body down after the heat from the sauna starts to feel uncomfortable. Often this is done by jumping into a pool or nearby lake. Those who take sauna very seriously, or who are simply hard core when it comes to experiencing cultural traditions, may roll around in the snow during winter or jump into an *avanto*, which is a hole cut into the ice of a frozen body of water. This heating-cooling cycle repeats itself for whatever duration is desired by each individual. Some engage in this process for 1–2 hours while others may call it quits after 30 minutes or so.

Afterward, sitting down to enjoy a drink and snack is customary. In Finland the sauna is highly revered by its people and the expectation is that those who use the sauna and interact with others will do so in a calm and respectful way. Conversation is assumed to be congenial and relaxed. Formalities and topics of conversation that might be controversial are left outside the door of the sauna.

Although a strong Finnish tradition, saunas are somewhat common in the United States. Many health clubs and some private homes have saunas. Regardless of its location, if you are in good health and are so inclined, enjoying a sauna just might help you sweat away your tensions and enter a calm, relaxed state.

FRANCE: VACATION

Americans are no strangers to the idea of vacation. Many of us take vacations throughout the year. But how much is allotted to us? Moreover, how much time do we take from what is allotted to us? Do we really know how to take full advantage of vacation time in order to relax? One culture that seems to understand the benefits of downtime in the form of vacation is the French.

France is known for many things: decadent food and drink, high fashion, Paris, fine art, and the French Riviera. Vacation, however, is not what usually comes to mind. The reality is that the French government understands the importance of time away from work so much so that they enforce a mandatory five weeks of vacation for those who work at least 35 hours a week—the equivalent of a full-time (i.e., 40 hour) work week in the United States. Those who work more hours than this standard are allowed even more time off. This is not only paid vacation, but it is above and beyond the numerous public holidays akin to things like President's Day or Memorial Day in the United States.

It is not uncommon for people in entry-level jobs in the United States to be allowed one to two weeks of vacation with the opportunity to earn four to five weeks of vacation after several years of service to their employer. To top it off, most workers in the United States take only about half of the paid vacation they are allowed, leaving over 50 billion dollars' worth of paid time-off unused. But in France, vacation time, and a lot of it, is a given. It would seem that even five weeks is not enough for many of the French as it is not uncommon for people to take up to two months off from work during the summer months. This is so common that the populace can be informally classified based on when they start their long vacations—either July or August.

Vacation time in France is sacred time. It is expected that the time will be spent relaxing, doing whatever one wants with whomever although that is usually family. When employees are on vacation (sometimes all at the same time so that the company shuts down for a month or so), the boss leaves them alone. There are no interruptions during one's vacation by phone calls from the boss or the expectation that one should be keeping up with email no matter where they are on the globe. The mantra for the French vacation is to be able to live life during that time as if you were not working at all. Perhaps the equivalent would be how Americans might spend their time during their retirement years: engaged in activities they have always wanted to do without the pressure of work looming. The French have ingrained in their culture that these activities should be enjoyed throughout one's life, and thus, they formally set aside time for that to happen.

The French enjoy the unstructured time of their vacations by reading books, going for walks, and enjoying long conversations and meals with friends and family. They rarely leave France (which would be like leaving one's home state in the United States) and instead elect to spend time at a vacation home out in the country. By contrast, Americans tend to leave the state, if not the country, and pack their vacations with activities to such an extent that a common refrain at the end of the vacation is *I need a vacation from my vacation*. Americans do not generally return from vacation refreshed and energized; rather they often return a day or two before work is to resume, feeling tired or exhausted. No doubt this is due in part to the fact that since Americans are generally not afforded much vacation time, and may even experience pressure to not take all of it out of fear of being perceived as a slacker, most of us try to pack in as many activities as possible because time is so limited and it is uncertain when there may be another opportunity to do these things again.

Even if you do not live in a country or work for a company with a generous vacation benefit, there are still ways to *vacation like the French*. Pick a destination that does not require too much time and effort to get to. Once there, resist the temptation to pack in as many scheduled activities as possible. Instead take advantage of the downtime by doing enjoyable activities you've been putting off until you have more time. If you're not sure what those activities are, then take your vacation time sitting by a fire or at the end of a dock jutting out into a lake to contemplate how you want to spend your leisure time. Keeping money in your pocket by not spending money on airfare for a whole family or high-priced activities means you can afford to rent accommodations that are spacious enough for all members of the family not for the purpose of enjoying where you are, but to enjoy time together.

INDIA: CHANTING

The word *chant* has its origins in the French word *chanter*, which means to sing. Chanting is not always singing in the sense that many of us think of: a wide range of notes sung with words and often accompanied by another instrument. Chanting can be considered singing with a restricted range of notes or a rhythmic type of speaking, but it can also involve much more complex arrangement of notes. Some ancient forms of chanting are believed to provide the musical roots of Western music that evolved much later.

Chanting is often conducted as part of a spiritual practice and as such can be practiced in a solitary fashion or as part of a group. Chanting is also associated with practices in a wide variety of cultures including African and Native American and various religions, including Lutheran, Eastern Orthodox, Roman Catholic, and Buddhism. One form of changing, *kirtan*, is associated with Indian culture (as in the country of India) and the word itself refers to adoration or praise of the divine. Kirtan chanting is a call-and-response type of chanting, meaning that there are paired phrases, each of which is sung, spoken, or played by a different person or instrument. The person performing the kirtan is referred to as a *kirtankara*. Often the practice of kirtan chanting does involve accompaniment by instruments, including the harmonium; tabla, a type of two-headed drum; or cymbals. It is also commonplace for storytelling and acting to be involved with kirtan.

The history of kirtan chanting is said to date back to the tenth century and is associated with the Hinduism movement of *bhakti*. In this movement kirtan is intended as a form of worship and glorification of Lord Krishna. Six centuries later kirtan became incorporated in the Sikh faith, in which the gurus of this tradition espoused the importance of kirtan as a form of workshop. During the fifteenth century in the Carnatic region of India, the mystic Tallapaka Annamacharya is said to have composed over 30,000 Sankirtanas as an expression of worship of the "deity of Seven Hills."

Kirtan chanting was not introduced to the West until the early 1900s. In 1923 Paramhansa Yogananda performed a kirtan chant entitled *Hey Hari Sundara*, or "Oh God Beautiful," at Carnegie Hall. In the 1960s the founding of a worldwide organization called the *International Society for Krishna Consciousness* helped to increase awareness of kirtan in the United States and other Western countries. Since that time an associated practice of yoga, which can involve chanting as part of the practice, has seen an increase in popularity.

Yoga itself has been studied by scientists and has been shown to have a multitude of benefits for the mind, body, and spirit such as improved mood and overall mental health and better sleep. Chanting per se has not received similar empirical attention; however, practitioners of this form of spiritual expression purport that it has numerous benefits. Some suggest chanting can help alleviate ailments such as depression and anxiety, and that it can facilitate the overall immune system functioning. They also indicate that practitioners of chanting can become more compassionate and more intuitive, feel more empowered, and feel soothed.

Depending on where one lives in the United States, it may or may not be easy to find a place of worship or other location that engages in chanting. Some Indian kirtan chanters have toured the United States much like mainstream music groups, and other performers go on tour and play for large audiences. If these opportunities are not readily available, it is certainly possible to play recordings of kirtan chanting via private Internet sites and social media. Additionally, given the ease with which audio files can be created and shared, songs and albums of kirtan chanting can be purchased via myriad outlets.

Whether one can experience kirtan chanting in person or via one's headphones, listening to this type of music can be soothing and can produce a sense of relaxation and peace. Given enough familiarity with a particular song and one's own comfort level with vocalization, it may even be worth chanting right along with the performers. You may need to be sure that you are either alone when you do or that your friends and family know what you're doing if this is not a practice in which they engage themselves. Either way the potential benefits make this particular practice worth trying out.

JAPAN: ROCK GARDENS

The Japanese word for rock garden is *karensansui*, which also means dry landscape. Rock gardens are also referred to as *Zen gardens*, which are typically small dry landscapes surrounded by a wall and best enjoyed from a particular viewpoint. Rock gardens usually include rocks that may symbolize the mountains, moss, pruned trees and bushes, a water feature, and sand or small rocks that are raked to look like ripples one might see in a slow-moving stream or after one tosses a small rock in a placid pool of water. The ancient tradition of rock gardening is simultaneously an art form and a mechanism for stress release.

Rock gardens are believed to date back in Japan to the late 700s to late 1100s. Japanese rock gardens were heavily influenced by gardens developed by the Chinese during the ancient Song Dynasty. The first book that was essentially a DIY publication of ancient Japanese rock gardens was called the *Sakuteiki*, which means the Records of Garden Keeping and was written in the late 1000s. This book was a how-to manual in that it provided detailed instruction on how and where to place rocks. Elements of Japanese rock gardens can have particular meaning depending on the religious or cultural tradition in which one learns and creates these gardens. The sand and gravel, for example, can represent purity or, in other traditions, can symbolize water or emptiness and distance. Regardless of the particular meaning of any feature or arrangement of the elements of each garden, rock gardens are universally used as places of meditation: a place to clear one's mind while walking through the garden or while rhythmically raking the sand and gravel.

The arrangement of the rocks in a Japanese rock garden is called *ishi wo tateru koto*, which means the act of setting stones upright. Since the rules as described in the *Sakuteiki* were quite specific, there was also an accompanying admonition that if the rocks were not placed properly in the garden, misfortune would befall the one who improperly built the garden. Rocks are usually grouped together rather than placed in symmetrical patterns. It is also important that the rocks selected for the garden vary in shape, size, color, and texture. The arrangement of the garden is often intended to be interpreted. Some gardens reveal their intended symbolism (e.g., journey through life) quite readily, whereas others are much more abstract and therefore it is much more difficult to decipher the intended meaning.

The most well-known Japanese rock garden, *Ryoan-ji*, is located in Kyoto, Japan, and was crafted in the late fifteenth century. This garden is believed to represent a purely abstract Zen garden. Thus, it was not constructed to look like an actual landscape. This garden is composed of 15 rocks of varying sizes, grouped and surrounded by white gravel. The groupings of rocks involved one group of five rocks, two groups of three rocks, and two groups of two rocks. These groupings are highlighted by the white gravel that is raked each day by the monks who reside at the temple grounds. As noted earlier, Japanese gardens of this nature are intended to be most appreciated when viewed from a particular locale. In this case, the garden was designed so that the most pleasing view would be while seated on the porch of the on-site residence.

Myriad examples of Japanese rock gardens can be found by conducting a simple Internet search for images. Results depict gardens using minimal materials arranged in simple designs, or those using a wider range of natural materials and designed to re-create certain landscapes. One can also take note of the raking that exists in all rock gardens. Some consist of straight lines running the length or width of the garden while others overlap the raking in both directions. Some include wavy lines that look much more like waves on water, and others use concentric circles that would seem to represent the ripples that form when a heavy object is dropped into a calm pond.

Within the last 100 years or so, Zen gardens have extended beyond the borders of Japan. Although large, traditional gardens can be viewed across this country and others, it is also possible to create one's own Zen garden for personal use. Desktop gardens can be readily purchased and usually consist of a small tray with sand, several rocks, and a small rake. Once the calming and meditative effects of Zen gardening was made known, these "portable" Zen gardens became somewhat of a hot ticket item and it became common to see small rock gardens on the desks of business executives and others. Personal Zen gardens like this are not as popular as they once were as other relaxation techniques have become en vogue; however, those who use them often report feeling a sense of calm and a clearing of the mind primarily when they rake the sand in slow, repetitive fashion. If you don't have the time, energy, or space to create a larger, outdoor authentic Japanese rock garden, the small desktop version just might be a rejuvenating alternative.

NEW ZEALAND: ZORBING

Many countries have favorite pastimes that help to relieve stress by simply having fun. In the United States we like our sports. Although many of us can get quite competitive when we watch or participate, if we are able to find a way to play a game of baseball, soccer, or football with friends and family without turning it into a hardcore competition, it is highly likely that the experience will be enjoyable and will result in an overall sense of well-being. Of course, many cultures enjoy a good game of football (i.e., soccer), but in New Zealand a particularly unusual and potentially fun activity has become popular in recent years. This activity is called

Zorbing and involves rolling down a hill while contained inside a large (very large) ball. Of course, this sort of activity is not for everyone and to date there is no science to suggest it will guarantee stress relief or relaxation, but by all accounts for the right type of person this activity could be quite enjoyable, which in and of itself can contribute to one's overall well-being.

If it is difficult to picture what Zorbing actually is, try to imagine a person inside the equivalent of a human being-sized hamster ball. Of course, the interior of contemporary Zorbing balls is more comfortable than the hard plastic of a rodent ball; however, early versions of the ball were not terribly successful. Although the history of the Zorb (the large human-sized orb) might date back to the early 1970s, it was not until the 1980s that a club based in the United Kingdom called the *Dangerous Sports Club* attempted to create an orb large enough for two chairs to fit inside. This club is also credited with inventing the modern version of bungee jumping, so pushing the limits of what human beings are capable of (club members also engage in BASE jumping) including Zorbing is par for the course.

The Dangerous Sports Club's original design of the orb was unsuccessful. It wasn't until the mid-1990s that some inventors in New Zealand devised the current version of the orb, which they eventually called a "Zorb." The Zorb itself is translucent or see-through and contains a smaller ball inside of a larger ball. In-between the two balls is a large space filled with air, which serves as a shock absorber. This is certainly necessary since not all hills are smooth and it is possible for the Zorb to become airborne. The Zorb is generally lightweight and made of a flexible plastic material. Some Zorbs allow the rider to be strapped in so they do not move around, while others allow for the person inside to roll or to be tossed around as the ball makes its way down the hill. Most Zorbs are about 10 feet across with the inner ball about six and a half feet across and can accommodate up to three people inside at the same time. A variation of Zorbing called Hydro-Zorbing involves being encased in the inner ball with several gallons of water allowing for a more slippery ride down the hill. Although Zorbing has historically been associated with individuals and companies that take risks, it was not until the late 1990s that the sport gained worldwide notoriety when it became a staple of extreme sport enthusiasts.

Although the world record for speed in a Zorb is about 32 miles per hour, Zorbing is meant to be done on a smooth, gentle slope that includes fences on both sides of the run and a place at the bottom of the hill where the Zorb can safely stop. All of this is in place to ensure the safety of the riders and to ensure maximum enjoyment. Given the unusual nature of this particular activity and the fact that the sport has seen a surge in popularity over the past 15 years, numerous videos of Zorbing are available on various social media sites. Watching these videos can give one a sense of how much fun the participants are having, but they also reveal that this activity is clearly not for everyone. Although Zorbing is most well known in New Zealand and the United Kingdom, this activity is becoming more popular around the world. Clubs and commercial venues are available in Australia, Sweden, Canada, Poland, Japan, Slovenia, and a multitude of other countries including the United States; however, only a handful of states including Wisconsin, Tennessee, Massachusetts, and Pennsylvania have entered into this market.

As already noted, Zorbing is not for everyone. The description above may have piqued your interest or convinced you that there is no way you would try this activity. Regardless of your initial reaction, Zorbing has grown in worldwide popularity over the last several years, and before long, participation may be available in more states in the United States, making it easier to try this sport.

RUSSIA: DACHA

Russian culture is perceived in the United States as a harsh, unforgiving lifestyle. Indeed, when some of the most familiar things about Russia are Siberian winters, which seem to last half the year, and *Gulag*, which is portrayed as a brutal prison system, it is easy to assume that Russians do not experience much by the way of pleasurable activities. The reality, of course, is that the Russian people have a rich culture that extends beyond what many know. Additionally, the people of Russia work, play, and relax as the rest of the world does. One of the things that aptly characterizes Russian relaxation is *dacha* (pronounced da-sha).

Dachas are what some New Englanders would call *camp*. They are second homes that may be equipped for year-round habitation or may be seasonal—that is, someone would be there only during the warmer months of the year. These homes are usually located far outside of city limits and can vary widely in terms of construction and luxury. To Americans the idea of a second or seasonal home invokes an image of wealth and prosperity. Indeed, when dachas originated during the seventeenth century, they referred to plots of land given by the Tsar to someone of importance or in favor with the Tsar. This early history also accounts for the meaning of the term *dacha*. Although the direct translation does not fully capture the spirit of dacha, it means to give. Moreover, the term is said to refer not just to the fact that one can exist on the plot of land but also to the lifestyle that accompanies it. Although some use their dacha for year-round living, and others for seasonal activities like hunting or gardening, many use their dacha as purely a place of leisure. Regardless, the dacha was a place to get away, to get out of the city and away from life in the city. A century later, dachas were more common and many in the elite and middle classes had a dacha. Homes were built on the plots of land at which it was common for their owners to have formal and informal social gatherings.

The early nineteenth century and the accompanying Russian Revolution saw a more equal distribution of these seasonal homes to the working class. As a result of this, numerous regulations were instituted to regulate not only how large a plot of land any one person or family could have but also how many stories this home could be. The plots of land were just large enough to grow and maintain a small garden that might be used to feed the family or supplement the family's income. The use of dachas as a place of leisure reached its height during the era of the Soviet Union; however, the shifting economic climate has once again made dachas a place of leisure rather than a more primary, permanent residence.

Since their emergence during the 1600s, regardless of the political and economic climate, dachas were still a status symbol and were given by the government to prominent Russian figures, including artists, scientists, and high-ranking officials. Depending on who received the gift, the maintenance of the dacha may have also been taken care of by the government. During the 1990s many people were able to take on full ownership of their dacha, making many of the once government-owned gifts (that could be taken away at any time) fully privately owned. Thus, it is not uncommon for a Russian family of nearly any economic class to have a dacha. With the boom of private dacha ownership since the existence of the former Soviet Union, many homes located in villages are being sold as dachas. This means that dachas are no longer just out in the country, but may be located in and among a neighborhood of other dachas.

Regardless of the physical location of the dacha or how large or luxurious it is, dachas have historically been and continue to be a way for many Russians to get away from their daily lives and engage in leisure and relaxation. Although certainly not as mainstream as it is in Russian culture, in some regions of the United States, it is common to have a small, simple seasonal dwelling (e.g., camps) that serves a similar purpose. Even if your family does not own such a thing, it may be worth looking into borrowing one from a friend or finding one for rent. Such homes can be quite inexpensive for a weekend or a week or two despite being situated on a lake. They can serve the same purpose of a dacha: a place for family and friends to gather away from the stressors of everyday life.

SPAIN: SIESTA

The word *siesta* has entered the lexicon of the English language in the United States; however, many who use the term may not fully understand or appreciate the cultural tradition and benefits that a true siesta can provide. Siesta is a Spanish tradition that most simply described is a nap taken during the middle of the day for the purpose of helping to reenergize in order to finish the obligations of the afternoon. When Americans are sitting at their desks with a sandwich in one hand and the computer mouse in the other as they work through their lunch break, many Spaniards are taking a siesta right after having eaten their mid-day meal. Although most commonly associated with Spain, siesta is common in other countries where the weather is particularly warm.

The word *siesta* is a derivative of the Latin term *hora sexta*, which means sixth hour—or mid-day (six hours from dawn). It is not uncommon in countries with the siesta tradition, or *riposo* as it is known in Italy, for establishments of all kinds to close down in the middle of the day to allow employees or proprietors to go home for lunch and a nap. In addition to the warm climate that seems to coincide with the taking of a siesta, this tradition also seems to not only follow the mid-day meal but a particularly large mid-day meal. Heat and a very full belly is an almost perfect recipe for being able to take and enjoy a long nap.

Taking a nap in the middle of the day may seem counterproductive to many living and working in the United States; however, scientists who study the body and the rhythms that regulate our sleep-wake cycle indicate that the middle of the day is an ideal time to take a rest. They note that when we wake up in the morning, our bodies are on the clock in terms of when we'll need to rest again. Many of us who work straight through the day may notice the difficulty we have staying energized and focused on work regardless of the size of our meal or the temperature outside. Sleep experts point to the body's circadian rhythm informing us that it needs to rest for a bit. Feeling awake, on the other hand, tends to coincide with early evening, a few hours prior to a typical bed time—which is why it can be difficult to go to bed and fall asleep too much earlier than normal.

Other sleep experts point to the soaring rates of sleep deprivation in this and other cultures. Those who are sleep deprived usually feel it the most in the middle of the afternoon. They indicate that around mid-day what is going on in the brain is that levels of certain neurotransmitters (i.e., brain chemicals) such as dopamine and serotonin start to drop. Since these chemicals are involved in part in the regulation of sleep, the drop in these chemicals means that we start to feel sleepy. This is the case for those who have gotten a normal amount of rest. For those who are already sleep deprived, this sleepy feeling will be experienced more intensely. As a result of these and other similar findings, scientists note that taking a rest during the middle of the day is likely to help workers be more productive. Additionally, and perhaps more importantly, safety can also be an issue. A dip in hand/eye coordination can occur along with a decrease in alertness during this time, making unrested employees a potential danger on some job sites.

Shifting the culture in the United States toward that of a siesta culture is a tall order. A particular value of this culture is that we work hard no matter what even if it means we get very little rest. Many employers reward workers who put in extra hours, don't take breaks, work through lunch, and come in early and stay late. The erroneous assumption is that this type of work ethic results in greater productivity. Sleep researchers strongly disagree, especially given the findings that the more sleep deprived we are, the more likely it is that we will make mistakes, which is, of course, counterproductive.

If you know that you would benefit from a mid-day nap (as many of us would), check with your employer about allowed breaks, including when, where, and how long they can be taken. Some progressive companies have ensured that there is ample time and comfortable spaces for their employees to rest as needed. While this is still relatively rare in the United States, it may be possible to create your own siesta without getting into trouble. If you can, make sure you can get as comfortable as possible in a quiet, cool place. And be sure to set an alarm in the event that you do not naturally wake up from your siesta.

SWEDEN: FIKA

Coffee breaks are commonplace among the workforce of the United States. In fact, employers are required to allow for at least a morning and an afternoon break in addition to one's lunch break. While some use these brief breaks to drink coffee, some use the time to smoke a cigarette, simply chat informally with coworkers, or spend time at one's desk not doing anything in an attempt to reenergize to keep up the work for the rest of the day—or at least until the next break. Some cultures, however, have elevated the coffee break to something of a social event. The Swedes, for example, have combined coffee breaks with snacking and informal social gathering.

When in Sweden you may take a *fika* (pronounced fee-ka)—which as implied above has its closest equivalent in American culture to a coffee break. For those living in the United Kingdom, fika might sound akin to afternoon tea. Regardless of what fika seems like and despite the fact that the word itself means to drink coffee, if you refer to fika as a coffee break in Sweden, you will likely be met with a shake of the head since fika is typically more than just taking a quick break to have a cup of coffee. At minimum it will also involve a sweet of some kind usually in the form of a cinnamon roll or other baked good. Additionally, the complexity of what fika is or is not can be illustrated by the fact that the term can be used as a noun or a verb: you can simply fika or you can take a fika. Although the tradition is associated with coffee in the context of taking a break from work or some other endeavor that might require a rest or break, Swedes will specify this by using *fikapaus*, literally translated to fika pause, or *fikarast*, meaning fika break. Thus, fika is more than just a *coffee break* from work.

The tradition is thought to have begun in the 1700s and currently usually involves a break from work in the morning and afternoon—but always with something to drink *and* something sweet to eat. Whereas Americans are likely to sweeten up their coffee and make the coffee a treat in and of itself, Swedes tend to prefer a much stronger blend, which likely complements the sweet bite to eat quite well. Generationally, there seems to be some differences in how the word *fika* is used. Older generations may use the word to literally mean just coffee, whereas when members of younger generations use the term, they are almost decidedly referring to specifically taking a break.

A fika as it seems to be taken in the present can certainly involve a cup of coffee or any other type of drink, but what makes this endeavor different than a run-of-the-mill coffee break is that it always involves something to eat—usually something sweet. Traditionally, cinnamon rolls are a staple during a fika; however, any sweet baked good is welcome and may even include candy. Regardless, an additional purpose of the fika is to gather with others. Although it is possible to take a fika as a solitary event or with one other person, typically a group of people are involved. The gathering itself is intended to be informal and topics of conversations are likely to be mundane and comprising small talk. Essentially, the fika is a low-pressure situation and any two people alone on a fika are assumed to be two friends taking a break together rather than having a romantic encounter.

Whether on the job or involved in some task for a long period of time, taking a break is often recommended. The next time you take one, consider turning it into something more than a brief period of time where you stop doing what you were doing. Consider following the lead of the

Swedes. Make sure you have your favorite drink, but be sure you've also brought along or can easily purchase a baked good. Despite the concern many American's have about consuming such foods, indulging in a small sweet snack can feel good, and if shared with a good friend or family member, the break can feel less like your run-of-the-mill coffee break and more like an event, not unlike the Swedish fika.

THAILAND: MASSAGE

Massage is certainly something that is not new to many Americans. Many get a massage to de-stress or to maintain their sense of overall well-being. It is common for athletes to get massages to help their bodies heal from injury or simply strenuous competition. There are also massages specifically designed for pregnant women. Couples can arrange to receive a massage simultaneously by two different masseurs.

The type of massage received can vary. Massage can be used with firm pressure in order to get to deep muscle tissue, or less pressure can be used along with long, slow movement along the length of major muscle groups. Although the choice is usually up to the person receiving the massage, it is common practice to be naked. Well-trained, professional masseurs are adept at maintaining one's modesty, but the lack of clothing, including underwear, allows the masseur to more effectively reach target muscles and tissue. The purpose of the massage can vary although many people want a massage to help them de-stress and relax. However, some massages are designed to stimulate one's senses and foster alertness and one's ability to concentrate. This type of massage would certainly be beneficial for those in the middle of a work day who need to remain energized and focused. Thai massage is different from the typical forms of massage readily available in the United States and is a form of massage that reenergizes and fosters mindfulness.

Thai massage, *nuat phaen thai* or *nuat thai*, is an ancient practice believed to be 2500 years old and developed by the Buddha's physician; however, Thai massage combines knowledge drawn from the practice of medicine in India, China, and Southeast Asia. Given these various influences it is believed that there is no one single way to practice Thai massage. Generally speaking, however, Thai massage incorporates yoga poses along with acupressure, reflexology, and stretching to help release tension and improve the functioning of various systems of the body. When receiving a traditional Thai massage, the recipient wears loose-fitting clothing and lies on a firm surface. The body is often manipulated into yoga poses throughout the massage, but primarily the masseur will employ deep pressure on particular areas of the body as well as deep rhythmic pressure.

The masseur achieves this type of pressure by being higher than the recipient (which is often why in this type of massage the recipient lies on a mat on the floor) and pressing down on the recipient's body with straight arms and locked elbows. Pressure on the body follows the Sen lines of the body.

Sen lines are believed to number in the tens of thousands. The idea is that as air is inhaled into the system, it travels throughout the body and can get trapped. Thus, these Sen lines are thought to represent energy pathways in the body and tend to follow the contours of various muscle groups; however, there is not complete agreement among various schools that teach this particular form of massage. Regardless, massage along the Sen lines is intended to release stored and blocked energy. The release of this tension is not only believed to help the body operate more effectively but can also help heal unexplained, nonphysical problems related to emotional pain, which in some cases reportedly reveals childhood issues that have been kept in one's unconscious. The manipulation of the body along Sen lines with the release of *blocked energy* improves circulation and flexibility, resulting in a relaxing of joints and tendons.

Sometimes a hot compress infused with herbs such as camphor, lemongrass, or turmeric is used along with the Thai massage. This compress is steamed, and when placed on the body, the herbs are intended to be absorbed throughout the skin. The hot compress is believed to help those experiencing migraines, back pain, inflammation of tendons, and overall tension. The result of the compress is usually a reduction in stress and anxiety and can help to address sleep problems.

Regardless of the form of massage, this type of treatment has been consistently found to help relieve pain, including headaches; improve sleep; help your immune system function at its best; and help you become and stay alert. For women it may help to alleviate the uncomfortable and painful symptoms that accompany one's menstrual cycle. Since pain and discomfort can accompany many typical (e.g., stress) and atypical (e.g., depression, medical illness) conditions, it is worth considering incorporating massage into your routine for taking care of yourself. Thai massage, while still difficult to find in the United States, may be worth pursuing if it sounds like the techniques used and potential benefits will address your particular needs. If not, any form of massage applied by a trained and credentialed masseur will undoubtedly help you feel better both mentally and physically.

WEST AFRICA: DRUMMING

For many individuals, drums call to mind the plastic and metal drum kit with a festive bow affixed to it lying in wait for a child's birthday or other holiday. When the child finally gets their hands on their drums, there is hardly much that is stress relieving about it—in fact, for many the stress increases. Drumming, however, has a very rich history, and depending on by whom it is practiced, it can evoke feelings of stress relief and an overall sense of a reduction in tension.

Drums are believed to be the oldest instrument in history. In Western Africa, in particular, drumming is not necessarily utilitarian and is often associated with entertainment. Other types of drums and drumming techniques by contrast are used like telephones to communicate messages to distant villages. The *talking drum*, for example, when used by an expert, can mimic the sound of language and therefore can result in conversations by drum between drummers. Other types of drums include the *sabar*, which can be played using one's hands or a stick; the *bougarabou*, which is a solo instrument but is played as a set in which each drum is uniquely tuned; and the *udu*, which are clay pots that are quite similar to water jugs that have a hole in the side and are played by hitting the hole with the palm of the hand, slapping the side of the vessel, or rubbing the body of the drum, which is textured and therefore produces a different type of sound. The drum that is most iconic of West African drumming is the *djembe*.

The djembe drum is made from a single piece of wood that is hollow all the way through and is in the shape of a goblet. The top is covered with an animal membrane traditionally from a goat or cow and fastened to the drum using natural materials such as shells, intestine, or rawhide. Although the method used and the location of striking the djembe produce a variety of sounds, it is predominantly a deep bass instrument. The tenor of the instrument is also affected by the density of the wood used to create the drum, any carvings on the outside of the drum, and the nature of the membrane used to cover the drum. The djembe has great significance to African culture and is thought to date back to the Mali Empire, which dominated Africa in the thirteenth and fifteenth centuries. This particular drum was initially crafted to be used in sacred ceremonies (e.g., rites of passage, healing ceremonies); however, it is most well known for its use as an instrument and tool to help tell stories, specifically that of the warrior who founded the Mali Empire. African drumming was introduced to cultures outside of West Africa during the 1950s when Les Ballets Africans toured various parts of the world and played their music. Djembe drumming is believed to have been introduced to the United States in the 1960s, and since then various drumming and dance companies have been formed to celebrate African culture, music, and drumming.

The use of drumming as a form of stress relief is not too much of a stretch for most people to imagine. Pounding or banging on a drum as hard as you can is bound to release some physical and emotional energy. It turns out, however, that there is scientific evidence that supports the practice of *group drumming* as a way to heal the body and de-stress. A study published in 2001 demonstrated that those who participated in organized group drumming compared to others who either simply rested or who listened to the drumming itself were shown to have a reduction in the production of stress hormones and an increase in cells that help boost immune system functioning. This study lends evidence to the healing power of drumming rituals that have been practiced for centuries in Africa and other cultures. Certainly those who have grown up with the use of drums or who have added drumming to their lives can attest to the benefits of this practice; however, science seems to have proven that drumming is an effective stress reliever and facilitator of relaxation.

Drumming of this variety is not what may come to mind when envisioning a child banging away on his or her first drum kit. There usually isn't too much about it that may seem relaxing. Rather, this type of drumming is purposeful, rhythmic, and creative. Even if there is no option to join a drumming class, you can easily purchase your own drum, watch a few videos, and learn what traditional African drumming looks, sounds, and feels like. When you're ready, invite some friends over to drum with you to fully experience the benefits of group drumming.

Part II

Scenarios

In this section, five different scenarios will be presented depicting someone struggling with stress or anxiety. The scenario itself will be described, which will then be followed by an interpretation of what was going on along with a recommendation for what would likely be most helpful.

Jamie Doesn't Want to Go to School

Jamie is a ten-year-old, fifth-grade boy. He has been attending the same elementary school since kindergarten, and although he has occasionally given his parents difficulty when going to school, neither his mother nor his father was concerned about this behavior. They assumed, rightly so, that most children do not want to go to school sometimes. Jamie's early school years revealed that he enjoyed learning and liked making new friends. Several weeks into his fifth grade year, however, Jamie began protesting more regularly about going to school. He began by saying that he was just too tired or that he did not feel well, but when pressed, he shared with his parents that he really did not like going to school anymore. Concerned, Jamie's parents spoke with his teacher and the school counselor about what they noticed with regard to his behavior. Both the teacher and the school counselor agreed that Jamie seemed different this year and that he did not seem to be as engaged with his classmates nor with the subjects about which his class was learning as he had been the previous years. Jamie's teacher also told his parents that he seemed anxious in class and consistently worried about the work he was expected to do both in class and as homework. Jamie's parents agreed that they had seen similar stress in their son when he attempted to complete work at home. The degree of worry and stress Jamie seemed to be experiencing lead to Jamie's parents keeping him at home on more than one occasion. They noticed, however, that Jamie protested more vigorously the next day when they tried to get him to school. Jamie was now in a pattern of missing school or being late nearly every day. His parents knew this was not okay but did not know what to do to help their son. The school counselor referred Jamie to a local pediatric psychologist who specialized in working with childhood anxiety.

Jamie met with the psychologist, who also worked with his parents to help them manage Jamie's behaviors. The psychologist helped Jamie describe how he felt both at school and at home. He also encouraged Jamie to describe how he felt physically when he was worried. Finally, the psychologist asked Jamie what he was most afraid would happen—or what his biggest worry was about school. Jamie was able to tell the psychologist that he was worried that his work would not be good enough or that he would answer a question wrong—ultimately he thought this would mean he wouldn't pass fifth grade. He also added that he did not want to be embarrassed in front of his classmates or to disappoint his teacher or his parents. He said that when he felt worried like this, he felt sick to his stomach and developed a headache.

The psychologist worked with Jamie on restructuring his thoughts and feelings about school. The psychologist helped him to identify where his thoughts were inaccurate (e.g., getting wrong answers meant he would fail the class) and to normalize what he was thinking and feeling (e.g., some of his classmates probably have similar concerns). He also taught Jamie some simple relaxation techniques he could do before going to school and that he could use during school should he feel anxious in class. Finally, the psychologist worked with Jamie's parents on how to get him to school on time every day.

Jamie's situation is not terribly uncommon. Children at any age can feel anxious about going to school. Some children may be worried about their ability to complete the work, like Jamie, whereas others may be concerned about how their peers are treating them. Regardless of the reason it is important for children to learn how to cope with this type of anxiety so that they can continue to attend school regularly.

It was useful for Jamie's parents to talk with both his teacher as well as the school counselor. Collectively, they could establish if the behavior was situation or location specific. Some children may experience signs of anxiety or stress only at home while getting ready for school or only while at school. Moreover, while at school a child may experience distress only in a particular class or when around particular peers. In Jamie's case, it was clear that his anxiety was more *global* in that he felt anxious about school-related activities regardless of where he was, which lead to his refusal to go to school. Since most parents want to find a way to help their children feel better, Jamie's parents did what many do, which was to allow him to stay home when his distress was high. Unfortunately, as expected, the result was that his anxiety was reinforced, ultimately leading to greater anxiety rather than helping it to abate.

When the situation that causes anxiety is avoided, it is communicated to the brain that the situation was bad enough so it was avoided, which provides brief respite from worry. The brain further understands that the person was "right" to fear the situation, so when the situation is experienced again, the anxiety response will likely be more intense than before since the brain and body are trying to protect themselves from harm. By contrast, experiencing the situation that causes anxiety communicates to the brain that nothing bad actually happened. Over time, this can lead to the person trusting that the situation is "not that bad" and therefore does not need to be avoided. As noted in the scenario, in addition to working with Jamie directly, the psychologist also worked with the parents providing education about the relationship between anxiety and avoiding the situation as well as specific strategies that helped them manage the occasions when Jamie refused to go to school. This work in many respects is as important as (if not more important than) the strategies Jamie learned. If the parents are unable to make him go to school, then the strategies that Jamie learned are effectively worthless.

Jamie's work with the psychologist allowed him to talk about what was bothering him. He was not only able to share his concerns with someone who could understand them but was also able to learn how to challenge these concerns in terms of their veracity. When his thoughts and feelings were overwhelming or he was unable to challenge his thoughts soon enough he also learned effective strategies to calm his physiology (e.g., deep abdominal breathing) so that he could slow down both his mind and body. This would then allow him to use his cognitive techniques and ultimately reengage with the class and the subject matter.

Warren's Devastating Medical Diagnosis

Warren is a 53-year-old married man who was recently diagnosed with lung cancer. He has a family history of various cancers, but as a younger man, he vowed to take care of his body by eating well, exercising, and not smoking. Despite his efforts, Warren developed an aggressive form of cancer. He has been the primary breadwinner in his family and has generally been relied upon by his wife to make most major decisions during their 30-year marriage.

Warren's wife has attended all physician appointments with him so that she can fully understand not only the course of Warren's cancer but also treatment possibilities and prognosis. She has been a diligent note taker at these meetings and has picked up on information relayed by the physician that Warren missed due to his being shocked and overwhelmed by his situation. Additionally, Warren's two adult children and their spouses, all of whom live within an hour of Warren, have been supportive by being physically present when possible and also by regularly checking in by phone and/or email.

Warren has been struggling to manage his reactions to his diagnosis as well as his prognosis, which is that his cancer is terminal and he will have, at best, one more year to live. He has also been consumed by worry about his wife and how she will carry on after he has died. Although they both have had wills prepared, Warren has been obsessed with reviewing all of his documents and scheduling multiple meetings with his lawyer to review the documents despite his lawyer's assurance that Warren's medical and financial wishes are clearly spelled out. Warren's wife has also been present at these meetings and is comfortable with the contents of all of the documents.

Warren's physician has spoken with him on several occasions reminding him that his time left is limited and that he highly encourages Warren to let go of his concerns and focus on spending quality time with his family. He has also encouraged Warren to consider having final "dream" experiences (e.g., travel) as soon as possible while he is still feeling well enough to enjoy them. Warren agreed but had great difficulty letting go of his concern for his wife's financial stability and as a result rejected any suggestion of doing something he would find enjoyable.

Things changed for Warren one evening when his wife displayed a combination of intense anger and sadness toward him for being so consumed by worry that he was not enjoying the time he had left with her and that her final memories of their lives together would be Warren in a constant state of worry. She also repeated something Warren's physician had said, which was that constant stress and worry had the potential to make his symptoms worse, which would almost guarantee he would be unable to enjoy any final activities and experiences. Warren became tearful and defensive but knew that his wife was right. He tried on his own to let go of his worries. He felt some relief but continued to experience intrusive, anxious thoughts (e.g., Does my wife know how to access the safety deposit box? Does she know how to withdraw money from the 401k?) and decided to learn more about how to relax and manage anxiety. He did an Internet search and found a few reputable websites that described relaxation techniques and identified some self-help books that provided more *detail about managing anxiety and worry. He also learned that these skills might also help him to manage pain and discomfort.*

Warren's situation is not that uncommon, not only in terms of receiving a devastating diagnosis but also in terms of experiencing significant worry and concern for loved ones' well-being once they are gone. Warren was fortunate in that he has a significant support system. Not only was he married with adult children, but that all were available for him as needed. His wife provided necessary support during his visits to his physician's office. As a result, she was not only able to provide emotional support, but as noted in the scenario, was also able to provide support in the form of knowing what the physician said and reminding Warren about it. Although more difficult to establish, his wife's presence at these meetings likely reduced Warren's overall anxiety because he did not have to manage his diagnosis and treatment information alone. He could rely on his wife for support in this way.

Warren's adult children were also able to reduce some of the burden of everyday life by taking care of small errands for their parents and for helping to keep their home clean and providing meals. Their children indicated that they would rather their father spend quality time with their mother rather than on mundane tasks and that they were happy to help in this way. Again, this series of gestures also likely contributed to a reduction in Warren's overall stress level.

Both Warren's wife's and children's ability to step up in ways that were needed helped to demonstrate the importance of social support. Warren initially took on sole responsibility for making sure everything would be taken care of before and after his death; however, he eventually realized that not only was this not necessary but that he felt worse (physically and emotionally) when he shouldered the burden entirely on his own. Being able to rely on capable people with whom one has mutual caring can help to reduce stress and the toll prolonged stress can take on the mind and body.

When Warren's wife finally got through to him, he was able to more fully rely on others for help. Freeing himself up in this way also allowed for more time and energy to be devoted to taking care of himself by learning how to calm his mind and body. When Warren regularly practiced his newly learned relaxation techniques, he found that he was, in fact, less worried and less stressed. He also realized that he was sleeping better and was much less irritable. This allowed Warren to more fully enjoy the time he had with his wife and children, as well as to quickly plan a trip oversees that he and his wife had dreamed of taking but never had.

Warren still struggled with concern for his wife but was able to better manage these feelings on his own. He did, however, also decide to meet with a counselor regularly to help him cope with the end of his life and to say good-bye in ways that were meaningful to him.

When the Pressure to Perform Is Too Much

Sarah is a junior in high school. She has been playing the violin since she was five years old and has realistic aspirations to attend college on a music scholarship. She has received private instruction since the fifth grade and worked her way to first-chair violinist in her high school's orchestra as a sophomore. She is repeatedly complemented by friends and family about how talented she is and hears similar accolades from her orchestra's conductor and private teacher. She routinely enters regional competitions and often performs well, placing consistently in the top three. Additionally, she has consistently been encouraged to audition for the nearby city's professional orchestra as a way of further establishing her talent.

Sarah has welcomed each challenge as it has been presented to her. She has eagerly awaited future announcements about competitions and has carefully considered with her private instructor whether or not it would be a good idea for her to try to play for the local professional orchestra. She regularly practices her technique and perfects the musicality with which she delivers both her section-based parts (i.e., music performed with the other first violinists) as well as the solos that are routinely awarded to her.

It has not been uncommon for Sarah to feel some nerves prior to performing, especially when she has a substantial solo; however, typically she has been able to work through her nervousness by distracting herself through talking with others backstage. Recently, however, she has noticed that she has not been able to so easily shake off her feelings of anxiety. In her most recent performance Sarah stated that she felt so nervous before going on, she drew a blank on the music she was about to play—music that she had previously memorized as she had for all other performances. After the performance she was certain she made so many mistakes that stood out and the entire audience heard. Her family and friends again complemented her on her talent and denied hearing any mistakes. Her conductor praised her as well but added that in one or two places he noticed she seemed off.

Now, approaching the end-of-the-year concert and important regional competition, Sarah expressed feeling nervous all the time. She stated that she could not stop thinking about what would happen when she made a mistake and she found it difficult to maintain her focus and concentration during rehearsals. As a result she made numerous errors in tempo and notes played, which caused her conductor to pull her aside after rehearsal to ask her what was wrong. At that point she became tearful and referred to herself as a failure and a fraud. Her conductor was unable to console or reassure her so he encouraged her to talk with the school counselor about what was going on. Sarah met with the school counselor, who taught her some basic relaxation techniques but recognized that Sarah might need specialized help. The counselor referred Sarah to a local psychologist who specialized in performance-based anxiety. The psychologist reinforced the relaxation techniques Sarah learned and included instruction in visualization. Working with the psychologist, Sarah developed a visualization script tailored to her situation including terminology and imagery familiar to her. Sarah learned to use the script at home and a shortened version was developed for her to use prior to her performances.

Sarah, like so many other adolescents, is involved in a performance-based activity. Some focus time and energy in sport, some in more academic pursuits, and others in the arts. Sarah seemed to have identified a passion for playing the violin when she was just a kindergartner. Although some children may feel pressure from adults (e.g., parents, teachers, coaches, etc.) to participate in one activity or another, Sarah seemed to genuinely enjoy practicing and playing the violin. It is possible that this authentic passion for her instrument contributed to the degree to which she excelled.

As noted in the scenario, it was not uncommon for Sarah to experience some nervousness prior to performing. This is, in fact, quite common for many performers and a certain degree of arousal like this may be important for some to perform at their best. Problems arise when anxiety and the physiological arousal that comes with it exceed optimal levels. This will vary from person to person; however, nervousness to the point of physically shaking or having difficulty concentrating or remembering can be signs that the individual is too aroused, and thus, their performance may suffer. This seems to have been the case for Sarah. She was unable to successfully use her usual coping strategies (i.e., distracting herself), which previously seemed to work more by accident than by intent. As a result, Sarah's self-report was that her performance suffered—which was mildly confirmed by her conductor.

Since Sarah was not used to entering a performance feeling that degree of nervousness, and since that resulted in a slightly poorer-than-normal performance, Sarah interpreted the experience in its entirety as an indication that she was in fact not good at playing the violin and therefore did not deserve the accolades she previously received. Sarah's confidence was supremely shaken, and it was revealed in her session with the school counselor that all she did now related to the violin was relive her mistakes (real and imagined) from all of her previous performances. The relaxation techniques Sarah learned with the school counselor helped her to physiologically calm down in the moment, but it did not take long for her mind to replay her perceived failures and therefore to re-arouse her mind and body. The school counselor recognized that Sarah might be dealing with clinical anxiety, but even if she was not, the counselor knew that she did not have experience helping students in performance-based situations regain their confidence and ultimately made the referral to a psychologist who did.

As noted in the scenario, the psychologist worked with Sarah on crafting a visualization script that involved her imagining a flawless performance. Although they needed some time to work through Sarah's self-doubt, eventually the script was effortless to craft since Sarah had an abundance of actual experiences from which to draw. She was able to imagine herself confidently poised on stage, holding a perfect posture, hitting every note, and using flawless technique. The end of her visualization involved a standing ovation by an anonymous audience. After one run through of the script, Sarah experienced a noticeable increase in confidence. She was instructed to use the script regularly to bolster her belief in herself and her ability, and to use the abbreviated script prior to performances should she feel like her confidence was wavering.

How Jessie Learned to Relax to Manage Everyday Stress Instead of Doing What Did Not Work

Jessie is a 32-year-old woman who is married, with three children under the age of 10. She has been working in sales for a local company for nearly 10 years. She and her husband live a modest lifestyle without very much discretionary spending. Most of the time they have enough money to pay their bills with a little extra left over to put in a savings account. Some months, however, especially when there is an unexpected expense, such as a major car repair or appliance replacement, they have to either drain the meager savings they have or use their credit card to cover the cost. As a result, over the last several years they have accumulated about $8,000 in credit card debit, which they are unable to pay down because all they can afford is the minimum payment and they often have to add to their debt due to unexpected expenses.

In addition to the stressors related to maintaining cars and a home, Jessie has found that attending to her children's needs has become taxing. All of her children are in school full-time, and while that frees up many hours during the day to focus on her work time at home, the after-work time is spent cooking meals, helping with homework, cleaning up, and making sure the children get to bed at a decent hour. Her husband assists with all of these tasks; however, Jessie feels an emotional burden as "mom" that she is the one who needs to be sure that their children are raised properly.

The last few years have seen Jessie consuming more caffeine than has been typical for her. She has not been sleeping well and therefore is tired most of the day. She drinks caffeine via strong coffee and soda throughout the day to stay alert and productive in her job. She continues to drink caffeinated beverages until the children are in bed, which can be as late as 10 or 11 in the evening depending on how cooperative the children are. This ongoing and late-into-the-evening caffeine consumption has meant that Jessie is wired before bedtime, making it difficult for her to fall asleep, thereby exacerbating her sleep deprivation. In the last several months Jessie has had a strong drink before bed to help her relax and wind down so she can fall asleep. She reports that this has worked for her and has recently found that consuming two alcoholic drinks before bed is even more effective.

Jessie still wakes up not feeling very rested and has found that she is more irritable than usual throughout the day. In the last couple of weeks, her alcohol consumption has increased and she has started to consume her alcoholic beverages with dinner to calm her nerves. This has made it so Jessie has not been able to help with the children's homework because she is drunk. Her husband has expressed concern for her well-being and her increase in drinking. Although reluctant to do so, Jessie agreed to meet with a local psychologist who specializes in treating individuals with drug and alcohol abuse or addiction. Jessie's husband explained to the psychologist her current pattern of behavior and what lead up to her current drinking habits. The psychologist recognized that Jessie is likely dealing with alcohol abuse at this point, which could quickly change to addiction should she not get her stress under control. In combination with psychotherapy, the psychologist worked with Jessie to identify her stressors and what, if any, can be eliminated or reduced. He also encouraged her to engage in regular progressive muscle relaxation as well as visualization, both of which are designed to help her get to a place of feeling calm and at peace.

Jessie's experience is not unlike that of many working adults with children. Although many have good, steady work, the pay is often such that it just barely covers expenses. Even with two wage earners, as is the case with Jessie and her husband, they make just enough to save a little each month only to see that savings disappear when a major expense is necessary. They are not overspending on vacations or extras (e.g., four-wheelers, top-of-the-line TV and sound system, high-end furniture and clothing, etc.). These stressors, in combination with raising children, have made it so Jessie has had a difficult time sleeping at night. As a result she found that she needed something to keep her awake enough to do her work during the day. Unfortunately her solution to drink a lot of caffeine started her on a cycle of being too awake at bed time, which left her even more tired during the following day, which lead to an even greater consumption of caffeine. Her solution to this problem was to have a night cap just to help her relax; however, this quickly turned into multiple drinks that started to interfere with her ability to take care of her nighttime responsibilities.

Jessie attempted to solve her fatigue issue with substances—both of which are legal and both of which ultimately made her situation worse. Like so many, Jessie focused her attention on the immediate issue (i.e., being tired during the day) rather than what might have caused the issue to begin with. In this case, either Jessie had too much going on, or her internal reactions to her responsibilities made her situation feel worse.

As already noted, Jessie and her husband did not dramatically overspend nor could they necessarily control what was needed by their children from one moment to the next. Through a few sessions of psychotherapy, however, Jessie recognized that not only was she unhappy with the state of their lives, but that there were ways to make it a little bit better in the short run. She also developed a plan for her to make things better in the long term. She and her husband reviewed their bills and identified a few areas in which they could reduce their spending. The dollar amount was not extraordinary, but it relieved some of the financial pressure they felt each month. Additionally, Jessie realized how unhappy she was in her current job. She also recognized that she could not just quit her job because finding another job would be quite difficult. Thus, she developed a plan for finding another job that included specific things she could do each week to work toward this goal.

Finally, Jessie faithfully practiced her progressive muscle relaxation, which she began to look forward to each day. She and her husband worked things out so that she could take time during the evening to do this and he would be sure that she would not be disturbed by the children. If she had a particularly stressful day, she would also use her visualization, which for her involved stilling on a tropical beach with her husband and no children. Both of these techniques in addition to specific problem solving allowed Jessie to invoke relaxation when she needed it. In time she found that her sleep improved and she was able to consume much less caffeine because she didn't need it. She stopped drinking alcohol unless she and her husband had a glass of wine with dinner.

Sally and the Principal

Sally is a 15-year-old sophomore in high school. She has consistently struggled with academics throughout her time in school. Her elementary school years were completed with some difficulty as were her junior high school years. Her first year in high school resulted in a slight improvement in academics, but since the beginning of her sophomore year she has struggled again to keep up with her classmates. She has received testing for a learning disability as well as attention deficit/hyperactivity disorder (ADHD) to determine if any of those issues could account for Sally's struggles. The results of the testing simply indicated that Sally's intellectual functioning was average to below average, which meant that it has been and will continue to be somewhat difficult for her to keep up with her work and perform at the level of her peers.

Although Sally has previously been able to manage her frustration with how difficult school has been for her, she was able to feel a sense of accomplishment in art class, where she seemed to excel. As is the case with most of her peers, Sally plans to attend college and has filled her schedule with academic-related courses (e.g., science, math, English, etc.) and has not taken any art classes since they will not prepare her for the rigors of college. Thus, the pressure on Sally to keep up has been more intense for her than it has been thus far in her schooling. She puts in several hours each week studying and reviewing the week's work, and her parents have hired a private tutor to help her with study skills and with learning requisite material. Sally's performance, however, has remained stagnant at best and has started to show signs of decline.

More recently, Sally has been unable to contain her frustration during class. She has become defensive and argumentative with her teachers and has taken to distracting her classmates by doodling in her notebook and showing others, and making sarcastic comments about the class content. She has been sent to the principal's office on more than one occasion with the warning that the next time she was sent she would be suspended. Sally was sent to the principal's office one more time, and although she knew what would happen if she was sent, Sally became enraged by being told that she was officially suspended for two days. She yelled at the principal and knocked some papers off his desk. This caused the principal to suspend her for a full week.

Sally's parents met with the principal to determine how to best help Sally at this point since she seemed to be self-destructing. He recommended that she receive counseling to help her manage her frustration and either receive another intellectual evaluation or have someone work with the family based on the previous evaluation to develop a plan for the remainder of Sally's time in high school.

Sally initially showed an increase in frustration again when told she had to meet weekly with a counselor. She felt like she was a freak and a mental case. The counselor worked with Sally on identifying what exactly frustrates her during school, and the psychologist who initially conducted Sally's assessment worked with Sally and her parents to develop a realistic plan for what courses to take in high school as well as discussing whether or not college was a reasonable path for her.

Unfortunately, Sally was dealing with something that many children, adolescents, and adults deal with: she is not able to do what her peers are able to do—at least not as easily. Her frustration and escalating behavioral outbursts are not that uncommon for students who do not have the skills to cope with failing to perform as they and/or others expect them to. Although Sally was tested for a learning disability and other possible diagnoses that might affect her ability to perform well in school, those results were negative but revealed that she simply did not have the aptitude for high performance in academics and that performing at an average level would take quite a bit of effort.

Despite this result, Sally continued to unfairly compare herself to her peers and thought that she should earn the same grades or not have to put in more time studying than they did just to earn lower grades. This, coupled with the added pressure of college aspirations, created a situation for Sally that almost guaranteed that she would self-destruct. She simply had expectations of herself that were neither reasonable nor fair to her. What also seemed to be overlooked initially was the fact that she had a proficiency in art. When discussing this with her counselor, it became clear that not only was she good at it (painting in particular) but that she also thoroughly enjoyed it. She responded to this realization by saying *I can't make any money as an artist so I have to go to college and study something normal.*

Sally and her counselor discussed the various ways training in art can lead to a paying job and that she could learn more about art schools that were not affiliated with a traditional college or university setting. They also discussed the importance of Sally finishing her high school education, which would continue to be challenging since she had well over two years remaining. The counselor consulted with the psychologist who completed Sally's previous assessment to determine what kind of support, if any, could be requested of the school.

With a plan in place for how she could graduate from high school while meeting the requirements but not overtaxing her, the counselor worked with Sally on how to manage what would likely be ongoing in class and at home frustrations related to academic work. The counselor used cognitive behavioral therapy to address Sally's thoughts related to her course work. The counselor helped Sally recognize that she was highly critical of herself when she didn't know an answer or how to solve a problem. The counselor helped Sally learn how to *reframe* these experiences in terms of the fact that it is just harder for her than others but that she is not *stupid* or a *failure* because it takes her longer. They also discussed Sally's hesitation with asking questions during class, concluding that if she did ask questions, she would likely understand the material better, resulting in a better performance in class and with her homework. Because Sally will encounter these types of struggles throughout the rest of her time in high school, she and her counselor worked in identifying ways she could remind herself that she plans to pursue art and that she needs to finish high school in order to do what she is really passionate about. Sally decided to create a collage of her own artwork that she could display in her room to add more over the next few years. This served as a visual reminder of not only what she plans to do with her future but also what she enjoys and where she excels.

Part III

❖

Controversies and Debates

Although relaxation is not an inherently controversial subject, this section includes three issues on which not all researchers or professionals agree. Each issue is put forth in the form of a question and two opposing responses are presented. These responses are written by professional scholars who engage in clinical practice or who conduct research. An introduction to each issue is provided prior to the responses.

Controversy #1: Do relaxation drinks actually work?

INTRODUCTION

As we in American culture and others similar to it go about our daily lives, we are bombarded by numerous expectations about how to live our lives, who should be in our lives, and how we should be feeling from one situation to the next. In and among these expectations there is no shortage of message telling us that we need more energy so that we can outperform those around us, while myriad other messages tell us we just need to relax and take things slowly. American culture in particular seems to value competition and being *the best* at whatever it is that we do. In order to achieve this standard, we need to have enough energy. The reality for many of us is that we are often under-rested and sleep deprived, which leaves us with low energy levels. As a result, many of us turn to stimulants of one variety or another to boost our energy levels. Caffeine in the form of coffee, soda, or tea is among the most common ways to reenergize; however, a market of consumables that has exploded in recent years are *energy shots* and *energy drinks*. These products are formulated and marketed for the explicit purpose of giving the consumer more energy. Although the FDA (U.S. Food and Drug Administration) cautions that these products do not allow you to function in the same way that consistently getting a good night's sleep would, these products collectively generate billions of dollars in sales annually.

By contrast, there are now products formulated to facilitate relaxation. They are often marketed as products that can help with studying or working (which is also what the energy drinks purport to help with) as well as sleeping. These *relaxation drinks* contain active ingredients that have otherwise been linked to being in a relaxed state or to helping people fall asleep (e.g., melatonin, kava) and are typically produced in the form of tea, dairy-based, or carbonated drinks. Although there are hundreds of relaxation drinks on the market, many people have never heard of them and very few stores carry them. Collectively, relaxation drinks have been described as a booming or growth market but are clearly not yet competitive with their energy drink counterparts.

Regardless of the size of this particular market, what remains somewhat debatable is the effectiveness and safety of consuming drinks formulated to help you relax. Neither energy drinks nor relaxation drinks are regulated by the FDA in the sense that the active ingredients do not require preapproval by the FDA in order to be included in the product. Thus, a manufacturer can include whatever ingredient they want in whatever amount they want as an active ingredient. The FDA gets involved only when there is a problem and it has to provide proof that the product is unsafe before it can be removed from store shelves. Relaxation drinks, in particular the typical active ingredients, have been found to lose effectiveness in liquid form, which means that the drink may have lost its effectiveness during production. Moreover, many active ingredients may not have been studied in terms of how they interact with other supplements or medications. When a medical provider asks what medications or supplements you are taking, your answers help them to determine what new medication is safe to prescribe as well as to identify known drug interactions that may present a problem. Without this information, due to a lack of scientific study medical providers are unable to accurately counsel their patients with respect to the safety of taking or otherwise consuming various substances at the same time.

With the uncertainty about and at times caution against consuming something to induce a particular physiological state (i.e., aroused/energized or calm/relaxed), it may just be worth saving your money (two to three dollars a drink) and trusting your body to take care of itself by giving it what it needs: a reasonably healthy diet, a reasonable amount of physical activity, and enough hours to get enough sleep. Of course, this may also mean that you have to re-prioritize what you have going on in your life, and that can be one of the most difficult things for us to do. Given the wonderfully democratic nature of our society, each of us gets to decide whether or not we want to spend our money on products such as these. In order to make such decisions, however, it is useful to be presented with as much information as possible on the benefits and drawbacks of a particular product. What follows in this section are two essays designed to provide you with such information. The first essay takes the position that relaxation drinks can be effective, while the second supports the position that relaxation drinks are not effective. Each reader is challenged to consider the information presented here and perhaps do some additional sleuthing on their own to determine if using relaxation drinks is right for them.

RESPONSE 1: YES, RELAXATION DRINKS WORK

Due to the lack of research on the effectiveness of relaxation drinks, it is difficult to argue that these drinks are successful or unsuccessful in promoting relaxation. Most of the evidence on whether these drinks work or do not is anecdotal, which is quite subjective in nature. However, many individuals who try these relaxation drinks endorse feeling calmer upon consumption. In fact, Benjamin Weeks (2009) mentioned that an unpublished study on relaxation drinks found that 52 of 61 people who drank one of the market relaxation drinks reported feeling relaxed, with 39 of those individuals feeling more focused during a variety of tasks. Other researchers have investigated more objective and physiological measurements of relaxation. According to Dr. Tasneem Bhatia, more objective measurements of relaxation including lowered heart rate, lower respiratory rate, and decreased blood pressure have been found within 30 minutes to an hour after ingesting a relaxation drink. However, a lack of formal clinical trials testing the effectiveness of relaxation drinks is perpetuating the current controversy regarding whether these drinks actually work.

Although there is not much research testing the effectiveness of relaxation drinks that are currently on the market, studies have shown that various ingredients used in relaxation drinks are effective in promoting relaxation. Therefore, there is empirical evidence that components of many of these relaxation drinks do, in fact, promote relaxation. For example, Dr. Bhatia explains that five common ingredients are found in relaxation drinks, including valerian root, L-theanine, gamma-aminobutyric acid (GABA), 5-HTP, and melatonin, that have all been shown to help with inducing relaxation in humans. Thus, the components of these drinks are known relaxants, which provides some preliminary evidence that these drinks likely work.

First, valerian root is a medicinal herb that has been used to treat sleep disorders and anxiety. FDA classifies valerian root as "generally recognized as safe" in the United States for food use. Valerian root has been safely used as an alternative to other pharmacotherapies as treatment for stress and anxiety. Valerian root is found in some relaxation drinks and has been shown to aid in relaxation as an over-the-counter medication. Therefore, relaxation drinks that contain valerian root may promote relaxation just as this herb does on its own.

Second, L-theanine is naturally found in black tea and has been shown to produce relaxing brain waves that provide relief from anxiety. Lu and colleagues (2004) have studied the effects of L-theanine on anxiety levels in humans. L-theanine has been shown to increase relaxation compared to placebo and a pharmacotherapy, alprazolam. Therefore, L-theanine, a component of some relaxation drinks, has demonstrated its ability to aid in relaxation among humans.

Third, GABA is a neurotransmitter that has been shown to increase tranquility. Abdou and colleagues (2006) showed that GABA induced relaxation and reduced anxiety through altering brain wave patterns. Additionally, they found that GABA can also be administered prior to a stressful event to combat the anxiety of that situation. For example, if individuals who are afraid of heights are given GABA prior to crossing a suspended bridge, they had lower stress response levels compared to individuals who did not receive GABA. As a result, GABA, which is found in some relaxation drinks, has a demonstrated ability to relax individuals and perhaps even lessen the effects of stressful situations.

Fourth, Birdsall (1998) found that 5-HTP, an amino acid that crosses the blood-brain barrier, increases serotonin levels, and therefore lessens the effects of anxiety. Lastly, melatonin, a hormone, has been shown to help individuals relax and be able to fall asleep and, therefore, improve their sleep quality. Melatonin has been implicated in various studies to affect sleep patterns in humans. Further, administering melatonin has been shown to be helpful in promoting relaxation with the goal of sleep induction.

Despite a lack of empirical evidence that determines whether relaxation drinks work or do not, there is an abundance of evidence that ingredients found in relaxation drinks do work. Therefore, additional research is needed to test whether relaxation drinks, which contain other ingredients besides these known relaxants, are effective in promoting relaxation. The evidence supporting the effectiveness of the ingredients in relaxation drinks suggests that relaxation drinks may also work by promoting relaxation and reducing anxiety.

Christine May, PhD

BIBLIOGRAPHY

Abdou, Adham M, et al. "Relaxation and Immunity Enhancement Effects of Gamma-Aminobutyric Acid (GABA) Administration in Humans." *Biofactors* (Oxford, England) 26, no. 3 (2006): 201–208.

Bhatia, Tasneem. "What You Need to Know about Relaxation Drinks." (2013) http://www.doctoroz.com/article/relaxation-drinks.

Birdsall, Timothy C. "5-Hydroxytryptophan: A Clinically-Effective Serotonin Precursor." *Alternative Medicine Review* 26, no. 4 (1998): 271–280.

Lu, Kristy, et al. "The Acute Effects of L-Theanine in Comparison with Alprazolam on Anticipatory Anxiety in Humans." *Human Psychopharmacology* 19, no. 7 (October 2004): 457–465.

Weeks, Benjamin S. "Formulations of Dietary Supplements and Herbal Extracts for Relaxation and Anxiolytic Action: Relarian." *Medical Science Monitor* 15, no. 3 (2009): RA256–RA262.

RESPONSE 2: NO, RELAXATION DRINK DO NOT WORK

Relaxation drinks are unlikely to be effective. While research focusing on this class of beverages is scarce, conclusions about effectiveness can be drawn based on our current understanding of human relaxation, product composition, and ingredient mechanisms of action. There is sufficient evidence to conclude that relaxation drinks fail to achieve their purported benefits, such as creating a sense of calmness, decreasing anxiety, and inducing sleep.

The majority of ingredients used to support claims of achieving calmness and tranquility are naturally produced in plants. Humans consumed these long before relaxation drinks hit store shelves. Of these ingredients, kava root boasts the most evidence in support of its effects on mild anxiety, as found by Pittler and Ernst. Despite this, the FDA issued warnings about consumption of kava use due to reports of toxic effects to the liver (including those published by Escher, Humberston, and Stickel). Valerian root has also been the focus of numerous clinical studies, some of which demonstrated improvements in sleep quality or reduction in anxiety. Nonetheless, some studies have had negative results. As with kava, adverse effects have been reported with valerian, including liver injury and gastrointestinal discomfort, shown by MacGregor and Chan.

Other ingredients, such as passion flower, L-theanine, rose hip, hops, and linden flower, are included for their traditionally alleged effects of inducing relaxation, yet uncertainty of effectiveness is a frequent problem with these naturally occurring products. They do not undergo the same rigorous analysis required for synthetic pharmaceutical compounds and their regulatory oversight is minimal.

Some ingredients in relaxation drinks mimic those naturally produced in the human body, such as melatonin. Most play various roles in nervous system regulation and are available as over-the-counter products in natural or synthetic form. Unfortunately, supplementing the body's normal production of these compounds does not necessarily enhance the effects. Though melatonin regulates the sleep-wake cycle, studies by Ardendt and Buscemi provided no clear evidence that taking it as a supplement improves sleep quality.

In addition to lack of confirmation of efficacy, ineffective ingredient dosages make it unlikely that relaxation drinks meet their claims. In many relaxation beverage products, the amount of each ingredient listed on the label is small enough that a single serving would not produce a significant response. Moreover, laboratory testing by Consumer Reports showed that the quantities of ingredients are often much smaller than those listed on the labeling. Some brands do not list the amounts used; rather, they use a propriety blend, leaving consumers unaware of how much of each ingredient is consumed.

Even if the ingredients were effective in inducing relaxation or reducing anxiety, many claims made on relaxation drink labeling would not be met. Product claims commonly go beyond the traditional uses of their ingredients, suggesting effects such as waking up feeling refreshed, enhancing ability to focus, and even achieving better grades in school. There is an inherent subjectivity to relaxation and its related moods and mental states. Objectively measuring the effects of relaxation drinks is difficult and, for some claims, unfeasible.

Relaxation drinks may interact with certain prescription medications, leading to unwanted and adverse health effects that would most likely increase, rather than decrease, anxiety. Some classes of psychiatric and neurologic drugs are contraindicated with the use of certain supplements, such as melatonin and kava, due to compound interactions, additive effects, and mechanisms of action similar to that of prescription drugs.

Most relaxation drinks contain multiple ingredients that can interact with medications and supplements.

Anxiety and sleep disruption are multifaceted problems that, as a result of our hectic lives and demanding schedules, are widespread. In some cases, these conditions are caused by underlying medical disorders and warrant the use of prescription medication and physician oversight. Some stress, though, is normal and can be controlled without medications or supplements. Lifestyle changes and adjustment to stressor responses can ease the overall burden of anxiety and tension. The effects of such actions are apt to produce a more profound and sustainable improvement than that which can be consumed from a bottle.

Relaxation drinks may provide an enjoyable experience and subjective improvement in mental state; however, evidence suggests they are unable to cause meaningful change in anxiety levels or a lasting relaxation effect. If used in moderation by healthy individuals, these beverages are unlikely to cause harm; nonetheless, at a steep price, frequently hefty sugar load, and generally poor nutritional composition, there are better choices. A glass of water and a conscious change in personal habits and attitude are likely to produce true relaxation.

Sylvie Stacy, MD, MPH

BIBLIOGRAPHY

Arendt, Josephine, and Debra Jean Skene. "Melatonin as a Chronobiotic." *Sleep Medicine Reviews* 9, no. 1 (2005): 25–39.

Buscemi, Nina, Ben Vandermeer, Nicola Hooton, Rena Pandya, Lisa Tjosvold, Lisa Hartling, Sunita Vohra, Terry P. Klassen, and Glen Baker. "Efficacy and Safety of Exogenous Melatonin for Secondary Sleep Disorders and Sleep Disorders Accompanying Sleep Restriction: Meta-Analysis." *British Medical Journal* 332, no. 7538 (2006): 385–393.

Chan, T. Y. "An Assessment of the Delayed Effects Associated with Valerian Overdose." *International Journal of Clinical Pharmacology and Therapeutics* 36, no. 10 (1998): 569–569.

Consumer Reports. "Relaxation Drinks: An Antifrazzle Fizzle." *Consumer Reports Magazine* (May 2013).

Escher, Monica, Jules Desmeules, Emile Giostra, and Gilles Mentha. "Hepatitis Associated with Kava, a Herbal Remedy for Anxiety." *British Medical Journal* 322, no. 7279 (2001): 139.

Humberston, C. L., J. Akhtar, and E. P. Krenzelok. "Acute Hepatitis Induced by Kava Kava." *Clinical Toxicology* 41, no. 2 (2003): 109–113.

MacGregor, F. B., V. E. Abernethy, S. Dahabra, I. Cobden, and P. C. Hayes. "Hepatotoxicity of Herbal Remedies." *British Medical Journal* 299, no. 6708 (1989): 1156.

Pittler, Max H., and Edzard Ernst. "Efficacy of Kava Extract for Treating Anxiety: Systematic Review and Meta-Analysis." *Journal of Clinical Psychopharmacology* 20, no. 1 (2000): 84–89.

Stickel, Felix, Hans-Martin Baumüller, Karlheinz Seitz, Dimitrios Vasilakis, Gerhard Seitz, Helmut K. Seitz, and Detlef Schuppan. "Hepatitis Induced by Kava." *Journal of Hepatology* 39, no. 1 (2003): 62–67.

Controversy #2: Does American culture encourage or discourage relaxation?

INTRODUCTION

There are probably few who would disagree with the idea that American culture is fast paced. We have a history of innovating and striving to be the best at whatever we set out to do. The advances in Internet resources and portable technology means that we can attend to whatever and whomever we want at any time of the day or night. While this certainly can be advantageous for many reasons, it can also mean that we may not take time to slow down and refuel ourselves physically, mentally, emotionally, or spiritually. This can certainly lead to a state of unrest. By contrast, the technological advances that have taken place over the last several decades (upward of 100 years) have meant that we are able to accomplish some tasks more quickly and efficiently than ever before. This frees us up so that we have more time to do whatever we want. For some of us that may mean taking time to spend on activities we enjoy or simply taking time to relax.

Most of us, however, lament how busy we are. Since we can easily take work home via portable work computers or access to work via our own smart phones, tablets, and home computers, it may seem as if we're more busy and working more because many of us do work while at home. This may, of course, mean that we're doing less work while at work. Since we also have easy access to technologically based leisure activities such as social media or the Internet for surfing, we may spend a few minutes here and there updating our various statuses and checking on others' or watching videos of humans or animals doing strange and funny things. Thus, for many of us, our work and leisure lives are intermingled. We no longer leave work at the office; we bring it home. We no longer reserve leisure activities for time away from work; we engage in it at work. This can leave us feeling like we are busier than we actually are. In terms of overall hours of work completed, American workers actually work fewer hours, on average, than we did throughout the 1950s, 1960s, and 1970s. Technology truly has freed up our time. The question, of course, is what are we doing with that free time?

Another factor that can contribute to us feeling as though we barely have time to breathe is the plethora of choices available to us when we do choose to engage in leisure activity. Since leisure is done in the context of a "be the best" culture, we often approach leisure activities in the same way. We do not want to be the one who does not know what is going on with a popular television show so we *have* to be sure we watch it (and if it is on a paid television or movie service, we may "binge watch" these shows, which can take hours or multiple days). Usually, of course, there is more than one *must see* show, which means we have to allow more time for this type of activity. If we prefer something like reading or picking up a new skill to do in our leisure time, again the choices are so vast that it can be difficult to decide what to read or what to do. As a result of a lot of readily available leisure options, leisure time can feel less like downtime and more like work.

Overall this can leave us feeling like our time is scarce and quite valuable. Despite this feeling, however, we do have more time available to us than we think. It is just so easy to fill that time, and once filled, we are left feeling like we have no time at all. Some employers have recognized the busy, hectic lifestyles many of us lead and have made changes in expectations on the job. For example, some employers allow *flex time*, giving us more freedom to leave work early or arrive to work late in order to take our time getting to the office or take time to do something enjoyable. Other employers encourage leisure time at work during the work day. They may provide a place designated for taking naps, encourage long lunch breaks, or have *play rooms* where recreational toys and games are available for employees at any point during the day. Of course, these opportunities do not rival the built-in cultural mandate of siesta in Spain; however, we may have the same opportunity. We just have to make it happen on our own.

So, does American culture encourage or discourage relaxation? The answer to this question for each of us might very well rest on how we choose to interact with American culture. What free time (i.e., time not accounted for by responsibilities and obligations) do we have? What do we do with it? Even if we have the time, are we truly encouraged to take it in the form of a relaxing activity? The two essays that follow offer opposing perspectives. The first essay takes a look at the ways in which American culture encourages relaxation, whereas the second essay postulates that American culture discourages relaxation. Readers are encouraged to carefully consider both points of view globally and in the context of their individual lives and decide for themselves whether or not this culture supports relaxation.

RESPONSE 1: AMERICAN CULTURE ENCOURAGES RELAXATION

Contemporary American culture encourages relaxation. The counterargument would point to a societal lack of support for relaxation, potentially citing evidence such as lack of federal policies regulating maximum work hours and mandatory leave for employees. Other industrialized, first-world countries, particularly those in Europe, have these kinds of regulations in place. However, a major cultural shift is in process within the United States, and the positive outcome is that twenty-first-century American culture encourages relaxation. In particular, trends in medicine, the culture of the workplace, and military training provide support for a culture that now recognizes the value and benefit of relaxation as a critical component of health promotion.

According to research from the American Psychological Association, 90 percent of adults understand that chronic stress is a contributor to many major illnesses, such as heart disease and depression. Research by the American Institute of Stress reports that between 75 and 90 percent of doctor's visits are due to conditions related to stress. The medical field understands that chronic stress is a major health risk, and doctors increasingly recommend stress management practices such as yoga and meditation to their patients. A "Yoga in America" report commissioned by the magazine *Yoga Journal* stated that six percent of Americans had tried yoga or meditation based on a recommendation from a medical professional. The National Institutes for Health, a scientifically rigorous component of the federal government that provides grant money to support research, has a subunit called the National Center for Complementary and Integrative Health (NCCIH). NCCIH supports research about the health benefits of stress management practices such as yoga and meditation. Research studies at Harvard University using magnetic resonance imaging, a technique for mapping the human brain, have shown that meditation physically changes the structure of the brain in beneficial ways. Continued research will help us to understand how relaxation and stress management strategies such as yoga and meditation improve health and well-being, but the evidence clearly supports that relaxation is an important part of promoting overall good health.

Within the workplace, the youngest generation currently in the workforce, the millennial generation (sometimes called generation Y), is a driving force of a cultural shift toward embracing relaxation. Millennials, the group of younger adults and older teen-agers born from approximately 1980 through 2000, have come into the workplace with expectations of work-life balance. Survey research has found that millennial employees, in particular, want to be judged for their impact, rather than hours at work, and prefer workplaces that support flexible schedules and flexible locations, through telecommuting and other forms of remote employment. Survey results also indicate that millennials come to the workplace with an expectation that their job will make the world a better place, and that they will experience work-life integration, which is an overall sense of balance and satisfaction with their work and their life. These expectations bring a new dynamic to the workplace, and many companies and corporations are taking action to support a better work-life balance for their employees. For instance, according to research by the Society for Human Resource Management, more than 85 percent of human resource professionals think that vacation time is crucial to support and promote employee morale and performance. Some companies offer relaxation and rest opportunities during the workday and at the workplace by providing employee benefits such as on-site fitness centers and fitness classes, meditation or nap rooms to allow employees to rest and recharge during the day, and flexible work schedules, which allow employees to choose their own work schedule or telecommute from home. Other companies have implemented even more proactive policies such as disallowing overtime, to enforce that employees need to have time for their personal lives, or creating open policies about vacation and time off, with no tracking or regulations around time away from work. These kinds of corporate trends reflect implementation of the findings from numerous research studies, which indicate that workers perform at higher levels and more effectively when they are rested and feel trusted by their employer.

Even the U.S. military now recognizes the value of relaxation and holistic well-being. The U.S. Army offers a mandatory training program for soldiers called "Comprehensive Soldier and Family Fitness." The program, developed by faculty members from the positive psychology program at the University of Pennsylvania, under the guidance of Dr. Martin Seligman, focuses on building resilience and enhancing performance. The program teaches soldiers about how to manage their thoughts, deal with stress, and use breathing effectively. Centers for Excellence at many military installations, including the U.S. Military Academy, offer training in mental skills such as focusing, relaxation, and visualization, to enhance performance. On many military posts, fitness centers offer yoga classes to both the military and their family members. Hospitals within the Veteran's Administration (VA) use meditation programs to help veterans with psychological disorders, including post-traumatic stress disorder. The VA Hospital system also conducts research studies on the use of stress management strategies in the treatment of psychological disorders. When military training includes a focus on holistic well-being and relaxation, relaxation has become an integrated aspect of our broader cultural expectations.

In conclusion, trends in medicine, corporate culture, and military training all reflect a growing societal understanding that relaxation is a vital component of both individual health and societal functioning. Individuals who have the opportunity to relax are more able to effectively interact with others and achieve high performance at work and within society. During the twentieth century, we saw a cultural shift within the United States as research provided evidence that cigarette smoking was unhealthy. We are in the middle of a similar cultural shift, as we increasingly understand the health hazards of chronic stress. Twenty-first-century American culture has evolved with the increased understanding of the importance of relaxation, and our society now recognizes relaxation as a fundamental aspect of health and well-being promotion for both individuals and society as a whole.

Kimberlee Bethany Bonura, PhD

BIBLIOGRAPHY

American Psychological Association. "Latest APA Survey Reveals Deepening Concerns about Connection between Chronic Disease and Stress." Last modified January 11, 2012. http://www.apa.org/news/press/releases/2012/01/chronic-disease.aspx.

Asghar, Rob. "What Millennials Want in the Workplace (And Why You Should Start Giving It To Them)." *Forbes*, January 13, 2014. Accessed January 20, 2015. http://www.forbes.com/sites/robasghar/2014/01/13/.

Katamura, Makiko. "Harvard Yoga Scientists Find Proof of Meditation Benefit." *Bloomberg*, November 21, 2013. Accessed January 20, 2015. http://www.bloomberg.com/news.

Miller, Stephen. "Unused Vacation Days Can Be Detrimental." *Society for Human Resource Management*, November 12, 2013. Accessed

January 20, 2015. www.shrm.org/hrdisciplines/benefits/articles/pages/unused-vacation-detrimental.aspx.

National Center for Complementary and Alternative Medicine, National Institutes for Health, U.S. Department of Health and Human Services. "Get the Facts: Yoga for Health." June 2013.

Seligman, Martin & Matthews, Michael (Guest Editors). "Comprehensive Soldier Fitness." *American Psychologist*, January 2011.

RESPONSE 2: AMERICAN CULTURE DISCOURAGES RELAXATION

American culture discourages relaxation. Our culture has created the antithesis of calm and tranquility, ease and comfort, peace and presence. Our current popular culture is based on constant and frequently cluttered thinking, relentless striving, continuous and oftentimes frenetic movement, and an incessant need to act and react. The result is a persistent state of worry, stress, anxiety, and tension.

This inability to achieve, much less sustain, a state of relaxation is evidenced by the multibillion dollar "relaxation-industrial complex" that includes anti-anxiety medication, corporate wellness programs, yoga studios, fitness clubs, meditation retreats, fad diets, and various forms of therapy including psychological, massage, and aroma. In the face of this culture, we pursue the increasingly elusive state of relaxation with tremendous vigor and at great expense, yet with so little success.

This culture of anxiety has been created and perpetuated by several factors external to and within us. The economic climate of the last two decades has contributed to this zeitgeist of anxiety. The financial crises of the last 20 years, including the Internet and real estate bubbles, as well as the Great Recession, have left many of us in dire straits caused by lost jobs, foreclosed homes, and diminished retirement savings. This economic instability has created an ongoing financial angst that is experienced by parents and their children. Many families have two working parents, some working more than one job, just to make ends meet, which means less quality time and influence over their children.

The emergence of the Internet and all that has accompanied it, including websites, mobile technology, social media, and the explosion of Big Data, is another cultural force that has dramatically altered our lives and made relaxation less attainable. These technological innovations have resulted in our being connected 24/7. This constant connectivity means that we are being bombarded by information almost every moment of our waking lives. Moreover, we feel pressure to process and then respond to all of that information.

You might suppose that all of the technological advances and conveniences of twenty-first-century life would make us more efficient and give us unprecedented time to pursue a stress-free life. Yet, life for many of us seems to be busier, more scheduled, and with less free time than ever before. And we tend to spend the free time we do have in ways that are neither leisurely nor relaxing.

The economic insecurity and the growing influence of the Internet on our lives has resulted in an attitudinal shift that makes it even more difficult to experience a sense of calm and contentment. Our popular culture, which is now driven by Big Business through popular media, the Internet, and advertising, has caused us to alter how we define success and happiness. Ours has become an aspirational culture in which what we have is never enough and more and better is always the goal. Success is defined in terms of wealth, status, power, and celebrity, all of which are largely unattainable for the majority of us. Happiness has become a goal to pursue rather than a feeling to experience. Moreover, popular culture has redefined what happiness is (e.g., conspicuous consumption, physical appearance) in a way that is also neither controllable nor attainable for most of us. As a consequence, we have lost touch with what really makes us happy and at peace (e.g., relationships, quiet time). The result is a constant state of tension between what we have and what we wish we had.

Another manifestation of this aspirational culture is a pressure to "keep up with the Joneses." Research has shown that we base happiness, in part, by comparing ourselves to those around us, which used to mean our neighbors and who we worked with. But the Internet and other forms of entertainment media have opened the doors to people's lives that are far removed from our immediate lives including, for example, the lives of the so-called rich and famous such as movie and television stars and professional athletes. This oftentimes intimate exposure to those we are really so distant from has raised our referential aspirations of what we should be, have, and do far above that of the past.

These distorted aspirations have also caused an imbalanced perception of time as another source of anxiety. No longer are we satisfied and at peace with our present, but rather are always regretting the past for what we failed to do and look to the future for the success and happiness we hope we will find, yet worry we will never attain. This other-focus prevents us from appreciating and relaxing into what we have now.

In conclusion, the idea that American culture encourages relaxation flies in the face of both scientific research and our everyday experiences. Our culture has created structural and attitudinal barriers that not only discourage the experience of relaxation but also seriously impede our efforts to pursue a state of calm and contentment.

Jim Taylor, PhD

BIBLIOGRAPHY

Accenture. "The Changing Future of Consumer Health." *Accenture*, March 24, 2014. http://www.accenture.com/us-en/Pages/insight-consumer-healthcare-market-high-performance-business-research-2013.aspx.

American Psychological Association. "Economy and Money Top Causes of Stress for Americans." *American Psychological Association*, June 4, 2008. http://www.apa.org/news/press/releases/2008/06/economy-stress.aspx.

The Blackrock Institute. "From Keeping Up with the Joneses to Keeping above Water: The Status of the US Consumer." *The Blackrock Institute*, September, 2011. http://www.blackrock.com/uk/intermediaries/literature/whitepaper/status-us-consumer.pdf.

Easterlin, Richard A. "Income and Happiness: Towards an Unified Theory." *The Economic Journal* 111, no. 473 (2001): 465–484.

Godelnik, Raz. "7 Things You Need to Know about Aspirational Consumers." *Triple Pundit*, December 12, 2012. http://www.triplepundit.com/2012/12/aspirational-consumers/.

Huffington Post. "Internet Stress Tops Workers' List of Anxieties, Study." *Huffington Post*, April 15, 2013. http://www.huffingtonpost.com/2013/04/15/internet-stress-tops-work_n_3084889.html.

Kasser, Tim, Richard M. Ryan, Charles E. Couchman, and Kennon M. Sheldon. "Materialistic Values: Their Causes and Consequences." In *Psychology and Consumer Culture: The Struggle for a Good Life In a Materialistic World*, edited by Tim Kasser and Allen D. Kanner, 11–28. Washington, DC: American Psychological Association, 2004.

Levine, Bruce E. "How Our Society Breeds Anxiety, Depression and Dysfunction," *Salon*, August 26, 2013. http://www.salon.com/2013/08/26/how_our_society_breeds_anxiety_depression_and_dysfunction_partner/.

Lyubomirsky, Sonja, and Lee Ross. "Hedonic Consequences of Social Comparison: A Contrast of Happy and Unhappy People." *Journal of Personality and Social Psychology* 73, no. 6 (1997): 1141–1157.

Robert Wood Johnson Foundation. "The Burden of Stress in America." *Robert Wood Johnson Foundation,* July 7, 2014. http://www.rwjf.org/en/research-publications/find-rwjf research/2014/07/the-burden-of-stress-in-america.html.

Controversy #3: Should taking medication or learning new behaviors be used to help people relax?

INTRODUCTION

Given the myriad reasons that people who live and work in American culture get stressed or have difficulty relaxing, and given the vast differences in terms of what works to help people de-stress, it makes sense that there are various options for learning how to relax. This book has covered numerous strategies for helping you to relax. Some of these techniques you may already do with some success whereas others you may have tried only to find that they did not work for you. Additionally, if you found strategies that work, you may have become frustrated by how much time and effort they take—you may prefer to find a strategy that is more easily executed. In our fast-paced culture, many of us have the expectation that whatever ails us not only has a solution but has a solution that can be found quickly and that will solve the problem quickly. It is not uncommon for people to say (sometimes in jest and sometimes not), *Is there a pill for that?* The previous two debate sections discussed the issues of whether or not we live in a culture that encourages us to relax and, when we need to relax, whether drinking something designed to induce relaxation will actually work. The issue in this section is whether taking a pill or learning new behaviors should be recommended for those who want to relax.

This debate in part has its roots in the medical model, which loosely defined means that when someone asks a professional for help, the problem is identified and the solution is applied in order to cure the problem. If you have asthma, you take asthma medication; if you have appendicitis, you have surgery to remove the inflamed appendix. Problem. Solution. For issues associated with *how* we live, the problems may not so easily be identified and the solutions not so easily applied. Concerns about taking medication, for example, to address something like stress or anxiety include the idea that while the medication may reduce the symptoms that are associated with the problem, the medication does not necessarily fix the problem to begin with. Thus, when the medication is discontinued, the antecedent problem (i.e., the thing that started it all to begin with) is still there and the symptoms will likely reemerge. Moreover, it is not uncommon for people taking medication to either discontinue the prescription because of unpleasant side effects or endure the side effects so they can experience some relief from their original problem. By contrast, however, making behavioral changes that might very well address the originating problem or cause of the stress/anxiety make take time to learn. Additionally, the improvements seen with these new behaviors may be small to begin with and can lead to people "giving up" and wanting something to work more quickly.

What is also relevant to this discussion is the idea of whether or not working with (and therefore paying) a trained professional is necessary for the recommendations on either side of this debate. Typically when speaking of medications, the term is used in reference to a substance prescribed by a medical professional—a substance you cannot get unless you have been evaluated by the professional and received a prescription for it. If the term medication is stretched to include any substance, then the gatekeepers to obtaining and using something that will help you relax diminish. As noted in the first debate, there are products called relaxation drinks. Although their effectiveness is not very well established, you do not need a prescription to try one—just a willingness to spend a few dollars. There are also "over-the-counter" supplements that are thought to help reduce stress and anxiety, which simply require spending money to buy them. Usually, the medications prescribed by a professional have been well studied and found to actually produce the effect they are purported to produce in many people. Some supplements have also been well studied and have been shown to have the effect they are marketed to have. Either way, this route involves ingesting some substance with the hope that it will help you relax.

Learning behavioral techniques is similar in that there are some techniques that are best learned under the guidance of a trained professional whereas others anyone can try at any time without much difficulty. Reading a book, for example, or going for a walk do not require specific training. However, some forms of exercise might, and in some cases, people need to know how often and in what intensity they can safely exercise. That kind of information is best gathered by a professional who can evaluate your unique needs and abilities. Cognitive behavioral strategies usually require the assistance of a trained professional. Certainly one can read a self-help book and apply the techniques to one's own life; however, a professional is helpful and sometimes necessary to identify road blocks when the techniques are not working and to help devise solutions to get around those obstacles. Similarly, autogenic training or progressive muscle relaxation are best learned in consultation with a professional.

Regardless of the need for a professional or not, the issue of whether or not one should use substances or learn new skills to foster a sense of relaxation is a personal one. Readers are encouraged to consider the positions taken by the authors of each essay and to learn more about any procedure, technique, or medication that may have been recommended to them by a professional or that they are simply considering pursuing for themselves.

RESPONSE 1: TAKING MEDICATION SHOULD BE USED TO HELP PEOPLE RELAX

Medications should be used to help people relax. There are many different reasons why it might be difficult for someone to relax. In order to help someone relax, it is first most important to understand the root cause of his or her agitation, as that information will most certainly guide treatment. The comprehensive assessment of a person who is having difficulty achieving a state of relaxation includes a careful review of biological, psychological, and social factors that may be causing the individual's state of unrest. For many people, multiple factors contribute to their inability to relax, and effective treatment should address each of these factors. Treatments with medication are most important when biological conditions are influencing a person's inability to relax, whether those conditions are psychiatric or non-psychiatric.

There are a number of psychiatric disorders driven by biological factors, which present with a fundamental inability to relax. There is an increasingly large body of evidence demonstrating alterations in brain chemistry that mediate symptoms of these disorders and the effectiveness of medications targeting particular neural circuitry. For example, children and adolescents who have a diagnosis of attention deficit hyperactivity disorder (ADHD) appear "hypermotoric," or unable to sit still or relax. Criteria for this diagnosis include such items as "on the go, acting as if driven by a motor" and "unable to play or engage in leisure activities quietly." The Multimodal Treatment of ADHD (MTA) Study was carried out at multiple sites across the country to evaluate the leading treatments for ADHD. Nearly 600 children were randomly assigned to one of four treatment groups, including behavior therapy alone, medication management alone, the combination of the two, and routine community care. According to the results, the children receiving medication, either alone or in combination with intensive behavior therapy, showed the greatest improvement sustained over a 14-month period. This study suggests that carefully monitored medications for ADHD are more effective than non-medication treatments alone.

Another class of psychiatric disorders classically presenting with an inability to relax is anxiety disorders. People who struggle with anxiety disorders such as generalized anxiety disorder, obsessive compulsive disorder, and social phobia suffer from a variety of emotional and physical symptoms that create great difficulty achieving a state of relaxation. Two landmark studies, the Pediatric OCD Treatment Study (POTS) and the Child/Adolescent Anxiety Multimodal Study (CAMS), examined the outcomes of children and teens who were treated with medication management alone, cognitive behavioral therapy alone, or a combination of the two for anxiety disorders. Both studies found that treatment combining both therapy and medication resulted in the greatest and most sustained reduction in symptoms. There are many similar studies demonstrating an important role for medications in treating anxiety disorders in adults. In addition, numerous other psychiatric disorders present with agitation as a primary symptom in youth and adults, and have been found in replicated studies to respond most robustly to medication management. Often these patients will find the combination of medication management and non-pharmacologic treatment most effective, but many are unable to learn new behavioral strategies for relaxation without the support of appropriate medication.

There is a wide variety of non-psychiatric conditions involving a number of organ systems that also present with an inability to relax and would require medication intervention. For example, people with thyroid disorders may feel their heart racing and may be sweaty or cold, shaky, worried about changes in weight or appetite, and unable to sleep. These conditions are most often diagnosed by a blood test and require medication to either increase or decrease their level of thyroid hormone, ultimately resulting in a reduction in their overall level of agitation. Likewise, any condition that affects how oxygen is distributed to the body and brain can cause a sensation of agitation and inability to relax. For example, asthma or other causes of obstructed airflow, blot clots, or other causes of interrupted circulation could result in a significant state of unrest. Just as in the case of thyroid dysfunction, primary management of these conditions would include the use of medication to treat the underlying cause.

An inability to relax has many possible causes and requires thorough evaluation for biologically based etiologies at the outset. Overlooking a biologically based cause for agitation could result in significant medical morbidity or mortality. Even in cases where there is no acute health risk, failing to address the biological aspects of treatment may reduce the effectiveness of non-medication interventions. After careful assessment of all biological, psychological, and social aspects contributing to a presentation of restlessness, a treatment plan should be developed to address all relevant factors utilizing a multidimensional approach. Clearly, the use of medication is often a critical component of comprehensive and individualized treatment for a wide variety of conditions interfering with the ability to relax.

Jessica Manaker, MD, and Sibel Algon, MD

BIBLIOGRAPHY

The MTA Cooperative Group. "A 14-Month Randomized Clinical Trial of Treatment Strategies for Attention-Deficit/Hyperactivity Disorder." *Archives of General Psychiatry* 56 (1999): 1073–1086.

Pediatric OCD Treatment Study (POTS) Team. "Cognitive-Behavior Therapy, Sertraline, and Their Combination for Children and Adolescents with Obsessive Compulsive Disorder: The Pediatric OCD Treatment Study (POTS) Randomized Controlled Trial." *Journal of the American Medical Association* 292 (2004): 1969–1976.

Piacentini, John, Shannon Bennett, Scott N. Compton, Phillip C. Kendall, Boris Birmaher, Anne Marie Albano, John March, et al. "24- and 36-Week Outcomes for the Child/Adolescent Anxiety Multimodal Study (CAMS)." *Journal of the American Academy of Child & Adolescent Psychiatry* 53 (2014): 297–310.

TADS Study Team. "Fluoxetine, Cognitive-Behavioral Therapy, and Their Combination for Adolescents with Depression: Treatment for Adolescents with Depression Study (TADS) Randomized Controlled Trial." *Journal of the American Medical Association* 292 (2004): 807–820.

RESPONSE 2: LEARNING NEW BEHAVIORS SHOULD BE USED TO HELP PEOPLE RELAX

The issue of medications versus psychotherapy using cognitive behavioral therapy (CBT) for anxiety is an important issue for individuals seeking treatment for anxiety. CBT is a form of treatment in which a person learns skills to modify thinking that leads to anxiety and to perform behaviors (e.g., relaxation skills) that reduce feelings of anxiety. Most individuals within the American health-care system are much more likely to have a connection to a primary care provider than to a psychotherapist who is capable of performing CBT. In fact, most antidepressant medications, many of which are used for anxiety treatment, are prescribed by primary care physicians (rather than psychiatrists) who may have limited training in treatment of mental health disorders. Patients are also less likely to receive concurrent psychotherapy, even though, as we shall see, psychotherapy using CBT has multiple benefits. In fact, from 1996 to 2005 the percentage of those receiving psychotherapy decreased from 32 to 20 percent. It is clear from these findings that patients need to be knowledgeable and assertive in order to receive CBT in the current American health-care landscape.

So what are the benefits of CBT? Do the benefits of CBT only as a primary treatment outweigh the benefits of medication only as a primary treatment? There are three major points that suggest that CBT may be superior to medication only in the treatment of anxiety. These are the long-term efficacy of CBT, relapse rates after discontinuation of medication, and side effects of medication.

What does the research say about the short- and long-term effectiveness of CBT and medication in treating anxiety disorders? It is clear from many research studies that both CBT and medications reduce symptoms of anxiety. CBT has shown superiority for certain anxiety disorders (obsessive compulsive disorder and social phobia) in which exposure treatment is a crucial component (facing a feared stimulus until fear is reduced). Though both CBT and medication show effectiveness in reducing symptoms in the short term, a major negative of medication is that it appears to suppress symptoms, but not impact a patient's functioning in the long term if medication is eliminated. Learning specific cognitive and behavioral skills is at the heart of a CBT treatment. A behavioral example would be learning relaxation skills that reduce feelings of anxiety. A cognitive example would be to learn to restructure anxious thoughts by looking at the evidence for and against an anxious thought and then coming up with a rational replacement thought. As you can see, CBT is a treatment in which specific psychological skills are taught that can decrease anxiety in the short and long term, as long as a patient continues to use these acquired skills.

Another issue that a patient needs to assess in choosing a treatment is the extent to which they may relapse after discontinuing a treatment. It makes sense that from the perspective of a patient, a treatment that continues to help one feel better after discontinuing would be superior. What happens after you discontinue medication versus discontinuing CBT? As mentioned in the previous paragraph, CBT skills when learned and practiced can be used for the rest of a person's lifetime. The effects of medications, in contrast, have been shown to suppress symptoms only while the medication is being taken. If a person stops taking them, the effect of the medication wears off. In other words, the chance of symptoms returning (relapsing) after taking medication for anxiety is higher. In CBT a person learns how to use a coping skills model that can be used after psychotherapy has ended, making the chance of relapse lower.

What about side effects of the different treatments? Side effects are an important thing for a consumer to consider when assessing any treatment. CBT has been shown to have no adverse side effects. Medications, in contrast, have multiple possible side effects. Serotonin-specific reuptake inhibitors (SSRIs), which are one of the most commonly prescribed medications for anxiety, have side effects including the following: nausea, nervousness, agitation, restlessness, dizziness, reduced sexual desire or difficulty reaching orgasm or inability to maintain an erection (erectile dysfunction), drowsiness, insomnia, weight gain or loss, headache, dry mouth, vomiting, or diarrhea. It should be noted that only a portion of individuals taking SSRIs will experience any of these side effects, and a portion of these side effects do decrease or stop with continued use of the medications. Despite this, it is clear that the potential side effects of medications should be considered when a patient is seeking medication for anxiety.

When assessing any treatment for anxiety, a patient should know and assess the possible benefits and risks of each treatment. The benefits for CBT include efficacy, lifelong skill acquisition, no side effects, and lower risk of relapse following treatment discontinuation. CBT has no apparent risks. Medication's benefits are that it has also shown efficacy; however, the risks include possible side effects, higher rate of relapse after the treatment is discontinued, and lower long-term treatment effectiveness. Each patient must assess these possible risks and benefits with their treatment provider prior to making a decision on a treatment. Patients should also be aware that these two treatment approaches can be combined and that this has shown better outcome in research trials than medication-only or CBT-only treatment. Patients need to remember that it is less likely, according to research, that a primary care provider will offer a CBT referral option, and patients need to be assertive with their prescriber in order to receive this treatment option.

Brian Selby, PhD

BIBLIOGRAPHY

Chambless, Dianne. L., and Thomas H. Ollendick. "Empirically Supported Psychological Interventions: Controversies and Evidence." *Annual Review of Psychology* 52 (2001): 685–716.

Haug, Tone Tangen, Svein Blomhoff, Kerstin Hellstrøm, Ingar Holme, Mats Humble, Hans Petter Madsbu, and Jan Egil Wold. "Exposure

Therapy and Sertraline in Social Phobia: 1-Year Follow-Up of a Randomised Controlled Trial." *The British Journal of Psychiatry* 182, no. 4 (2003): 312–318.

Hollon, Steven. D., Michael O. Stewart, and Daniel Strunk. "Enduring Effects for Cognitive Behavior in the Treatment of Depression and Anxiety." *Annual Review of Psychology* 57 (2006): 285–315.

Mayo-Wilson, Evan, Sofia Dias, Ifigeneia Mavranezouli, Kayleigh Kew, David Clark, A. E. Ades, and Stephen Pilling. "Psychological and Pharmacological Interventions for Social Anxiety Disorders in Adults: A Systematic Review and Network Meta-Analysis." *The Lancet Psychiatry* 1, no. 5 (2014): 368–376.

Mojtabai, Ramin. "Increase in Antidepressant Medication in the US Adult Population between 1990 and 2003." *Psychotherapy and Psychosomatics* 77, no. 2 (2008): 83–92.

Montgomery, Stuart A., Rico Nil, Natalie Dürr-Pal, Henrik Loft, and Jean-Phillippe Boulenger. "A 24-Week Randomized, Double-Blind, Placebo-Controlled Study of Escitalopram for the Prevention of Generalized Social Anxiety Disorder." *Journal of Clinical Psychiatry* 66, no. 10 (2005): 1270–1278.

Mörtberg, Ewa, David M. Clark, and Susanne Bejerot. "Intensive Group Cognitive Therapy and Individual Cognitive Therapy for Social Phobia: Sustained Improvement at 5-Year Follow-Up." *Journal of Anxiety Disorders* 25, no. 8 (2011): 994–1000.

Norton, Peter J., and Ester C. Prince. "A Meta-Analytic Review of Adult Cognitive-Behavioral Treatment Outcome across the Anxiety Disorders." *Journal of Nervous and Mental Disease* 195, no. 6 (2007): 521–531.

Olatunji, Bunmi O., Josh M. Cisler, and Brett J. Deacon. "Efficacy of Cognitive Behavioral Therapy for Anxiety Disorders: A Review of the Meta-Analytic Findings." *Psychiatric Clinics of North America*, 33, no. 2 (2010): 557–577.

Olfson, Mark, and Steven C. Marcus. "National Patterns in Antidepressant Medication Treatment." *Archives of General Psychiatry* 66, no. 8 (2009): 848–856.

Pilling, Stephen, Evan Mayo-Wilson, Ifigeneia Mavranezouli, Kayleigh Kew, Clare Taylor, and David M. Clark. "Recognition, Assessment and Treatment of Social Anxiety Disorders: Summary of NICE Guidance." *British Medical Journal* 346 (May 22, 2013): f2541.

Roth, Anothony, and Peter Fonagy. *What Works for Whom? A Critical Review of Psychotherapy Research, Second Edition*. New York: Guilford Press, 2005.

Stein, Dan J., Marcio Versiani, Tanya Hair, and Rajinder Kumar. "Efficacy of Paroxetine for Relapse Prevention in Social Anxiety Disorder." *Archives of General Psychiatry* 59, no. 12 (2002): 1111–1118.

Stewart, Rebecca E., and Dianne L. Chambless. "Cognitive-Behavioral Therapy for Adult Anxiety Disorders in Clinical Practice: A Meta-Analysis of Effectiveness Studies." *Journal of Consulting and Clinical Psychology* 77, no. 4 (2009): 595–606.

Thase, Michael E., and Ripu D. Jindal. "Combining Psychotherapy and Psychopharmacology for Treatment of Mental Disorders." In *Bergin and Garfield's Handbook of Psychotherapy and Behavior Change*, edited by Michael J. Lambert, 767–804. New York: Wiley, 2004.

Directory of Resources

The Association for Applied Psychophysiology and Biofeedback, Inc.
http://www.aapb.org/
This is an organization for biofeedback professionals. The website has links to information about biofeedback credentialing and a link to find a biofeedback provider.

Association for Behavioral and Cognitive Therapies
http://www.abct.org/home/
This is an organization for professionals who practice cognitive behavioral therapy (CBT). The website has links to finding a CBT therapist.

Good Relaxation
http://www.goodrelaxation.com/
This website offers "Only no-nonsense health, relaxation and stress relief tips."

Quitting Smoking
http://smokefree.gov/
An resource developed by the U.S. Department of Health and Human Services, the National Institutes of Health, the National Cancer Institute, and USA.gov.
This online resource is for those who have relied on smoking as a source of stress management and who are interested in trying to kick the habit.

Rethinking Drinking: Alcohol and Your Health
http://rethinkingdrinking.niaaa.nih.gov/Support/
SelfHelfStrategiesForQuitting.asp
An online resource developed by the National Institute on Alcohol Abuse and Alcoholism.
This online resource offers tips, printables, and answers to commonly asked questions about quitting drinking.

Teens + Relaxation
http://mayoclinichealthsystem.org/~/media/Local%20Files/Cannon%20Falls/Documents/Health%20Coaching/Sleep/TeensRelax.pdf
Published by the Mayo Clinic
This resource is recommended specifically for teens who may feel stressed and are looking for ways to feel more calm and relaxed.

Worried No More: Help and Hope for Anxious Children, 2nd Edition
By Aureen Wagner, 2005
This book is recommended for parents, school personnel, as well as healthcare professionals who work with anxious children.

Glossary

Acupressure: An intervention associated with traditional Chinese medicine that involves applying pressure on certain parts of the body for the purpose of healing ailments including pain and tension.

Acupuncture: An intervention associated with traditional Chinese medicine that involves the use of small needles that penetrate the skin at certain points on the body for the purpose of healing aliments including headaches and tension.

Anti-anxiety Medications (Anxiolytics): A class of psychiatric medications used to treat symptoms related to clinical anxiety.

Autonomic Nervous System (ANS): The branch of the peripheral nervous system that regulates organ function involuntarily. The ANS is subdivided into the sympathetic and parasympathetic nervous systems.

Bereavement Overload: A term created over 40 years ago to describe the situation when an individual experiences losses so close in succession that they are not able to fully grieve one loss before they experience the next.

Biofeedback: A technique used to give feedback to an individual on how their autonomic nervous system is functioning. This feedback helps the individual learn to control these physiological responses.

Chanting: Syllables or words that are sung or spoken using the same note or a restricted range of notes; often associated with spiritual belief systems.

Cognitive Behavioral Therapy (CBT): A common form of therapy that addresses an individual's maladaptive thoughts and behaviors and replaces them with adaptive thinking and behaving.

General Adaptation Syndrome (GAS): A syndrome, identified by Hans Selye, that describes what happens when we experience prolonged periods of stress. Experiencing all three stages (i.e., alarm, resistance, and exhaustion) can result in a greater susceptibility to illness and, in extreme cases, death.

Imagery: A technique used to help people relax in which the individual mentally pictures a scene that is peaceful and soothing; effective imagery involves the use of as many senses as possible.

Karoshi: A Japanese term coined in the 1980s that refers to literally working one's self to death.

Learned Helplessness: A result of prolonged exposure to unpleasant or painful situations over which one has no control. The result is that the individual or animal learns that they are helpless to stop the discomfort and therefore give up.

Operant Conditioning: A form of learning that involves the use of reinforcement and punishment to shape behavior.

Parasympathetic Nervous System (PNS): A branch of the autonomic nervous system that has a calming effect on the body.

Progressive Muscle Relaxation (PMR): A technique designed to induce relaxation by tensing and relaxing major muscle groups throughout the body.

Relaxation Drinks: A relatively new line of products intended to have a relaxation effect by including natural substances known to produce feelings of calm.

Sauna: A practice interwoven in the culture of Finland involving sitting in a small wooden room or building that is heated to over 170 degrees; water is poured on the heating element to produce steam and birch branches are often used to gently beat the skin to stimulate and relax the muscles.

Siesta: A mid-day rest or nap usually taken after the mid-day meal and often associated with Spain but is also practiced in many parts of the world that have warm climates.

Sympathetic Nervous System (SNS): A branch of the autonomic nervous system that has an arousing effect on the body.

Zorbing: A sport with roots in the United Kingdom and New Zealand that involves climbing into a large, cushioned, plastic ball and rolling down a hill.

Bibliography

"African Drums and Drumming." *The Drum Dr*. Accessed January 6, 2015. http://www.drumdr.com/african-hand-drums.html.

Alzheimer's Association. *2014 Alzheimer's Disease Facts and Figures*. Chicago, IL: Alzheimer's Association, 2014. http://www.alz.org/downloads/Facts_Figures_2014.pdf.

Ameli, Rezvan. "Progressive Muscle Relaxation." In *25 Lessons in Mindfulness: Now Time for Healthy Living*, edited by Rezvan Ameli, 90–94. Washington, DC: American Psychological Association, 2014.

American Psychiatric Association. *Diagnostic and Statistical Manual of Mental Disorders, Fifth Edition*. Arlington, VA: American Psychiatric Association, 2013.

Barbara Woodward Lips Patient Education Center. *Teens + Relaxation: Patient Education*. Rochester, MN: Mayo Clinic, 2012.

Barlow, David H. *Clinical Handbook of Psychological Disorders: A Step-by-Step Treatment Manual, Fifth Edition*. New York: Guilford Press, 2014.

Barrett, Paula M., and Thomas H. Ollendick, eds. *Handbook of Interventions That Work with Children and Adolescents: Prevention and Treatment*. West Sussex, UK: Wiley, 2003.

Bates, Claire. "How Hugging Can Lower Your Blood Pressure and Boost Your Memory." *DailyMail*. January 22, 2013. http://www.dailymail.co.uk/health/article-2266373/Hugging-lower-blood-pressure-boost-memory.html.

Benson, Herbert. *Beyond the Relaxation Response*. New York: Berkley, 1985.

Benson, Herbert, and Aggie Cassey. *Stress Management: Approaches for Preventing and Reducing Stress*. Boston: Harvard Medical School, 2011.

Benson, Herbert, and Miriam Z. Klipper. *The Relaxation Response*. New York: Harper Torch, 1976.

Bhasavanija, Tirata, and Tony Morris. "Imagery." In *Routledge Companion to Sport and Exercise Psychology: Global Perspectives and Fundamental Concepts*, edited by Athanasios G. Papaioannou and Dieter Hackfort, 356–371. New York: Routledge/Taylor & Francis Group, 2014.

Bittman, Barry B., Lee S. Berk, David L. Felton, James Westengard, O. Carl Simonton, James Pappas, and Melissa Ninehouser. "Composite Effects of Group Drumming Music Therapy on Modulation of Neuroendocrine-Immune Parameters in Normal Subjects." *Alternative Therapies in Health Medicine* 7, no. 1 (2001): 38–47.

Blumenstein, Boris, Tsung-Min Hung, and Iris Orbach. "Self-Regulation and Biofeedback." In *Routledge Companion to Sport and Exercise Psychology: Global Perspectives and Fundamental Concepts*, edited by Athanasios G. Papaioannou and Dieter Hackfort, 356–371. New York: Routledge/Taylor & Francis Group, 2014.

Chiang, Li-Chi, Wei-Fen Ma, Jing-Long Huang, Li-Feng Tseng, and Kai-Chung Hsueh. "Effect of Relaxation-Breathing Training on Anxiety and Asthma Signs/Symptoms of Children with Moderate-to-Severe Asthma: A Randomized Controlled Trial." *International Journal of Nursing Studies* 46 (2009): 1061–1070.

Chiedozie, Anjus. "The History of African Drumming." *eHow.com*. Accessed January 6, 2015. http://www.ehow.com/about_5366218_history-african-drumming.html.

de Belloy, Alexis. "In France, Expect Beaucoup de Vacation." *CNN.com*. May 25, 2011. http://www.cnn.com/2011/TRAVEL/05/25/france.long.vacations/.

Dmitriev, Oleg. "Of Russian Origin: Dacha." *Russiapedia*. Accessed January 6, 2015. http://russiapedia.rt.com/of-russian-origin/dacha/.

Drexler, Peggy. "The Case against Staying Calm." *Psychology Today*. February 27, 2014. https://www.psychologytoday.com/blog/our-gender-ourselves/201402/the-case-against-staying-calm.

Dusek, Jeffrey A., Out H. Hasan, Ann L. Wohlhueter, Manoj Bhasin, Luiz F. Zerbini, Marie G. Joseph, Herbert Benson, and Towia A. Libermann. "Genomic Counter-Stress Changes Induced by the Relaxation Response." *PLoS ONE* 3, no. 7 (2008): e2576.

George, Emma, Richard R. Rosenkranz, and Gegory S. Kolt. "Chronic Disease and Sitting Time in Middle-Aged Australian Males: Findings from the 45 and Up Study." *The International Journal of Behavioral Nutrition and Physical Activity* 10 (2013): 1–8.

Harvard Medical School. *Stress Management: Approaches for Preventing and Reducing Stress*. Cambridge, MA: Harvard Health Publications, 2013.

"The Healing Powers of Thai Massage." *Health24.com*. last updated March 4, 2013. http://www.health24.com/Natural/Therapies/The-healing-powers-of-Thai-massage-20130228.

Heffner, Michelle, Laurie A. Greco, and Georg H. Eifert. "Pretend You Are a Turtle: Children's Responses to Metaphorical versus Literal Relaxation Instructions." *Child & Family Behavior Therapy* 25, no. 1 (2003): 19–33.

Hoch, Daniel B., Alice J. Watson, Deborah A. Linton, Heather E. Bello, Marco Senelly, Mariola T. Milik, Margaret A. Baim, Kamal Jethwani, Gregory L. Fricchione, Herbert Benson, and Joseph C. Kvedar. "The Feasibility and Impact of Delivering a Mind-Body Intervention in a Virtual World." *PLoS ONE* 7, no. 3 (2012): e33843.

Huffpost Healthy Living. "Relaxation Tips: De-Stressing Wisdom from around the Globe." *Huffingtonpost.com*. March 14, 2013. http://www.huffingtonpost.com/2013/03/14/relaxation-tips-de-stress_n_2859585.html.

Inoue, Kazuo, and Masatoshi Matsumoto. "Karo Jisatsu (Suicide from Overwork): A Spreading Occupational Threat." *Occupational and Environmental Medicine* 57 (2000): 284.

Jacobson, Edmund. *Progressive Relaxation, Second Edition*. Oxford, UK: University of Chicago Press, 1938.

Kanai, Atsuko. "'Karoshi (Work to Death)' in Japan." *Journal of Business Ethics* 84, Suppl 2 (2009): 209–216.

Kendall, Philip C. *Coping Cat Workbook*. Philadelphia, PA: Workbook Publishing, 1992.

"La Siesta." *donQuijote.org*. Accessed January 6, 2015. http://www.donquijote.org/culture/spain/society/customs/siesta.

Leung, Rebecca. "France: Less Work, More Time Off." *CBS News.com*. June 27, 2005. http://www.cbsnews.com/news/france-less-work-more-time-off/.

Lin, Jue, Elissa S. Epel, and Elizabeth H. Blackburn. "Telomeres, Telomerase, Stress, and Aging." In *Handbook of Neuroscience for the Behavioral Sciences, Volume 2*, edited by Gary G. Berntson, 1280–1295. Hoboken, NJ: John Wiley & Sons, 2009.

Locker, Melissa. "Oreos May Be as Addictive as Cocaine." *News-Feed.Time.com*. October 16, 2013. http://newsfeed.time.com/2013/10/16/oreos-may-be-as-addictive-as-cocaine/.

McConnell, Allen R., Christina M. Brown, Tonya M. Shoda, Laura E. Stayton, and Colleen E. Martin. "Friends with Benefits: On the Positive Consequences of Pet Ownership." *Journal of Personality and Social Psychology* 101, no. 6 (2011): 1239–1252.

McGonignal, Kelly. "How to Make Stress Your Friend." *TED*. June 2013. http://www.ted.com/talks/kelly_mcgonigal_how_to_make_stress_your_friend?language=en.

Miller, William R., and Stephen Rollnick. *Motivational Interviewing: Preparing People for Change, Second Edition*. New York: Guilford Press, 2002.

Morris, Tracy L., and John S. March, eds. *Anxiety Disorders in Children and Adolescents*. New York: Guilford Press, 2004.

National Center for Chronic Disease Prevention and Health Promotion. *National Diabetes Statistics Report, 2014*. Atlanta, GA: Centers for Disease Control and Prevention, 2014. http://www.cdc.gov/diabetes/pubs/statsreport14/national-diabetes-report-web.pdf.

Norris, Jeffrey. "Aging, Chronic Disease and Telomeres Are Linked in Recent Studies." *University of California San Francisco*. February 3, 2011. http://www.ucsf.edu/news/2011/02/9353/aging-telomeres-linked-chronic-disease-and-health.

Palazzolo, Rose. "Sleep Experts Call for Siestas." *ABC News*. October 31, 2014. http://abcnews.go.com/Health/story?id=117147.

Pappas, Stephanie. "Oreos as Addictive as Cocaine? Not So Fast." *LiveScience.com*. October 16, 2013. http://www.livescience.com/40488-oreos-addictive-cocaine.html.

Park, Elyse R., Lara Traeger, Ana-Maria Vranceanu, Matthew Scult, Lonathan A. Lerner, Herbert Benson, John Denninger, and Gregory L. Fricchione. "The Development of a Patient-Centered Program Based on the Relaxation Response: The Relaxation Response Resiliency Program (3RP)." *Psychosomatics* 54, no. 2 (2013): 165–174.

Pedersen, Traci. "For Some, Relaxation Triggers Anxiety." *PsychCentral*. December 13, 2012. http://psychcentral.com/news/2012/12/13/for-some-relaxation-triggers-anxiety/49051.html.

Pikul, Corrie. "De-Stressing Secrets from around the World." *Oprah.com*. May 23, 2012. http://www.oprah.com/world/Global-Relaxation-Secrets-De-Stressing-Advice-from-Around-the-World.

Ratini, Melinda. "Acupressure Points and Massage Treatment." *WebMD.com*. March 18, 2013. http://www.webmd.com/balance/guide/acupressure-points-and-massage-treatment?page=2.

Relax Kids. "Doctors Say Relaxation Will Help Teems Manage Stress." *RelaxKids.com*. June 10, 2013. http://www.relaxkids.com/UK/Blog/Relaxation_prescribed_for_teenagers_/604.

"Rock Gardens, Dry Landscapes, Hill Gardens, Karesansui, Kasa, Tsukiyama, Others." *OnMarkProductions*. Accessed January 6, 2015. http://www.onmarkproductions.com/html/japanese-gardens.shtml.

Samuelson, Marlene, Megan Foret, Margaret Baim, Jonathan Lerner, Gregory Fricchione, Herbert Benson, Jeffery Dusek, and Albert Yeung. "Exploring the Effectiveness of a Comprehensive Mind-Body Intervention for Medical Symptom Relief." *The Journal of Alternative and Complementary Medicine* 16, no. 2 (2010): 187–192.

"Sauna Health Benefits: Are Saunas Healthy or Harmful?" *Harvard Health Publications*. November 1, 2005. http://www.health.harvard.edu/press_releases/sauna_health_benefits.wp.

Selye, Hans. "The General-Adaptation-Syndrome in Its Relationships to Neurology, Psychology, and Psychopathology." In *Contributions Toward Medical Psychology: Theory and Psychodiagnotic Methods, Volume 1*, edited by Arthur Weider, 234–274. New York: Ronald Press Company, 1953.

Seven, Richard. "Thai Yoga Massage: A New Twist." *Seattle Times.com*. June 21, 2008. http://seattletimes.com/html/health/2008008836_thaiyoga21.html.

Shockey, Debra P., Victoria Menzies, Doris F. Glick, Ann Gill Taylor, Amy Boitnott, and Virginia Rovnyak. "Preprocedural Distress in Children with Cancer: An Intervention Using Biofeedback and Relaxation." *Journal of Pediatric Oncology Nursing* 30, no. 3 (2013): 129–138.

Smith, Jonathan C. *ABC Relaxation Theory: An Evidence-Based Approach*. New York: Springer, 1999.

Somasundaram, Daya. "Cultural Relaxation Methods for Minor Mental Health Disorders." *Sri Lanka Journal of Psychiatry* 3, no. 2 (2012): 3–6.

Stack. "10 Athletes and Teams You Might Not Think Would Practice Yoga." *Stack*. September 17, 2012. http://www.stack.com/2012/09/17/yoga-athletes/.

Stamatkis, Emmanuel, Josephine Y. Chau, Zeljiko Pedisic, Adrian Baouman, Rona Macniven, Ngaire Coombs, and Mark Hamer.

"Are Sitting Occupations Associated with Increased All-Cause, Cancer, and Cardiovascular Disease Mortality Risk? A Pooled Analysis of Seven British Population Cohorts." *PLoS ONE* 8, no. 9 (2013): e73753.

Thies, William, and Laura Bleiler. "2013 Alzheimer's Disease Facts and Figures." *Alzheimer's & Dementia* 9 (2013): 208–245.

"Understanding the Stress Response." *Harvard Health Publications*. March 1, 2011. http://www.health.harvard.edu/staying-healthy/understanding-the-stress-response.

University of California–Irvine. "Stress Significantly Hastens Progression of Alzheimer's Disease." *ScienceDaily.com*. August 30, 2006. http://www.sciencedaily.com/releases/2006/08/060830005837.htm.

U.S. Food and Drug Administration. "Energy 'Drinks' and Supplements: Investigations of Adverse Event Reports." *FDA.gov*. November 16, 2012. http://www.fda.gov/Food/NewsEvents/ucm328536.htm.

Velden, Dana. "Do You Fika? A Swedish Custom." *The Kitchn*. Accessed January 6, 2015. http://www.thekitchn.com/do-you-fika-175755.

Vranceanu, Ana-Maria, Jeffery R. Shaefer, Ashkan Fahandej Saadi, Ellen Slawsby, Jaya Sarin, Matthew Scult, Herbert Benson, and John W. Denninger. "The Relaxation Response Resiliency Enhanced Program in the Management of Chronic Refractory Temporomandibular Joint Disorder: Results from a Pilot Study." *Journal of Musculoskeletal Pain* 21, no. 3 (2013): 224–230.

Wagner, Aureen P. *Worried No More: Help and Hope for Anxious Children*. Apex, NC: Lighthouse Press, 2005.

About the Author and Contributors

Christine L. B. Selby, PhD, earned her doctoral degree in Counseling Psychology at the University of North Texas in 2000 and earned her master's degree in Athletic Counseling in 1994 from Springfield College. She is an Associate Professor of Psychology at Husson University and maintains a small private practice in which she primarily works with adults. She is a Certified Eating Disorders Specialist with the International Association of Eating Disorders Professionals and is a Certified Consultant with the Association of Applied Sport Psychology. Dr. Selby's publications include articles and book chapters primarily in the area of athletes with eating disorders, and her presentations at local, national, and international meetings focus on eating disorders and the inherent complexities they present.

Sibel Algon, MD, received her medical degree from Robert Wood Johnson Medical School. She completed her residency in psychiatry with the University of Pennsylvania's hospital and was a fellow at Children's Hospital of Philadelphia, where she was Chief Resident of Research. Dr. Algon currently works in a community mental health setting.

Kimberlee Bethany Bonura, PhD, is a fitness and wellness consultant with decades of experience teaching the benefits of physical and mental health to elite athletes, higher education institutions, nonprofit community organizations, and corporations. She earned her PhD in Educational Psychology, with a research emphasis in sport and exercise psychology, from Florida State University. Her doctoral dissertation won national awards from the American Psychological Association (Division 47) and the Association for Applied Sport Psychology. Dr. Bonura is a triple-certified yoga instructor, registered with the Yoga Alliance, and a member of the International Association of Yoga Therapists. She also holds certifications as a personal trainer, group fitness instructor, kickboxing instructor, tai chi and qigong instructor, senior fitness specialist, weight management instructor, and prenatal and youth fitness specialist. Dr. Bonura is a peer reviewer for journals including the *Journal of Aging and Physical Activity*, *The Journal of Alternative and Complementary Medicine*, and the *Journal of Sport & Exercise Psychology*. She currently serves on the editorial board of the *International Journal of Yoga Therapy*.

Jessica Manaker, MD, is a Board Certified Child and Adolescent Psychiatrist in private practice in Bangor, Maine. Dr. Manaker is a graduate of the Medical University of South Carolina, where she earned her medical degree in 1998 and completed her adult psychiatry residency in 2002. She completed a Child and Adolescent fellowship at Brown University, and has been practicing outpatient psychiatry for the past 10 years in her home state of Maine. She has worked primarily in a community mental health setting, and enjoys collaborating with other providers and educators to serve families using a team-based approach. Dr. Manaker carefully considers all of the factors contributing to emotional and behavioral distress, and partners with families in developing strategies to improve functioning and overall well-being. She has experience treating a wide range of issues affecting children and teens, including anxiety, depression, attention deficit disorder, trauma, autism/developmental delays, and bipolar illness.

Christine May, PhD, earned her doctoral degree in Psychology from Case Western Reserve University in 2015. She is currently a Post-doctoral Research Fellow at the University of Massachusetts Medical School in the Division of Preventive and Behavioral Medicine. Dr. May's research focuses on obesity and health behaviors, including physical activity and eating patterns. She is also interested in using technology to better understand health behaviors and to aid in interventions to combat and prevent obesity. Dr. May is a member of the Society of Behavioral Medicine and the American Psychological Association.

Brian Selby, PhD, is a licensed psychologist in private practice in Bangor, Maine. He graduated with both his Master of Science in Counseling Psychology and his PhD in Counseling Psychology from the University of North Texas. He completed a post-doctoral residency in the Department of Psychiatry at the University of Rochester. Dr. Selby spent several years in a community mental health setting where he worked with individuals of all ages, families, and couples with varying degrees of mental illness. During the last eight years, Dr. Selby has worked in private practice where he has developed a specialty as a pediatric psychologist working with children diagnosed with anxiety and related disorders.

Sylvie Stacy, MD, received her Medical Doctorate from the University of Massachusetts Medical School and Master of Public Health from the Johns Hopkins Bloomberg School of Public Health. She is board certified in preventive medicine and public health. She has volunteered as a research team leader for the International Cancer Advocacy Network and serves on the physician panel for Doximity, Inc. As a result of her professional interest in the safe and appropriate use of pharmaceuticals and medical products, a portion of her research has concentrated on functional foods and beverages and their potential role in the field of prevention. Her published works include a scientific article entitled *Relaxation Drinks and Their Use in Adolescents* and a book chapter titled "Mental Exercises."

Jim Taylor, PhD, is internationally recognized for his work in the psychology of performance in business, sports, and family. He received his bachelors degree from Middlebury College and his master's degree and PhD in Psychology from the University of Colorado. He is a former associate professor in the School of Psychology at Nova University in Ft. Lauderdale and a former clinical associate professor in the Sport & Performance Psychology graduate program at the University of Denver. He is currently an adjunct professor at the University of San Francisco and the Wright Institute in Berkeley. A former U.S. top-20 ranked alpine ski racer who competed internationally, Dr. Taylor is a certified tennis teaching professional, a second-degree black belt and certified instructor in karate, a marathon runner, and an Ironman triathlete. He is the author of 13 books and the lead editor of two textbooks, has published more than 700 articles in scholarly and popular publications, and has given more than 1,000 workshops and presentations throughout North America, Europe, and the Middle East.

Index

Abdomen, 13, 66
Acupressure, 102–3, 117
Acupuncture, 102–3
Acute stress disorder, 34, 36
Adjustment disorders, 34, 36
Adolescents, 85, 88, 90–95, 126–28, 131–33, 152
Africa, 118–20
Aging, 34, 38, 46, 52–54; life span, 48. *See also* Death
Agoraphobia, 36–38
Alarm phase, 31; general adaptation syndrome (GAS), 31, 43
Alcohol, use of, 39–42, 53–55, 104, 128–30
All Blacks, 9
Allostasis, 69
Allostatic load, 69
Alzheimer's Association Report, 33
Alzheimer's disease, 33–34
American culture, 135, 142–47, 150
American Institute of Stress, 144
American Psychological Association, 144

Amygdala, 84
Anxiety: acute stress disorder, 34, 36; in adolescence, 126–28; in adults, 123–26; agoraphobia, 36–38; and American culture, 147–50; Attentional Behavioral Cognitive Relaxation Theory (ABC Theory), 73; and biofeedback, 20; and chanting, 108; in children, 85–90, 121–23; cognitive behavioral therapy, 22–25; and deep abdominal breathing, 14; and exercise, 11; and generalized anxiety disorder (GAD), 36, 38, 153; how your body responds to anxiety, 48; and how your mind responds to relaxation, 49–51; and hugging, 5; and massage, 10, 118; and medication vs. CBT, 150–58; and meditation, 11; mental health effects of, 34–39; in older adults, 95, 98; panic disorder, 36–38, 49; physical health effects of, 31–34; physiological response to, 27–31;

posttraumatic stress disorder (PTSD), 20, 34–36; and relaxation across the life span, 81–85; and relaxation drinks, 137–42; Relaxation Response Resiliency Program (3RP), 68–69, 72; social anxiety, 36–37; things we do to relax that may harm us, 55–56; and unhealthy behaviors, 40–41; and when recommended types of relaxation can backfire, 57–60; and yoga and stretching, 9

Arousal, 36, 57–58, 74, 127; Yerkes-Dodson Inverted-U, 57–58

Art: creativity, 6–8, 76, 98; drumming, 118–20; painting, 7, 94, 132. *See also* Music

Asthma, 33, 48, 150, 153

Attention Behavioral Cognitive (ABC) Relaxation Theory, 73–79

Attention deficit hyperactivity disorder (ADHD), 131, 152

Autogenic training, 65, 151

Autonomic nervous system: and exercise, 11; how the body responds to relaxation, 45; physiological response to stress and anxiety, 27–29; Relaxation Response, 64–65. *See also* Parasympathetic nervous system; Sympathetic nervous system

Avanto, 105

Balloon breathing, 89
Bath houses, 8
Baths, long hot, 8
Belly breathing, 13. *See also* Deep abdominal breathing
Benson, Herbert, 61–68, 73, 75
Benzodiazepines, 41
Bereavement overload, 96
Bhakti, 107
Biofeedback, 20–22, 64
Black-and-white thinking, 24

Blackburn, Elizabeth, 52–53

Blood pressure: and cardiovascular disease, 47; and diabetes, 33; and heart disease, 32; and hugging, 5; and meditation, 11; and nicotine, 40; and pets, 5; physiological response to stress and anxiety, 29; and relaxation drinks, 137; Relaxation Response, 65; and sauna, 104

Bougarabou, 119; drumming, 118–20

Brain: and American culture, 144; amygdala, 84; and Attentional Behavioral Cognitive (ABC) Relaxation Theory, 75, 78; and biofeedback, 20–21; central nervous system, 28; and creativity, 8; and exercise, 11–12; and guided relaxation and imagery, 19; and how your mind responds to relaxation, 50; and the life span, 81–84; and medication, 152–53; medulla oblongata, 28; and physical health effects of chronic stress and anxiety, 33–34; and physiological response to stress and anxiety, 28–31; and relaxation in adolescents, 90–91; and relaxation in children, 86, 88, 90, 123; and relaxation drinks, 138; and Relaxation Response, 64; and Relaxation Response Resiliency Program (3RP), 69; and siesta, 114; and things we do to relax that may harm us, 56; and unhealthy behaviors, 39–42; and yoga and stretching, 9

Brain, pleasure centers of, 40, 56
Brain waves, 138; central nervous system, 28. *See also* Brain
Bronchi, 29–30, 33
Buddhism, 10, 64, 107

Caffeine, use of, 128–30, 136
Cancer, 46, 48, 60, 68, 102, 123–24

Index 177

Cannabis, 39, 41
Cardiac Wellness Program, 68
Cardiovascular disease, 9, 47. *See also* Blood pressure
Catastrophic thinking, 49–51, 77
CBT. *See* Cognitive behavioral therapy (CBT)
Center for Disease Control (CDC), 33
Central nervous system, 28
Centre for Brain Research at the Medical University of Vienna, 5
Chanting, 10, 57, 107–8
Child/Adolescent Anxiety Multimodal Study (CAMS), 153
Children, 35, 82, 84–90, 121–23, 152–53
China, 102–3, 117
Chinese medicine, 102–3
Christianity, 10
Chromosomes, 52; telomeres, 52–53
Chronic illness, 34, 53, 68
Chronic stress, 31–39, 52, 54, 70, 144, 146
Classical conditioning, 81–82
Cocaine, 41–42
Coffee break, 115–17
Cognitive behavioral therapy (CBT), 21, 22–25, 48–51, 67, 88, 133, 153–58
Comfort food, 56; stress eating, 56; use of food, 41–42, 56
Comprehensive Soldier and Family Fitness, 145
Consumer Reports, 140
Coping Cat Workbook, 89
Counselor, 126, 132–33; mental health professional, 22–23, 37; school counselor, 88, 121–22, 127–28
Creativity, 6–8, 76, 98

Dacha, 112–13
Dangerous Sports Club, 111; Zorbing, 110–12

Death, 27, 31, 34–35, 37, 43, 54, 62, 95–96, 125; bereavement overload, 96; *Karo-jisatsu*, 43; *karōshi*, 43
Deep abdominal breathing, 13–14; in adolescents, 94; and biofeedback, 21; in children, 89, 123; and cognitive behavioral therapy, 22–23; and guided imagery and relaxation, 20; how your body responds to relaxation, 47; in older adults, 99; and progressive muscle relaxation, 15; relaxation response, 66; when recommended types of relaxation can backfire, 59
Deep breathing, 13; balloon breathing, 89. *See also* Deep abdominal breathing
Dementia, 33, 60, 97–98; Alzheimer's disease, 33–34
Depressed mood, 12, 37; depressive episodes, 37; major depressive disorder, 36–37. *See also* Depression
Depression: and acupressure and acupuncture, 102; and American culture, 144; and chanting, 108; in children, 86; and cognitive behavioral therapy, 22–24; and how your mind responds to relaxation, 51; and *karo-jisatsu* and *karōshi*, 43; major depressive disorder, 36–37; and massage, 10, 118; and meditation, 11; and mental health effects of chronic stress and anxiety, 36–38; in older adults, 95, 97; Relaxation Response Resiliency Program (3RP), 68, 72; and yoga and stretching, 9
Depressive episodes, 37
De-stress, 5, 101, 117, 120, 150
Diabetes, 33, 42, 56
Diagnostic and statistical manual of mental disorders (DSM), 34, 38, 41

Diaphragmatic breathing, 13; balloon breathing, 89. *See also* Deep abdominal breathing

Disinhibited social engagement disorder, 34–35

Distress: in adolescents, 92, 94–95; Attentional Behavioral Cognitive (ABC) Relaxation Theory, 77–78; in children, 85–89, 122–23; effects of relaxation on life expectancy, 52; forms of relaxation, 3; how the body responds to relaxation, 48; *karojisatsu* and *karōshi*, 43; massage, 117; mental health effects of chronic stress and anxiety, 35–36, 38; N-States, 77–78; in older adults, 96–97; relaxation across the life span, 82–84; Relaxation Response Resiliency Program (3RP), 69; things we do to relax that may harm us, 54–55; when recommended types of relaxation can backfire, 60

Djembe, 119; drumming, 118–20

Dopamine, 40, 114

Drugs: alcohol, 39–42, 53–55, 104, 128–30; cannabis, 39, 41; cocaine, 41–42; heroin, 41; illegal substances, 41, 55; nicotine, 39–41, 55–56; OxyContin, 41; prescription medication, 33, 41, 54–55, 140–41, 151; psychoactive drugs, 39, 41

Drumming, 118–20

Either/or thinking, 24

Electroencephalograph (EEG), 20

Electromyography (EMG), 20, 21

Ellis, Albert, 73, 76

Energy drinks, 136; relaxation drinks, 135–42

Energy shots, 136; relaxation drinks, 135–42

Exercise, 11–12: and acupressure and acupuncture, 102–3; in children, 89; and effects of relaxation on life expectancy, 53; and guided relaxation and imagery, 19; and how your body responds to relaxation, 47; and medication vs. learning new behaviors, 153; in older adults, 97–98; and progressive muscle relaxation, 15–18; Relaxation Response, 62, 64, 66, 68; and when recommended types of relaxation can backfire, 59–60; and yoga and stretching, 9

Exercise abuse, 60

Exercise addiction, 60

Exercise dependence, 60

Exhaustion phase, 31; general adaptation syndrome (GAS), 31, 43

FDA, U.S. Food and Drug Administration, 136, 138, 139

Fear, 37–38, 48, 59, 70, 78, 82–84, 87–90, 98, 106, 123, 155

Feedback thermometer, 20

Fight or flight: deep abdominal breathing, 14; exercise, 11; how your body responds to relaxation, 45; how your mind responds to relaxation, 50; and physical health effects of chronic stress and anxiety, 31–32; and physiological response to stress and anxiety, 29–31; Relaxation Response, 63–64, 69; when recommended types of relaxation can backfire, 57

Fika, 115–17

Fikapaus, 116; Fika, 115–17

Fikarast, 116; Fika, 115–17

Finland, 103–5

5-HTP, 138; relaxation drinks, 135–42

Flex time, 143; American culture, 135, 142–47, 150

Food: and classical conditioning, 16, 82; and FDA, 136, 138; and fika,

115–7; and France, 105; stress eating, 56; taste, 18; use of, 41–42, 56
France, 105–7

Gamma-aminobutyric acid (GABA), 138; relaxation drinks, 135–42
Gastro-esophageal reflux disease (GERD), 32; gastrointestinal problems, 32, 46–48, 92, 140
Gastrointestinal functioning, 46
Gastrointestinal problems, 32, 46–48, 92, 140
Gastrointestinal system, 47–48
General adaptation syndrome (GAS), 31, 43
Generalized anxiety disorder (GAD), 36, 38, 153
Generation Y, 145
Genetics, 33, 42, 46–47, 84
Group drumming, 120; drumming, 118–20
Guided relaxation and imagery, 18–20; visualization, 18, 127–28, 129–30, 146

Haka, 9
Hanging out on the couch, 4–5
Harvard Medical School, 46
Harvard University, 144
Headaches: and acupuncture, 102; and baths, 8; and biofeedback, 20; and massage, 118; physical health effects of chronic stress and anxiety, 33; and relaxation in adolescents, 92; and Relaxation Response Resiliency Program (3RP), 68
Health psychologist, 53; sport psychologist, 58. See also Psychologist
Heart attack, 32, 43, 47–48. See also Heart disease
Heart disease, 32–33, 42, 56, 60, 62, 144
Heroin, 41

Hinduism, 10, 107
Holistic medicine, 102, 145–6
Hops, 140; relaxation drinks, 135–42
Hot stone massage, 8
Hugging, 5, 35
Hydro-Zorbing, 111; Zorbing, 110–12
Hypertension, 32–33, 42, 47, 62, 67–68. See also Blood pressure

Illegal substances, 41, 55; cannabis, 39, 41; cocaine, 41–42; heroin, 41
Imagery: and adolescents, 127; and biofeedback, 21; and cognitive behavioral therapy, 23; and guided relaxation, 18–20; how your body responds to relaxation, 49; and relaxation in children, 89; and relaxation in older adults, 99; when recommended types of relaxation can backfire, 59
Immune system, 29, 31, 48, 108, 118, 120
Independence, 91, 95–96
India, 107–8, 117
Inflammation, 33, 46–48, 118
Insomnia, 48, 156
International Society for Krishna Consciousness, 108
Involuntary actions, 28–29
Irritable bowel syndrome (IBS), 32, 48; gastrointestinal problems, 32, 46–48, 92, 140
Ishi wo tateru koto, 109; rock gardens, 108–10
Islam, 10

Jacobson, Edmund, 14–15
Japan, 43, 65, 108–10, 112
Japanese Ministry of Health, Labor, and Welfare, 43

Kanai, Atsuko, 43
Karensansui, 108; rock gardens, 108–10
Karō-jisatsu, 43

Karōshi, 43
Kava root, 136, 139–40; relaxation drinks, 135–42
Kirtan, 107–8
Kirtankara, 107–8

Lashing out, 42
Learned helplessness, 38, 43
Learning theories: classical conditioning, 81–82; operant conditioning, 63–64
Leisure, 96, 107, 113, 142–43, 148, 152
Les Ballets Africans, 119; drumming, 118–20
Life span, 48. *See also* Death
Linden flower, 140; relaxation drinks, 135–42
Little Albert, 82
Loss, 36, 75, 95–97, 99
Loyly, 104
L-theanine, 138, 140; relaxation drinks, 135–42

Major depressive disorder, 36–37. *See also* Depression
Mali Empire, 119; drumming, 118–20
Marijuana, cannabis, 39, 41
Massage, 8, 9–10, 98, 102–3, 117–18, 147
McGonigal, Kelly, 53
Medical Symptom Reduction Program, 68
Meditation, 10–11; and American culture, 144–47; Attentional Behavioral Cognitive (ABC) Relaxation Theory, 78; how your body responds to relaxation, 46, 48–49; Relaxation Response, 63, 65; and rock gardens, 109
Medulla oblongata, 28
Melatonin, 136, 138, 140; relaxation drinks, 135–42
Memory, 12, 33, 60, 84

Mental health: and chanting, 108; and cognitive behavioral therapy, 22–23; and effects of chronic stress and anxiety, 34–39; and effects of relaxation on life expectancy, 53; and forms of relaxation, 3; and learning new behaviors to help people relax, 155; and Relaxation Response Resiliency Program, 72; when recommended types of relaxation can backfire, 60. *See also specific mental health diagnoses*
Mental health professional, 22–23, 37
Mental practice, 18; guided relaxation and imagery, 18–20; visualization, 18, 127–28, 129–30, 146
Mental rehearsal, 18; guided relaxation and imagery, 18–20; visualization, 18, 127–28, 129–30, 146
Millennial generation, 145
Miller, Neil, 63–64
Mind-body connection, 63–64
Motivational interviewing, 93–94
Multimodal Treatment of ADHD (MTA) Study, 152
Music, 7–8, 12, 20, 59, 83, 94, 98, 107–8, 119, 126

National Center for Complementary and Integrative Health (NCCIH), 144
National Center for Sleep Disorders Research, 48
National Institutes of Health (NIH), 48, 144
Nausea, 33, 37, 41, 68, 102–3, 156
Nervous system, 21, 28, 40, 140; central nervous system, 28; peripheral nervous system, 28–29. *See also* Autonomic nervous system; Parasympathetic nervous system; Sympathetic nervous system
Neurotransmitters, 114; dopamine, 40, 114; gamma-aminobutyric acid

(GABA), 138; serotonin, 40, 114, 140, 156
New Zealand, 9, 110–12
Nicotine, use of, 39–41, 55–56
Nonprescription substances, 54–55; alcohol, 39–42, 53–55, 104, 128–30; cannabis, 39, 41; cocaine, 41–42; heroin, 41; nicotine, 39–41, 55–56
N-States, 77–78
Nuat phaen thai, 117; Thai massage, 117–18
Nuat thai, 117; Thai massage, 117–18

Obsessive-compulsive disorder (OCD), 153, 155
Older adults, 52, 85, 95–99
Operant conditioning, 63–64
Overeating, 48, 53; comfort food, 56; use of food, 41–42, 56
Over-exercise, 60
Oxygen, 11, 13–14, 29, 33, 40, 53, 64–65, 153
OxyContin, 41

Pain: and acupressure and acupuncture, 102–3; and biofeedback, 20; and guided relaxation and imagery, 18; how your body responds to relaxation, 47; and massage, 10, 118; mental health effects of chronic stress and anxiety, 37, 38; physical health effects of chronic stress and anxiety, 32, 33; and relaxation in children, 87; and relaxation in older adults, 96–97; Relaxation Response Resiliency Program (3RP), 68, 72
Pain management, 18, 41
Painting, 7, 94, 132
Panic attacks, 37–38
Panic disorder, 36–38, 49
Paradox of passivity, 73

Parasympathetic nervous system: Attentional Behavioral Cognitive (ABC) Relaxation Theory, 74; exercise, 11–12; how your body responds to relaxation, 45–46, 48; physiological response to stress and anxiety, 27–31; Relaxation Response, 65
Passion flower, 140; relaxation drinks, 135–42
Pavlov, Ivan, 16, 81–82
Pediatric OCD Treatment Study (POTS), 153
Performance, 14, 18–19, 37, 56–58, 85, 94, 126–28, 131–33, 145–46
Peripheral nervous system, 28–29. *See also* Autonomic nervous system; Parasympathetic nervous system; Sympathetic nervous system
Pet therapy, 5
Pets, time with, 5–6
Play rooms, 143; American culture, 135, 142–47, 150
Posttraumatic stress disorder (PTSD), 20, 34–36
Premature death, 34, 54; *Karō-jisatsu*, 43; *Karōshi*, 43
Prescription medication, 33, 41, 54–55, 140–41, 151; benzodiazepines, 41; cannabis, 39, 41; OxyContin, 41
Progressive muscle relaxation (PMR), 14–18; in adults, 129–30; Attentional Behavioral Cognitive (ABC) Relaxation Theory, 78; how your body responds to relaxation, 49; medication or learning new behaviors, 151; in older adults, 97; Relaxation Response, 66
Psychoactive drugs, 39, 41
Psychologist, 61, 82, 88, 92, 122–23, 127–28, 129, 132; mental health professional, 22–23, 37

Qi, 102
Qigong, 102–3

Racing thoughts, 23, 49, 51
R-Attitudes, 74, 76–77
R-Beliefs, 74, 76–77, 78
Reactive attachment disorder, 34–35
Relaxation: in adolescents, 90–95, 126–28, 131–33; in adults, 123–26, 128–30; and American culture, 142–50; around the world, 101–20; in children, 85–90, 121–23; effects on life expectancy, 52–54; and genetics, 46–47; how the body responds to, 45–49; how the mind responds to, 49–52; and medication vs. CBT, 150–58; in older adults, 95–99; and relaxation drinks, 135–42; theories about, 61–79; things we do that may harm us, 54–56; throughout the life cycle, 82–99; ways you already relax, 3–12; what the professionals recommend, 12–25; when recommended types can backfire, 56–60
Relaxation attitudes, 74, 76–77
Relaxation beliefs, 74, 76–77, 78
Relaxation drinks, 135–42
Relaxation-induced anxiety, 60
Relaxation Response, 46–47, 54, 61–67, 73, 75
Relaxation Response Resiliency Program (3RP), 67–73
Relaxation states, 74, 76–78
Resiliency, 68–71; Relaxation Response Resiliency Program (3RP), 67–73
Resistance phase, 31; General adaptation syndrome (GAS), 31, 43
Retirement, 95–97, 106, 147
Riposo, 114; Siesta, 114–15, 143
Rock gardens, 108–10

Rose hip, 140; relaxation drinks, 135–42
R-States, 74, 76–78
Russia, 112–13
Russian Revolution, 113; Dacha, 112–13
Ryoan-ji, 109; rock gardens, 108–10

Sabar, 119; drumming, 118–20
Sakuteiki, 109; rock gardens, 108–10
Sandkühler, Jürgen, 5
Sauna, 8, 103–5
Sauvasauna, 104
School counselor, 88, 121–22, 127–28
School phobia, 87–88
Seligman, Martin, 145
Self-esteem, 4, 5
Self-fulfilling prophecy, 50
Selye, Hans, 31
Sen lines, 118; Thai massage, 117–18
Serotonin, 40, 114, 140, 156
Serotonin-specific reuptake inhibitors (SSRIs), 156
Siesta, 114–15, 143
Skinner, B. F., 63–64
Sleep: in adults, 125, 129–30; Attentional Behavioral Cognitive (ABC) Relaxation Theory, 75–76; and chanting, 108; and creativity, 8; and hanging out on the couch, 4; and how your body responds to relaxation, 48–49; insomnia, 48, 156; and massage, 118; and medication for relaxation, 153; and mental health effects of chronic stress and anxiety, 37; and progressive muscle relaxation, 16; relaxation in adolescents, 92; and relaxation drinks, 135–41; relaxation in older adults, 97; Relaxation Response, 62, 65; Relaxation Response Resiliency Program (3RP), 68; and siesta, 114–15; and when recommended types of relaxation can backfire, 57

Smith, Jonathan, 61, 73–79
Smoking, 40, 53, 55, 146; nicotine, 39–41, 55–56
Social anxiety, 36–37
Social phobia, 59, 153, 155
Society for Human Resource Management, 145
Somatic nervous system, 29; peripheral nervous system, 28–29
Soviet Union, Russia, 112–13
Spa, 8; bath houses, 8
Spain, 114–15, 143
Specific phobia, 59
Spinal cord, 28–29; central nervous system, 28
Sport psychologist, 58; health psychologist, 53. See also Psychologist
Stress: in adults, 124–25, 128–30; and American culture, 144–49; Attentional Behavioral Cognitive (ABC) Relaxation Theory, 76–79; and biofeedback, 20–21; in children, 122; and cognitive behavioral therapy, 22–25; and dacha, 113; and deep abdominal breathing, 13–14; and drumming, 119–20; and effects of relaxation and life expectancy, 52–54; and how your body responds to relaxation, 47–48; and how your mind responds to relaxation, 49–50; and *karōshi* and *karo-jisatsu*, 43; and massage, 117–18; medication or learning new behaviors, 150–51; mental health effects of, 34–39; perception of, 53; physical health effects of, 31–34; and physiological response to, 27–31; and progressive muscle relaxation, 15; and relaxation in adolescents, 90–95; and relaxation in children, 85–90; and relaxation drinks, 138, 141; and relaxation in older adults, 95–99; Relaxation Response, 61–64; Relaxation Response Resiliency Program (3RP), 68–72; and rock gardens, 109; and sauna, 104; things we do to relax that may harm us, 55–56; and unhealthy behaviors, 39–43; ways you may already relax, 3–12; when recommended types of relaxation can backfire, 57; and Zorbing, 110. See also Distress
Stress eating, 56; use of food, 41–42, 56
Stress management, 34, 47–48, 53, 62, 68, 72, 93–94, 144, 146
Stress related illness, 31–32, 38, 63; gastrointestinal problems, 32, 46–48, 92, 140. See also Headaches; Heart disease
Stress relief, 55, 111, 119
Stretching, 8–9, 117
Stroke, 33, 43, 62, 95
Sweden, 112, 115–17
Swedish massage, 10
Sympathetic nervous system: exercise, 11; how your body responds to relaxation, 45; how your mind responds to relaxation, 50; physiological response to stress and anxiety, 27, 29–31; Relaxation Response Resiliency Program (3RP), 69; things we do to relax that may harm us, 55

Talking drum, 119; drumming, 118–20
Taoism, 10
Telomeres, 52–53
Temperament, 86, 91
Tension: and American culture, 147–48; Attention Behavioral Cognitive Relaxation Theory, 75, 78–79; and baths, 8; and biofeedback, 21; and how the body responds to relaxation, 48; and how the mind responds to relaxation,

49, 51; and massage, 10, 117–19; and progressive muscle relaxation (PMR), 14–15, 18; and relaxation in adolescents, 92–95; and relaxation drinks, 141; relaxation in older adults, 98–99; Relaxation Response, 65; and sauna, 105; and things we do to relax that may harm us, 55; and when recommended types of relaxation can backfire, 60. See also Hypertension

Thai massage, 117–18. See also Massage

Thailand, 117–18

Transcendental meditation, 65

Udu, 119; drumming, 118–20

Ulcers, 32, 48; gastrointestinal problems, 32, 46–48, 92, 140

U.S. Food and Drug Administration (FDA), 136, 138, 139

U.S. military, 144–45

Vacation, 51, 105–7, 129, 145

Valerian root, 138, 139–40; relaxation drinks, 135–42

Vasta, 104–5; sauna, 8, 103–5

Vihta, 104; sauna, 8, 103–5

Visualization, 18, 127–28, 129–30, 146; guided relaxation and imagery, 18–20

Voluntary actions, 28

Vomiting, 33, 102, 156. See also Nausea

Watson, John, 82

West Africa, 118–20

Yerkes-Dodson Inverted-U, 57–58; arousal, 36, 57–58, 74, 127

Yoga, 8–9, 46, 63–65, 108, 117, 144, 146–47

Zen gardens, rock gardens, 108–10

Zorbing, 110–12